PUBLIC HISTORY,
PRIVATE STORIES

PUBLIC HISTORY, PRIVATE STORIES

Italian Women's Autobiography

Graziella Parati

University of Minnesota Press
Minneapolis
London

Grateful acknowledgment is made for permission to reprint excerpts from the following works: Valeria Finucci, "The Italian Memorialist: Camilla Faà Gonzaga," in *Women Writers of the Seventeenth Century,* ed. Katharina M. Wilson and Frank J. Warnke (Athens and London: University of Georgia Press, 1989), copyright 1989 the University of Georgia Press; Fausta Cialente, *Le quattro ragazze Wieselberger* (Milan: Arnoldo Mondadori Editore, 1976), copyright 1976 Arnoldo Mondadori Editore s.p.a.; Rita Levi Montalcini, *Elogio dell'imperfezione* (Milan: Garzanti Editore, 1987), copyright 1987 Garzanti Editore; Luisa Passerini, *Autoritratto di gruppo* (Middletown, Conn.: Wesleyan University Press, 1994), copyright 1988, 1994 Giunti Gruppo Editoriale, Florence, by permission of the University Press of New England.

Published by the University of Minnesota Press
111 Third Avenue South, Suite 290, Minneapolis, MN 55401-2520
Printed in the United States of America on acid-free paper

Library of Congress Cataloging-in-Publication Data

Parati, Graziela.
    Public history, private stories : Italian women's autobiography /
Graziela Parati.
        p.   cm.
    Includes index.
    ISBN 0-8166-2606-5 (hc). — ISBN 0-8166-2607-3 (pb)
    1. Italian literature—Women authors—History and criticism.
2. Autobiography in literature.   3. Women in literature.   I. Title.
PQ4055.W6P37   1996
850.9-9287—dc20   95-39547
                                                        CIP

The University of Minnesota is an equal-opportunity educator and employer.

A mia madre, Maddalena Degiovanni
a mia sorella, Elena Parati

Contents

Acknowledgments

I would have never been able to complete this book without the constant help of friends, colleagues, and colleagues who are friends. I want to say thank you here to Barbara Spackman, who has taught me how to feel comfortable in an American academic environment and has given me her friendship; to Rebecca West, who has been a mentor, friend, and patient reader of my work; and to Pia Friedrich, who turned my initial voluntary exile from Italy into a pleasant experience. I owe a lot of gratitude to Françoise Lionnet, Tilde Sankovitch, Carol Lazzaro-Weis, Michal Ginsburg, Lea Melandri, Luisa Muraro, Maria Rosa Cutrufelli, Larry Kritzman, Lynn Higgins, Keith Walker, Renate Holub, Giovanna Miceli Jeffries, and Albert Ascoli; their work has been a source of inspiration, and their friendship has been very important in confirming the career path I have chosen. I thank also the women who have supported me and helped me rewrite without becoming discouraged: Marianne Hirsch for being, first and foremost, one of my intellectual mothers. I am especially grateful to her for asking me the necessary theoretical questions at crucial moments in the writing of this book. I thank also Mary Jean Green, chair in French and Italian and currently dean of faculty at Dartmouth College, for her constant interest, support, and enthusiasm for my work. I thank Kate Conley, Liz Constable, Faith Beasley, and Irene Kacandes, who had to tackle the task of refining my English. My colleagues in Italian at Dartmouth College, Keala Jewell and Walter Stephens, have been enormously patient friends.

I want to express my appreciation to Luisa Passerini and Rita Levi Montalcini, who read and commented on the chapters in which I discuss their texts, and to Lionella Terni, who read the chapter about her mother, Fausta Cialente, and supplied me with valuable information. Thanks to Dartmouth College for granting me the Burke Award, which allowed me to complete the research for this book. I also thank Biodun Iginla and Elizabeth Knoll Stomberg for their valuable assistance and their immediate response to my many inquiries. Finally, I thank Anthony Tamburri, who has treated me as a valuable colleague and a friend from the very beginning of my career.

I am certain that all my friends who have helped me with this project know who they are and know how grateful I am to them for their contribution to this critical effort.

Introduction

I am permanently troubled by identity categories, consider them to be invari-
able stumbling blocks, and understand them, as sites of necessary trouble.
                        JUDITH BUTLER[1]

In 1622, but we are not even certain about this date, Camilla Faà wrote what
has been considered the first autobiography in prose composed by a woman
in the Italian literary tradition. Faà narrates the story of her life as a young
girl, a very young bride and mother who is deprived of her son because her
husband, Ferdinando Gonzaga, duke of Mantua, needs to acquire a new wife.
This new wife, Caterina de' Medici, will allow him to create the desired alliance with the Florentine Medici family. Faà's "metaphor of truth" about
her life and Mantua's history at the beginning of the seventeenth century
spans from her sixteenth birthday to her life in the monastery of Corpus
Domini in Ferrara, where her husband wanted her to disappear and be
silent.[2] In a few years Camilla is transformed from a *Dama di Corte*, a lady-
in-waiting, into the unacceptable wife of the duke, who it seems, fascinated
by her beauty, had secretly married her. She describes her unhappy life with
Ferdinando and ends with the ceremony in which she is forced to enter the
convent. The story acquires a rhythm through different rites of passage that
allow Camilla to abandon a private sphere, where she has the passive role

1

of daughter of a count and future wife of a minor member of the local aristocracy, in order to enter the public sphere of the court with a marriage that can potentially raise her to the role of duchess. She finally returns to a stifling corner of the private sphere in the seclusion of a cloister. It is within the enclosed environment of the convent that Camilla Faà Gonzaga writes a retrospective account of her multiple roles and identities and justifies her decision to write her own life. In the isolated domain of the convent, Camilla Faà undertakes the public act of writing what she calls "the truth," but disguises her intention by demanding secrecy. She paradoxically writes for a public interested in her private and public life but requests, simultaneously, the absence of such a reading public. Her private autobiographical act, she says, could have a powerful impact on the public sphere defined as the realm of "powerful people." The humble assertions of her ignorance and of her literary limitations hide her consciousness of the power of both the written word and the tale of her life.

I have always been fascinated by Camilla Faà Gonzaga's act of writing her life and by her story, which initially suggests a Cinderella-like ending and instead comes close to resembling a gothic novel and is concluded without any possibility of happy ending. Maybe the interest of feminist critics in Camilla's life supplies the delayed happy ending of this tragic woman's story. I position her at the beginning of this book on women's autobiographies because she symbolizes both the silence that has surrounded women's lives and roles in history and women's struggle to disseminate their autobiographical voices as transgressive acts of resistance throughout the centuries. I do not have the ambitious goal of defining what women's autobiographies are, because that would involve a process of universalization and essentialization of women's writing. My interest both in Faà's seventeenth-century narrative and in twentieth-century women's autobiographies is motivated by my desire to explore a few women's representations of private and public events and their use of autobiography as a means to define their identities as women in the private and public domains.

Autobiography as a genre allows for a constant redefinition of its boundaries and limitations.[3] Autobiography is a hybrid and malleable genre that partakes of other genres and becomes a literary space where a woman can experiment with the construction of a female "I" and, sometimes, a feminist identity. Autobiography also becomes a realm where women can construe a discussion on the boundaries of the domains that they have traditionally inhabited. The public act of writing a private life is the locus where women writers can seek to come to terms with the still contradictory relationship between the role of women in the public and private spheres.[4] In the different autobiographies I examine, women writers construct individual selves and create independent female identities in both spheres. Autobiography also becomes the medium in which the problematic points of contact between private and public realms are discussed.

In the twentieth century, Italian women writers such as Enif Robert, Fausta Cialente, Rita Levi Montalcini, and Luisa Passerini succeed in finding "relative" and temporary solutions to the complex problem of portraying the two spheres in their autobiographical writings. I find in Enif Robert's *Un ventre di donna: Romanzo chirurgico* (A Woman's Womb: A Surgical Novel) (1919), Fausta Cialente's *Le quattro ragazze Wieselberger* (The Four Wieselberger Girls) (1976), Rita Levi Montalcini's *Elogio dell'imperfezione* (In Praise of Imperfection) (1987), and Luisa Passerini's *Autoritratto di gruppo* (Group Self-Portrait) (1988), resistances to reconciling the representation of public and private realms.[5] Each author, in fact, contributes to the already complex definition of both public and private individual female selves and of the transgressive roles that they attempt to acquire. They strive, however, to construct new (as opposed to those traditionally predetermined by patriarchy) individual female roles.[6] Robert, Cialente, Montalcini, and Passerini share the same class origins: they belong to middle- or upper-middle-class families. Faà, instead, was part of a prebourgeois society. This aristocratic woman introduces my study of autobiographical texts because she points to similar ways in which women autobiographers throughout the centuries use strategies of "concealment and disclosure" in portraying their identities, their lives, and their stories within History.[7]

The writers I analyze, diverse in background, narrate their life stories and the historical events of this century, sharing an interest in exploring the relationships between the public and private selves, within and across national boundaries. Enif Robert, a controversial figure in Italian futurism, wrote her first and only novel, her autobiographical *A Woman's Womb*, in 1919. Little is known about her and about her literary activities after the publication of her book in 1919. Fausta Cialente (1898–1994) published a considerable number of novels and short stories between 1926 and 1976. Her literary career began in Italy and developed in Egypt, where she spent many years. Her final novel is an autobiographical text entitled *The Four Wieselberger Girls*, which recounts and concludes her long career as a self-exiled writer. Rita Levi Montalcini's autobiography spans most of this century: from the Great War to the late eighties. A Nobel Prize winner for medicine in 1986, Montalcini published *In Praise of Imperfection,* her only text of fiction, in 1987 (translated into English in 1988).

James Olney has defined autobiographies as contexts in which metaphors of selves are performed. The concept of truth in autobiography is therefore displaced into a discourse on metaphors of truth refined through the deforming filter of memory, what Lea Melandri calls "the crooked eyes of memory."[8] I consider autobiography as fiction, as a narrative in which the author carefully selects and constructs the characters, events, and aspects of the self that she or he wants to make public in order to convey a specific message about her or his past and present identity. The issue of truth is therefore not at all an issue in my discourse of women's autobiography. However, truth resurfaces in Montalcini's text not in regard to the "reliability" of her narrative, but in her relationship with the ideas of truth in the scientific world, ideas that she attempts to reconceptualize. Well known all over the world by medical researchers (and in Italy even by laypeople), Montalcini is still active in her field; after returning from the United States, where she spent about twenty years of her life, she now works and lives in Rome. Luisa Passerini's *Group Self-Portrait* narrates a woman's involvement in the movements of the sixties and seventies. After working for years as professor of methodology of historical research at the University of Turin, Passerini is now a history professor at the European University in Fiesole, Tuscany. Her texts mediate between her theoretical professional interest and her private identity as a woman, a daughter, and, at times, a feminist.

In *Private Woman, Public Stage,* Mary Kelley defines a few eighteenth-century women writers as "literary domestics."[9] Kelley argues that "these women reported on their own phenomenon and became unwitting witnesses to both the public event and their own private experiences."[10] Eighteenth-century literary criticism treated them as unusual occurrences and placed these "scribbling women outside of history."[11] Kelley adds that the "result has been not only to place them outside of history—recalling the fact that until recently most women have been outside of history—but also implicitly to deny the existence of positive and substantive elements in the domestic experience and thus in women's experience."[12] Most of the women writers in this book begin their autobiographical narratives by describing the female and familial nineteenth-century or early twentieth-century past in order to draw the reader's attention to the changing socioeconomic conditions in twentieth-century Italy. In her book *Gender and History,* Linda Nicholson affirms, "We need to think about gender and female devaluation historically."[13] The women autobiographers I study contribute to the discussion on gender and history by defining their difference from their foremothers. They resist sameness by stressing their successful struggles to be recognized in the public sphere of literary fame or, in the case of Rita Levi Montalcini, of medical history.

In parts of their narratives, Cialente, Montalcini, and Passerini perpetuate the nineteenth-century myth of the superiority of the public (i.e., male) sphere over the female private realm. Until the 1970s, female scholars considered the separation between private and public spheres necessary to facilitate the study of women's identities throughout the history of female oppression. In 1974, Michelle Rosaldo defended such a position by stating that "an opposition between 'domestic' and 'public' provides the basis of a structural framework necessary to identify and explore the place of male and female in psychological, cultural, social and economic aspects of human life."[14] This "useful" opposition reveals its limitations, and Rosaldo herself, in an article published in 1980, retraces her steps and redefines her position vis-à-vis the discussion on "wom[e]n's place in human social life," adding in the same article that "the significances women assign to their activities of their lives are things that we can only grasp through an analysis of the relationships that women forge, the social contexts they (along with men) create—and within which they are defined."[15] By dispensing with the rigid division between the public as male and the private as female, Rosaldo opens the doors to a redefinition and renaming of positions—an issue that the women in this book discuss within the context of their autobiographies.

In the construction of their identities and roles, Robert, Cialente, Montalcini, and Passerini seem to proceed along a line parallel to the developments and changes in the evolution of the theories on public and private domains. Their initial solutions tend to privilege the acquisition of visibility through a process that is imitative of male models, as in the case of Enif Robert, who attempts to mimic Marinetti's futuristic style in order to acquire an equal standing within the futurist movement. In her article "Women and the Public Sphere: A Modern Perspective," Joan Landes states: "As Michel Foucault has repeatedly argued, modernity has been sustained by drawing the self systematically into the orbit of social discipline."[16] Foucault stresses that movement within modernity that brings the private into the public. In such a shift, the public realm is privileged as the dominant realm in the oppositional structure of the two spheres. This one-way movement described is problematized in many women's texts where they either perform the opposite operation or attempt to create alternative models that go beyond the rigid separation between male and female models or public and private stereotypes and, drawing from both, construct individual identities based on the opposite of separatism.

At the beginning of their narratives, each woman writer defines the public and private spheres as culturally and politically divided. According to Fausta Cialente, the "public sphere" is the realm that includes History and dominating ideologies, such as *irredentismo* and fascism. The public world of a literary movement at the beginning of the century is the public sphere that Enif Robert unsuccessfully attempts to enter. The realm of science and the alternative, but still male, narrative of the student movement in the sixties are elements of the public sphere that are appropriated and rewritten by Montalcini and Passerini, respectively. These four autobiographies include definitions of woman as prisoner of the private sphere. The authors then portray, in different ways, their struggles to escape from the limitations imposed on them as women within the private realm. However, Luisa Passerini describes her "awakening" to the private world of the unwritten history of women when feminism in Europe becomes a force separated from the male movements in the sixties and the seventies. The privileged public realm, the space to conquer in order to be equal to men, becomes secondary in Passerini's experience to the rediscovery of the "private realm," intended as a non-homogeneous space, as a fragmented entity that cannot be defined only as the confining space in which women were and are marginalized and silenced. Private space is also meant to be the space of women's history in which women have been kept silent (but they cannot be completely silenced), a world to be charted in its many forms. It is from the private sphere that women's voices from the past can surface. Ignored because hidden in the womb-like recesses of the private, texts like Camilla Faà Gonzaga's autobiography are kept "alive." Preserved in the private library of a convent, Faà's transgressive narrative of her life with the duke of Mantua survives *because* it was overlooked and disregarded by public history. Therefore, the private sphere can be described, in some instances, as the protective shell of unspeakable words. Once made public, Faà's words have a visible impact on revising and proposing challenging questions to the official history: the voice that, according to Kelley, had been kept out of history comes back to challenge history itself.

The private sphere as inhabited by Woman as wife, daughter, mother, or sister represents only a component, what I would call the *matroneum,* of the realm that is completed by the privileged "space of privacy" inhabited by Man.[17] Within the *matroneum,* women are "named" according to their familial relationship to men. It is the realm where the convenient myth of the biological woman, the "natural" mother, becomes synonymous with femininity and womanhood. *Matroneum* is intended as a "space within a space," as a limited realm whose boundaries are defined by patriarchy but whose inner dynamics cannot be totally controlled. In such a space, women have influence, but not the power to redefine its boundaries. In his article "Private Selves and Public Parts," Alan Ryan presents a portrait of the private sphere as the "backstage area where one [Man] can wipe off the greasepaint, complain about the audience, worry about one's performance and so on."[18] It is the place where men "engage in repairs and rehabilitation, chew over performances and think how to improve them, and even rethink the whole play in which we [men] are engaged."[19] The public "play" in which men are engaged is arbitrarily left behind to retreat into "privacy," into the "male" private sphere that man can abandon or reenter.

The portrayals of the "mobile" man versus the "immobile" woman, as gendered in the private sphere, are challenged by the four women autobiographers presented here. Critics have defined women's relationships to the public realm as "indirect," because they are limited and controlled by patriarchy. Carol Pateman states, "The way in which women are included [in public life] is grounded, as firmly as their position in the domestic sphere, in patriarchal beliefs and practices."[20] I do not use the term "domestic sphere" as a synonym with "private sphere." "Domestic sphere" recalls the space of the *domus;* it is a realm with almost physical boundaries, which, however, still encompass both male and female spaces. *Domus* is also used in Latin to mean "country" (*pro domo,* for example). Such a term establishes a space of discourse with acquired connotations that go beyond the private sphere and invade the public realm of history and of the body politic. *Matroneum,* that "sphere within a sphere," is a term that allows me to ignore the physical boundaries of the "home" in order to privilege the investigation of the limiting discourses of female "spaces" and feminine roles. This *matroneum* can be also visualized by imagining it mirrored in architectural spaces in churches, usually located above the lateral aisles, called "women's galleries," places where women were kept separated from men but were still the object of male gazes and supervision. (In this discussion on spaces, I borrow and adapt the term *matroneum* because it allows me to talk about the private as a space at the same time connected to and separated from the public sphere.) In the *matroneum* of the private sphere, such a physical distance can transform itself into a marginal kind of independence from which Kelley's "literary domestics" could record their words on paper.

The transgressive words, which are not uttered by the foremothers of the women discussed in this book, become ventriloquized in autobiographical contexts that narrate the daughters' lives beyond the *matroneum*. These daughters struggle to create what Patricia Meyer Spacks calls "imagined female selves" beyond the limited female roles as "honorary men" in the public sphere.[21] Carolyn Heilbrun defines women who become "honorary men" as tolerated guests who achieve their position by imitating men and adopting "the play in which men are engaged" in an attempt to appropriate and experiment with men's power and leave women's limited influence behind in the abandoned *matroneum*.[22]

Women's presence in the public domain needs to be situated in a discussion on the heterogeneity of public space. Jürgen Habermas's *Structural Transformation of the Public Sphere*, published in German in 1962 but only translated into English in 1989, is helpful in defining the discourse of public women.[23] In his introduction to *Habermas and the Public Sphere* (1992), Craig Calhoun argues that Habermas's text elaborates on and is in opposition to Kant's definition of the bourgeois public sphere. Calhoun continues by adding that the "transformations of the public sphere that Habermas describes turn largely on its continual expansion to include more and more participants. . . . He suggests that ultimately this inclusivity brought degeneration in the quality of discourse."[24] The public sphere is intended by Habermas as "the sphere of private people come together as a public."[25] Such private people "soon claimed the public sphere . . . to engage [public authorities] in a debate over the general rules governing relations."[26] In the space of such a political debate, women remain excluded. Habermas explains that in the bourgeois public sphere, women can acquire a role outside the private if their goal is to access the literary domain, but even in such a context their role appears to be passive: "Female readers as well as apprentices and servants often took a more active part in the literary public sphere than the owners of private property and family heads themselves."[27] Habermas elaborates on his definition of a "more active part" for women in literary public spheres, but he seems to consider such a role an appendix to the still passive role of women as spectators. Allowed to peruse, but not to criticize or write about, texts of which men are often the authors, they are not totally excluded from the world of letters.

In "Rethinking the Public Sphere: A Contribution to the Critique of Actually Existing Democracy," Nancy Fraser criticizes Habermas's conception of "one" public sphere and also reveals her concern for the use of the expression "public sphere" within contemporary discourses and, in particular, feminism.[28] She notes a "confusion" in the use of "public sphere": "This expression has been used to refer to everything that is outside the domestic or familial sphere. Thus 'the public sphere' in this usage conflates at least three analytically distinct things: the state, the official economy of paid employment, and arenas of public discourse."[29] In my discussion of autobiography as a special kind of arena for women's public discourse about their public and private identities, Fraser supplies the landmark definition of not one but rather "a multiplicity of publics" that "must countenance not the exclusion, but the inclusion, of interests and issues that bourgeois, masculinist ideology labels 'private' and treats as inadmissible."[30]

It is by defining the differences among the "private people" who, according to Habermas, "come together as a public" that Fraser's fragmentation of the public sphere becomes the theoretical code with which to interpret women's autobiographical constructions of their selves that take into consideration their private origins and their "unusual" roles in *a* public. In Habermas, the fragmentation of the public sphere marks its degeneration. Fraser argues, instead, that the creation of a "subaltern counterpublic," that is, "alternative publics" created by those who are considered "others," allows these "others" to "formulate oppositional interpretations of their identities, interests and needs."[31] She cites as an example the network of feminist bookstores, academic departments, and publications, which constitute an "alternative public." This issue is further complicated by the relationships between the different publics. Fraser returns to Habermas's definition of "public sphere" as a "body of private persons assembled to form a public" in order to discuss the different public or publics a person can inhabit. She traces the differences between "weak publics" and "strong publics." The former indicates "publics whose deliberative practice consists exclusively in opinion formation and does not encompass decision making."[32] The latter defines "publics whose discourse encompasses both opinion formation and decision making."[33] "Weak publics" appear to be closely related to the *matroneum* in which women have influence and not power. It is in order to construct their identity in the public, or sometimes the limited corner within a "weak public," that women autobiographers like Cialente, Montalcini, and Passerini reexamine the familial collective *matroneum*. They retrace their steps and, by connecting to the sphere they left behind, attempt to explore the boundaries of the "weak" roles they have acquired.

In my interest in autobiographical texts that develop nonseparatist portrayals of public and private, I privilege those female autobiographies based upon the construction of nondichotomized portrayals of maternal and paternal roles. In the preface of her book *Gender Trouble*, Judith Butler succinctly summarizes a Foucauldian redefinition of genealogy:

> To expose the foundational categories of sex, gender, and desire as effects of a specific formation of power requires a form of critical inquiry that Foucault, reformulating Nietzsche, designates as "genealogy." A genealogical critique refuses to search for the origin of gender, the inner truth of female desire, a genuine or authentic sexual identity that repression has kept from view; rather genealogy investigates the political stakes in designating as an *origin* and *cause* those identity categories that are in fact the *effects* of institutions, practices, discourses with multiple and diffuse points of origin.[34]

Within certain autobiographical contexts, the search for origins and a personal genealogy reveals an antiessentialist, discontinuous connection with both the maternal and the paternal. The multiplicity of "points of origin" makes the construction of a uniquely matrilinear connection with the past impossible. The critical attention shifts from a separation between multiple spheres, between spheres within spheres, and turns toward a decentralization of a single discourse, origin, influence, and inheritance. In short, it turns toward a construction of hybrid, or braided, genealogies. In their attempt to rewrite the traditional relationship between female and male roles in the public and the private spheres, these autobiographers share the feminist agenda defined by Carol Pateman: "Feminists are trying to develop a theory of social practice that, for the first time in the western world, would be a truly general theory—including women and men equally—grounded in the interrelationship of the individual to the collective life, or personal to political life, instead of their separation and opposition."[35]

Thanks to the fictional construction of a personal mixed genealogy, the narrators create new roles that allow the protagonists of the autobiographical acts to partake of both spheres. My interest in the construction of braided genealogies echoes Françoise Lionnet's work on *métissage* among cultures. Lionnet uses the concept of the *métisse* in a postcolonial context to talk about the destruction of cultural and racial dichotomies in order to privilege a "trans-cultural," linguistic hybridity: literary *métissage*.[36] I have attempted to construct a minimal translation of her techniques of *métissage* in my analysis of autobiographical narratives in which the selves created do not rely on "'pure' or unitary origin," but instead on "indeterminacy, hybridization, and fragmentation."[37] In such a context, the female characters become *métisses*, hybrid, the result of an intertwining of paternal and maternal traces. They are hybrid entities that provoke a "degeneration" of the rigid dichotomy between male and female, paternal and maternal traces.[38] To weave a personal past by rewriting the paternal and maternal inheritance means using the space of autobiography as a locus where women can elaborate on the public and private roles played by the fathers and mothers. In these narratives in which private lives are translated into the public realm of the literary world, women's voices investigate the possibility of weakening the traditional oppositions in order to redefine the space in which to inscribe their own voices. Within such a space they go beyond their construction of themselves as the result of the mere mixing of opposites: they create "imagined selves" that are different from both the opposites that they had attempted to hybridize.

In discussing genealogy, Foucault supplies the background for the construction of disparate genealogies: "Genealogy," writes Foucault, "does not pretend to restore an unbroken continuity," and searches not for fixed origins but for "disparity."[39] Within a braided genealogy, a woman's past is structured in a form of textual *métissage*, intended as a plot in which maternal and paternal images are closely interwoven. Sidonie Smith's *Poetics of Women's Autobiography* also sees male and female traces as intertwined and thus attempts to "elaborate . . . a theoretical framework through which to understand women's self-writing."[40] In the introductory chapter of her book, Smith supplies her definition of a woman's past as a polyvalent metaphor that owes its articulation to a mixing of traces:

> The woman who chooses to write her life story must negotiate the figures of "man" and the figures of "woman" promoted by the cultural discourses that surround her. . . . This framework posits certain dynamics that structure women's life writing, including [the] way in which the autobiographer who is a woman must suspend herself between paternal and maternal narratives, those fictions of male and female selfhood that permeate her historical moment.[41]

Disparate genealogies are that "suspended" space. In Foucault's terms, it is an "interstice," in which these oppositional traces can coexist in a fiction that allows the narrator to "invade" history and write her "historical experience" at the same time as her personal story.

To rewrite the private and the public means for many women writers to construct the autobiographical space as an "in-between" realm, a marginal space where public and private spheres and roles can be represented and stripped of the traditional connotations of superiority and inferiority. In naming spheres, Habermas states that "the sphere of the family, as the core of the private sphere, we call the 'intimate sphere.'"[42] The "core" of my discourse is not the family but rather the *matroneum*, not an "intimate institution," but rather, mirroring Fraser's fragmentation of the public, a weak private. The *matroneum* is the "sphere within a sphere" that the women writers analyzed in this book reshape from a level in a hierarchical structure into an independent "plane" whose boundaries women can appropriate and modify. To eliminate the traditional boundaries of the *matroneum* means to supply alternative, transgressive signifieds to the signifier "mother." The convenient myth of the biological woman is abandoned and replaced by women's attempts to inscribe the construction of "matrilinearism" within the narratives of women's lives.[43] The creation of braided genealogies relies on an initial matrilinear structure that I call *gynealogy*. Gynealogies are genealogies that women autobiographers create to recuperate the silenced voices of their mothers, but they are also constructions that open themselves to revision and expansion toward a nonseparatist concept of women's personal narratives. Gynealogical techniques allow women writers to concentrate on the mothers as mirror images of the daughters, to create connections exclusively with the *matroneum* in order to reject its isolation, but also to treasure the female history enclosed within its boundaries. In emphasizing gynealogies as the basis for braided genealogies, I underscore not only the matrilinear links to the past, but also the "gyn," the presence of female narrators and protagonists in these autobiographies. These female-authored texts and genealogies depart from a rereading of the maternal roles in the *matroneum,* fragmenting the past and inscribing it into braided genealogies as heterogeneous systems.

Gynealogies need to augment themselves, starting from such a matrilinear foundation, in order to become hybrid genealogies, which I also call disparate and braided. The creation of an exclusively matrilinear link to the past tends to create a homogeneous concept of a female past that traps women in a potentially essentializing genealogy. Within Italian feminism, Adriana Cavarero and Luisa Muraro theorize a "concept of female genealogy to transmit knowledge and empower women and . . . a political separatist context from which a new female epistemology will derive."[44] Luisa Muraro has enunciated the possibility of creating a symbolic order of the mother capable of replacing the symbolic order of father.[45] In her essay "The Narrow Door," Muraro argues that through her privileging of the maternal she can also create, as secondary, a "practice of sharing that renders, for example, nonantagonistic the relationship with the other sex." She further explains that the "rendering of man-woman relations more just and good is not a goal but a consequence. For us, female freedom is the content of a political project in and of itself, autonomous."[46] In this context, one center is replaced by another: the maternal becomes "center"; woman acquires visibility in the public discourse on literary and social theory. This substitution, which is also the core of a gynealogical construction, creates, however, a new binary opposition that imitates the old one and that, by debunking the paternal, forms new margins yet does no more than mirror old dichotomies. Lea Melandri criticizes Muraro's symbolic order because it is an "order" created through a process of analogy with the male hierarchical order that it attempts to undermine. Melandri adds that in the symbolic order of the mother is the inherent possibility of remaining trapped within the system women strive to negate.[47]

The Muraro-Melandri debate is relevant to my discussion of disparate genealogies, because Melandri proposes an alternative by experimenting with nonauthoritarian, nonhierarchical relationships among women and between women and men. Her position is also very critical toward another concept within Italian feminism that is linked to Muraro's idea of the symbolic order of the mother: that of *affidamento,* or entrustment. In *Non credere di avere dei diritti,* critics theorize the possibility of creating a mother-daughter relationship between two women.[48] Carol Lazzaro-Weis summarizes that such a relationship

> redefines the mother-daughter relationship as a symbolic one: the "symbolic mother," usually but not necessarily an older woman, functions to sustain and recognize the gendered nature of the thought, knowledge and experience of another, less experienced woman who has entrusted herself to her. The mentor-guide relationship between two women facilitates the "vertical" (Muraro avoids the word "hierarchical") transmission of knowledge and authority from woman to woman and the recognition of individual difference.[49]

This order allows women to construct female models through which they can access the public sphere. However, such a structure, which is called "vertical" but has a hierarchical distribution of roles, reestablishes a one-way movement: awareness is transmitted from the more experienced woman to the other. Furthermore, such a construction does not take into consideration issues of class and race.

Melandri tends to reject the notion of separation between women because that would imitate the separation and hierarchization that are the basis of patriarchy. Lazzaro-Weis agrees with my interpretation of Melandri's thought when she writes that "Melandri analyzes how female dependency and alienation are the result of patriarchal ideology that separates the personal from the political, sentiment from reason, politics of the mind from that of the heart."[50] Melandri's position as "bad daughter" within the symbolic order of the father translates into a position equivalent to that of the transgressive daughter even within the context of matrilinearism. In *Come nasce il sogno d'amore* (How the Dream of Love Is Born), Melandri creates a critical text that attempts to collapse the separation between Sibilla Aleramo's work and her critical approach to the writer's text.[51] Aleramo's language is appropriated by Melandri, who draws Aleramo's autobiographical writing into her own critical text, which includes the critic's (Melandri's) own autobiographical contribution. This nonhierarchical relationship to a literary mother undermines the concept of "order," of a vertical transmission of knowledge, and of mentor-guide relationships as two different women's life experiences are placed on the same plane, in the same autobiographical context.[52]

Muraro and Melandri formulate theoretical positions from different points of view in the public sphere. Muraro's voice surfaces within an academic environment where, however, Muraro stresses, she has never acquired a male-like academic power position. While Muraro occupies a marginal position within the public realm of academia, Melandri speaks from a context in which, through her teaching at the Libera Università delle Donne (Free University of Women) in Milan, she has attempted to create an alternative to the traditional academic learning centers and to the figures of authority in the Italian educational system. Yet they both share an interest in creating public theories that draw the autobiographical into the theoretical realm, and vice versa. Muraro begins her discussion of the symbolic order of the mother by describing her experience as an apprentice philosopher in Italian academia and her "unconscious will to invalidate the maternal authority and actions."[53] She also notes that feminists have attempted to "unlearn" patriarchal culture, but she adds that, speaking from an autobiographical point of view, she cannot completely discard her background as a philosopher, in which she was trained to think within male theory and philosophy.[54] She continues by stating that "not everything is second-rate and . . . everything I have learned can be of use to me" and that, autobiographically speaking, the problem for her can be phrased simply, "because in my case it has to do with unlearning what I have never succeeded in learning."[55] By defining her identity as fundamentally incompatible with her education, Muraro declares the uselessness of attempting to attack patriarchal thought: "By criticizing patriarchy I have gained self-consciousness, but not the ability to freely signify female greatness, which I encountered and fully recognized in the first months and years of my life."[56] The alternative is to privilege the creation of a symbolic order of the mother by reopening a dialogue and constructing a relationship with the mother, a dialogue and relationship that had been "culturally repressed."[57]

In this debate on women's positions and roles within the public sphere, the discourse is often brought back to the definition of female margins, power, and influence. Muraro's present interest in the relationships between authority and power and Melandri's work on mother-son relationships seem to reopen the discussion and negotiate differences in order to find a way to develop a theory that transcends separatism. Within gynealogy, such a universal quest cannot be solved. In the limited field of autobiographical writing, disparate or braided genealogies are created by means of a genealogical zigzagging through fragmented paternal and maternal lines. What is privileged in this context is not so much "difference" but rather "differences" and an exploration of both female margins and male subjectivities at the margin. A fragmented past is handed down into the present through traces. I privilege the term *traces* instead of *lines* because the former conveys the fragmented nature of the components of paternal and maternal genealogies, which are subjective charts that map individual female pasts. Talking about paternal and maternal traces avoids any discourse on parallel but separate connections between past and present and on an uninterrupted continuity between past and present. In my discussion of differences, I also emphasize differences among women, between mothers and daughters. Diotima, a group of Italian women philosophers who have published a number of books on feminist thought, insists, in its discussion of feminist practices, on the concept of a fragmentation of difference that is necessary for my construction of disparate genealogies.[58] In her article on Italian postmodernism and Italian feminist thought, Renate Holub summarizes Diotima's position:

> The mother has been excluded from the symbolic and it is unlikely that a woman gains presence in, and access to, social reality if she identifies with an absence in that reality, with her mother and other women. Diotima suggests to take recourse to a different relation, not to identification and fusion with the mother, but to a relation that stresses difference, distantiation, and differentiation. Indeed, it is a relation of difference between symbolic mothers and daughters which powerfully creates the condition of new and liberatory possibilities. By positing herself not as the same but as different from the other woman, who is in any event "the other" of male discourse, by positing, that is, herself as similar but not as the same, woman creates the condition for exploiting the double alterity inscribed in woman's condition. She is at once "the other" of male discourse, but also the "similar other" of a feminine discourse.[59]

Braided genealogies embrace such a position with a twist, because, in the construction of a past, women writers attempt to locate paternal differences and transgressions that are not silenced in the construction of a text that focuses on women's double alterity. Even the concept of gynealogy as matrilinear past is nonlinear and nonhomogeneous as it deals not only with the affinities but also with the differences between mothers and daughters.

Women confront the paternal in similar ways: aware of the evident separations, they explore the male past in the familial sphere in order to search for points of contact, for relative sameness to the fathers. Through the revision of the fathers, women autobiographers construct models that allow them to abandon the immobility of that female sphere within a sphere and gain access into the public realm where they have to face, once more, the dilemma of either accepting male models of power or creating alternative models of authority. The female protagonists of disparate genealogies in autobiographical texts attempt to enter the public sphere and to confront, not reflect, male power. Muraro talks about *potenza materna* (which can be translated as "maternal power, strength, might") that has been controlled by men and that needs to be rediscovered in order to "translate the old relationship with the mother in [your] adult lives to make her again come to life for you as the principle of symbolic authority."[60] Power and authority become synonymous in this context and need to be examined. Melandri addresses this problem and therefore criticizes the concept of female authority in Muraro's work. Melandri has, in fact, experimented with the translation of her theory into practice by attempting to create nonauthoritarian relationships in her role as a teacher both in Italian public schools and in her Libera Università delle Donne.

If, however, we consider the idea of authority as a concept different from "power," the terms of Melandri's critique of Muraro can be redefined. Hannah Arendt's interest in power and authority can be of help in reconciling the concept of braided genealogies with both Muraro's and Melandri's positions and also in connecting it with Fraser's preoccupation with "weak publics," the space in which the opinions created cannot be translated "into authoritative decisions."[61] In "What Is Authority?" Arendt separates authority from power by establishing a difference between tradition and past.[62] Tradition is "the thread which safely guided us through the vast realms of the past, but this thread was also the chain fettering each successive generation to a predetermined aspect of the past."[63] Arendt stresses the need to reconceptualize tradition without completely debunking its position as one source of information, one mode of reading the past. The loss of tradition, which she detects in modern times, is accompanied also by a loss of religion that Arendt also defines as the "crisis of institutional religion."[64] Consequently, Arendt notes the disappearance not of "authority in general," but of a "very specific form" of authority, which "gave the world the permanence and durability which human beings need precisely because they are mortals."[65] In defining the difference between tradition and past, Arendt creates a historical analysis of Greek and Roman times and traces the connection between authority and tradition. Authority linked to tradition is defined as different from institutional power (*potestas*) and the recognized forms of government.[66] "All prototypes by which . . . generations understood the content of authority," writes Arendt, "were drawn from specifically unpolitical experiences, stemming either from the sphere of 'making' and the arts, where there must be experts and where fitness is the highest criterion, or from the private household community."[67] In the construction of gynealogies, authority has its source within the private *matroneum* to which women turn to find an unexplored tradition linked to influence and not power. "The word *auctoritas*," adds Arendt, "derives from the verb *augere*, 'augment,' and what authority or those in authority constantly augment is the foundation."[68] If we consider that the foundation of hybrid genealogy, that is gynealogy, is within the influence of the *matroneum*, female authority is based on an "augmentation" and modification of such influence, an influence limited by the male *potestas* within the private sphere. The aim is to create a concept of female authority through the construction of a braided genealogical past that can access and expand or, to echo Calhoun's words, can create a degeneration of the public sphere and consequently a weakening of the concept of power figures as models. The aim is also to create authoritative figures who are visible, accessible, and recognizable within the public sphere, but whose empowerment is not carried out at the "daughter's" expense. The emphasis can shift from the maternal teaching to a woman's active and subjective appropriation of the authoritative model, whose role is to supply "a mere advice, needing neither the form of command nor external coercion to make itself heard."[69]

Autobiography lends itself to a study on the relations between power and authority and, of course, between author and authority. Arendt supplies the connections with her analysis of the body politic and the sphere of literary writing: "*Auctores* can be used as the very opposite of the *artifices*, the actual builders and makers, and this is precisely when the word *auctor* signifies the same thing as our 'author.'"[70] The women autobiographers studied in this book both author and authorize a theory and practice in the construction of female identities that become revisable models in further developments in the construction of future hybrid genealogies. In her autobiography, Fausta Cialente creates a representation of her self as a literary model in an innovative postcolonial context that is named as such only years later. Montalcini's elaboration of the concept of "imperfection" as a model in the public sphere of scientific research creates a female voice of authority that contributes to the discussion on women in science. Passerini's attempt to "personalize theory" and inscribe her body and female identity in the academic field of historical research adds to the other models of "vulnerable authority," because she modifies her recognized public success in the public sphere in order to experiment with changing the rigid separation of her private identity as a woman and her public role as a university professor. She attempts to create a gentler model of intellectual authority for men and women alike.

The problem is to find a possible definition of such an authority that cannot reconstruct vertical or rigid hierarchical structures. Lazzaro-Weis's observations on theories of the maternal can be of help in this context as she states, following Marianne Hirsch and Jane Gallop, that "although contemporary theories of the maternal posit the mother as a privileged dissident, when she becomes a real figure she loses her status as a powerful goddess and repeats her traditional vulnerability."[71] In this attempt to construct alternative models of authority, the emphasis is not on the loss of the powerful goddess-like status, but rather on that "real figure" that reveals its vulnerability. A vulnerable authority is a weak form of authority that questions itself and is always under revision. Authority—that has an inherently nonegalitarian component—is weakened in such a model by the fact that it does not claim to exist in one form but in a plurality of vulnerable authoritative practices. This postmodern plurality redefines traditional strong models and welcomes the construction of an authority that does not have the power to silence.

Paradoxically, the first two chapters of my study of autobiography deal respectively with Camilla Faà Gonzaga, a female voice that can surface as an authoritative voice only centuries later when she has a sympathetic public, and with Enif Robert's attempt to acquire the power to become a futurist writer. Consequently, she wants to distance herself from the "unworthy" nonfuturist women.

If we consider autobiography a "retrospective narration in prose," as defined by Philippe Lejeune, we can safely state that the first female Italian autobiographical text was written by Camilla Faà Gonzaga at the beginning of the seventeenth century (circa 1622).[72] My first chapter is devoted to this seventeenth-century memoir. Yet can one apply the modern definition of private and public spheres to the historical context in which (or at the margins of which) Faà Gonzaga writes her life? I am interested in analyzing similarities and differences among the various strategies employed by women in their construction of female selves and identities—strategies that sometimes reveal similarities in works written in totally different socioeconomical and cultural contexts. I also focus on Faà Gonzaga's struggle to redefine the boundaries of the spaces that she is allowed to inhabit. Her attempt to transgress creates the detailed portrayal of the limitations imposed on her identities as "unofficial" duchess, daughter, wife, mother, and, finally, unwilling nun. This first autobiographical act in prose highlights the definition of limited spaces, of malleable female identities, and of the silencing power of the men who create History. Her attempt to define the male power that silenced her voice and isolated her in a convent creates a pre-text to the twentieth-century autobiographical acts in which women writers continue to struggle to define and redefine the boundaries that limit women's roles and suffocate their voices.

In my second chapter, I study an autobiography written at the beginning of the twentieth century. Published in 1919, *A Woman's Womb: A Surgical Novel* is the autobiography of a woman who struggles to create a self independent from the expectations of the bourgeois class to which she belongs. She attempts, in fact, to escape from the private sphere, where she is identified as mother and widow destined to remarry. In her autobiography, Enif Robert reveals her desire to construct a new personal identity as an active member of a literary movement. The text of her life is introduced by the futurist women's manifesto, which develops the theoretical agenda for the subsequent autobiographical work. However, her creation is repeatedly interrupted by the male writing hand: Marinetti completes the book by supplying the text with a male metaphor of a female self.

In her "Manifesto of Futurist Women," which is included in *A Woman's Womb*, Robert attempts to create a female alternative to the male agenda of the futurist movement. With the formula "CORAGGIO + VERITÀ" (COURAGE + TRUTH), Robert strives to enter the public sphere of a literary movement by writing about her fight to overcome cancer of the uterus. Marinetti contributes to the autobiography by gaining control of the narrative—the locus, again, of male creativity. In fact, Marinetti invents a futurist cure for a female disease and becomes the epistemological hero within the narration. His epistemological approach to a woman's, that is, to Robert's, body aims to construct a new definition of her "wound," which becomes the mirror image of the trenches, the wounds on the womb of the earth. Only the soldier, the futurist warrior, can succeed in controlling both a woman's disease and the earth's disruption. World War I becomes a public event rewritten by the male leader of the futurist movement, within a "tentative" autobiographical act by a woman writer. *A Woman's Womb* becomes the space where Man triumphs over the "weak" female voice, which is silenced as Marinetti constructs his version of "her" private story and of public history. The mutilated and scarred womb of a woman is reflected in the mutilated construction of a self, which becomes an empty signifier. Marinetti supplies the male signifieds for the empty shell of a female identity.

Enif Robert's work exemplifies a literally mutilated attempt to create a narrative space where a woman can come to terms with a private role as mother and a public role as member of a literary movement. This is an autobiographical text that embodies the concept of failed autobiographical projects. In fact, Marinetti directly intervenes in Robert's writing in order to transform her "disease" and her search for an independent identity into a threat to male virility and power. The image of the sick woman becomes the image of Woman as a potentially castrating and contaminating presence in the public sphere. Her "creative" presence is interpreted as a threat to the male predominance in the literary movement and must, therefore, be controlled by the futurist *Uebermensch*.

The third chapter is devoted to Fausta Cialente's *The Four Wieselberger Girls*. Cialente rereads and rewrites historical events in the twentieth century: the Great War, fascism, and World War II. Her agenda is to explore traditional public and private realms in order to, first, concentrate on the portrayal of the muted members of her family inside the *matroneum*. She later focuses on weakening paternal power in order to access the public sphere and articulate her identity as transgressive daughter of both the father(s) and the mother(s). Cialente's autobiography contains constructions of both her personal and her familial past that allow the author to transform genealogy into gynealogy, and consequently into a hybrid genealogy. I aim to define the tension between personal and public history that generates the basic structure for Fausta Cialente's reconstruction and revision of Memory (i.e., History) and personal memories. Third-person narration dominates the first of the four sections into which the book is divided, sections that also reveal the problematic relationship between author, narrator, and characters within the autobiographical act. Through a fragmented interweaving of official history and personal "life/lines," Fausta Cialente rereads her family's past, the bourgeois life of the four sisters, and official history, the irresponsible *irredentismo* of Trieste's middle class, in order to recreate her own gynealogical private story and later write an alternative narrative on public history.[73]

Male characters dominate the beginning of the autobiography. The first chapters of the book contain an extensive description of the grandfather's active *irredentismo*. In the intermediate chapters of Cialente's autobiography, the author introduces the problematic representation of the father who is feared, but also admired, for his anti-*irredentismo*, antimilitarism, anti-*interventismo* in the Great War, and antifascism. In fact, Fausta Cialente succeeds in presenting an alternative version of those gloriously patriotic times of the unification of Trieste with Italy and reveals the blindness of fanatic *irredentisti*. In the final pages of the book, the images of the father disappear, and the narrator's personal memories are integrated in the portrayal of the female figures of the past. In this new world of "doubles," as Fausta Cialente describes it, happiness cannot be found. Yet there is "calm" and "continuity in life."[74] In this context, even death, the death of the mother, becomes acceptable, because it is not "lost" in a male-dominated past, but becomes part of a gynealogy. Yet in this newly created personal history, traces of the father can still be found. The construction of a braided genealogy allows the author to reconsider the father and to create a form of textual *métissage*, which consists of an interweaving of paternal and maternal images and messages, of fragments and traces. The binary opposition between fear of the father and pity for the mother, which is the leitmotiv of much of the autobiography, is transformed in the context of a disparate genealogy.

The Four Wieselberger Girls and *A Woman's Womb* are two very different autobiographical texts, which nevertheless share the agenda of a construction of female selves in relation to new roles in the public and private spheres. At the same time, these two works approach the unresolved problem of the "language" in which to write a woman's life. As Cialente discovers that the language of the mother is even more a patriarchal ideological construction than the traditional paternal language, she reveals linguistic problematics particular to women's autobiographies. *A Woman's Womb* contains a futurist woman's attempt to negate the traditional language of literature; she adopts, however, the experimental language of the male-dominated futurist movement, in which she becomes silenced again.[75] Fausta Cialente is torn between the binary oppositions of the language of the father (Italian) and the maternal dialect. "Triestino" is the language spoken by the maternal side of the family, but it is also the lingua franca of the *irredentisti*, that obtuse bourgeoisie that Cialente rejects. It is the language of the father that the narrator adopts, for it is standard Italian that Fausta Cialente will use as a writer in her lifelong, voluntary exile from the fatherland.[76] In her autobiographical work, Enif Robert uses language as an attempt to create an independent female formula to establish the "Manifesto of Futurist Women." This experimental introduction is followed by a very traditional beginning of an autobiography in which linguistic experimentation becomes successful only when stimulated by a male avant-garde writer. In her letters to Marinetti, Enif Robert adopts the technique of *parole in libertà* (words in freedom), which becomes part of the futurist "talking cure"—a cure able to heal the scarred womb of the futurist woman. Enif Robert finds herself trapped in the order she is trying to negate by adopting an avant-garde experimental language invented and controlled by the leader of the futurist movement.

The strategy of imperfection presented by Rita Levi Montalcini in her *In Praise of Imperfection*, analyzed in the fourth chapter of this book, suggests a temporary solution to the problematic choices in the use of language in an autobiographical text—a language into which a woman inscribes her self. Scientific language, English, Italian, and Piedmontese, and quotations from Yeats and Primo Levi are mixed together in Montalcini's book. *In Praise of Imperfection* is Rita Levi Montalcini's only nonscientific, fictional book, introduced by the author's elaboration of the concept of "imperfection." Yeats's statement on the poet's "perfection of the life, or of the work," is transformed into Montalcini's decision to privilege "the imperfection of the life and of the work."[77] Montalcini expresses the idea of the imperfection of the work as the modus operandi to reach the traditional "perfection," in her case the Nobel Prize for medicine, by describing the failures and setbacks in her career. The characters of mentors and assistants, friends and coworkers, dominate most of the autobiography. Rita Levi Montalcini's success is reflected in and shared among the people with whom she has collaborated throughout her career. The narrator disguises her "self" and her achievements amid the many figures from her past. She thus repeatedly privileges the technique of hiding her self in the characters of her personal past-present story.[78]

The narrator's metaphor of her search for a personal and professional "Ariadne's thread" is also the metaphor of the construction of a female self and new roles in the public and the private spheres. The autobiography begins with a dedication to her sister as well as to the father whom she has begun to love only after his death. Her autobiography is the thread that links her to paternal traces and allows her to accept her paternal heritage. In this context, Turin and its patriarchal society, which prevented women from acquiring the same education as men; World War I; fascism and the 1938 racial laws; World War II; and her postwar research in St. Louis can all find a proper location in Montalcini's narration of her private and public "lives." She introduces herself as a woman, a scientist, and a Jew and analyzes her life under fascism in the thirties and forties, when the doors of an academic career were closed to her because of her "Jewishness." In fact, after entering the public domain of scientific research, Rita Levi Montalcini is, because of the racial laws, expelled from the world she has come to know. She becomes segregated into a private realm and trapped in imposed roles that she can never accept. Expelled from the University of Turin, exiled from her city, and deprived of her name, which she has to replace with an Aryan family name, Montalcini continues her research in an improvised and tentative laboratory in her room in Florence.

In her final chapter, in an epilogue dedicated to Primo Levi, Montalcini comments on her struggle to continue her research within the familial sphere and her "imperfect" success in the public. Levi's comment on the role of the writer as "weak messenger," the carrier of only relative "truth," becomes the symbol of Montalcini's struggle to make her voice heard in a hostile, prejudiced, and racist public sphere.[79] Primo Levi is the last of the male characters to appear in *In Praise of Imperfection*. The narrator presents male figures as mentors and friends with whom she establishes relationships "governed by profound admiration and affection, which would not, however, influence in our search for our (Rita and her sister's) identities."[80] These scattered traces of positive paternal images allow Rita Levi Montalcini to reaccept the paternal heritage and to dedicate the literary construction of her self both to her sister and to the previously rejected father.

In *In Praise of Imperfection*, the narrator describes recent history up to 1986 and her winning the Nobel Prize. The student movement and 1968 also briefly appear in Rita Levi Montalcini's autobiography to describe the difficulty of scientific research in that "nihilistic" period. Those years and the following *anni di piombo* (lead years), the years of Terrorism in Italy, are the core of Luisa Passerini's autobiographical act and the focus of the fifth and final chapter of this book. In *Group Self-Portrait* (1988), the narrator attempts to write a group autobiography using interviews with the ex-leaders of the 1968 movement, pages from her personal diary from those years, and memories of her involvement in the political activities of the sixties. Passerini looks back on her involvement in the *movimento studentesco* (student movement) from the perspective of the psychoanalytic sessions that are narrated in her diary. In order to destroy the unchallenged superiority of the public sphere, Passerini experiments with the translation of the theory created in her role as an academic and historian into autobiographical practice. Her "personalization" of theory attempts to weaken the traditional movement from private to public, a one-way movement that allows women to acquire a relative "visibility." Passerini's critical approach to the public sphere reproblematizes the definition of women's roles even within the male transgressive movements of the sixties. In her autobiography, the public is gradually drawn into the private, since the initial project of creating a collective document as the mirror of an era is transformed into a personal autobiographical act where women's transgression is explored. Through memory, she creates a link between the present and that rebellious past. She looks back on the past from opposite points of view: both as a university professor and as a patient in therapy who reads her involvement in the historical past through her present personal loneliness and confusion. In her role as a university professor, she considers this autobiographical work as a creative parenthesis for which she almost apologizes. Her narrative creation of a self ends with a promise to the reader that the narrator will return to her learned publications enriched by well-researched notes. Passerini, therefore, re-presents an irreconcilable dichotomy between her public roles and the autobiographical creation of a self—a dichotomy that she is actively attempting to weaken now that she is approaching her autobiographical text from a critical point of view and is consequently writing about her own self-portrait.

Luisa Passerini begins her autobiography by considering it as a mirror that distorts the images from the past. This mirror is the reflection of her attempts to create a new role in the public and private realms and a new self that can freely float between the two spheres in search of a plastic intermediate space. Such space is inherent in her hybrid autobiography as the narration moves between historical events and personal crisis, between an initial firm belief in a woman's role in a Movement and later doubts about the risk of entrapment in a totally male-dominated ideology. *Group Self-Portrait* is a fragmented "story" in which the personal past is interwoven with the description of "public memory." The individual chapters demonstrate the narrator's desire to rewrite her personal past, to separate herself from the "parents" and declare herself an intellectual and ideological orphan. To reject traditional paternal and maternal traces is an act of transgression that allows Passerini to articulate, within an autobiographical context, her past and her present. It also makes it possible to invent acceptable maternal and paternal figures that are complementary to the female self that Passerini creates.

Passerini writes a woman's life and at the same time personalizes within an autobiographical text her theories of history in order to reconstruct the "history" that she has witnessed. This "theoretical plot," which is absent in the other autobiographies analyzed in this book, defines Passerini's original approach to her construction of a public and a private self, and weakens the separation between the theoretical and the personal. *Group Self-Portrait* is both the construction of personal "life/lines" and an analysis of how to read a woman's autobiography. It can be considered an attempt to answer Carolyn Heilbrun's question of "how to write a woman's life?" by redirecting the question into the plural as Passerini writes her lives, her changing identities, and claims the right to partake of all spheres.[81] Passerini creates an autobiographical act that contains both theory and practice; it is, in fact, the construction of a woman's self and the critical analysis of how to rewrite a woman's private story and transgressive roles in public history. The final part, however, entitled "Peonie," is a *Kammerspiel*, a private sonata in which Luisa Passerini expresses her impatience with public history as a sphere in which personal roles meet with limitations and where women's roles acquire boundaries that women cannot control.

In my study of Passerini's autobiography, I succeed only in problematizing even further the complex definition of public and private spheres and the creation of female selves in relation to new roles in both realms and in the hybrid space consequently created. Even Passerini's conscious attempt to construct a theory of autobiography within the narration of her subjectivity reveals the impossibility of finding definite and universal solutions for the construction of a woman's self. However, by reinterpreting history and inventing independent selves, Fausta Cialente, Rita Levi Montalcini, and Luisa Passerini succeed in displacing the privileged position of the public sphere within modernity. They create new definitions of female selves that are not trapped within a "space" in that sphere within a sphere, which I have named the *matroneum*. These women writers construct an intermediate sphere that partakes of both and becomes a new female realm created through a *métissage* of traces borrowed from the two oppositional, and traditional, "male" and "female" worlds. They also attempt to go beyond "modernity" by creating a fictional "floating" self, a hybrid creation that partakes of both paternal and maternal heritages in order to construct an alternative to oppositions.

I began this introductory chapter by quoting Judith Butler on "identity categories," a quotation taken from an essay in which Butler focuses on theories of lesbian identities. Her interest in the limitations of the constructions of identity categories is useful in concluding this section, in which I struggle with using and translating, from Italian into English, nouns and adjectives such as *female* and *feminine*. The issue is complicated by the fact that Italian *femminile* means both female and feminine. Butler states that "identity categories tend to be instruments of regulatory regimes, whether as the normalizing categories of oppressive structures or as the rallying points of a liberatory contestation of that very oppression."[82] In the same vein, I define the social construction of femininity as a category that contains a long tradition of essentialist definitions about women (i.e., Woman) and as the ground that breeds both homologation and resistance to the same. By privileging the distance of some autobiographical "I" from any enforced models of femininity, I will describe the separation between autobiographical constructions of subjectivity and the overcodified concept of femininity that they had to resist. I suggest that the consent created is not to femininity but rather to a revisionary fragmentation into women's identities and female subjectivities. Problems arise in an autobiographical context (such as Enif Robert's book) in which resistance to femininity is combined with an incorporation of its construction so that transgression and regression become inseparable. It is Teresa de Lauretis who, in defining the limitations of the concept of "sexual difference," calls for the exploration of a "subject, therefore, not unified but rather multiple, and not so much divided as contradicted [or contradictory, in Robert's case]."[83] The point that I am trying to make is that by rejecting the use of the "feminine" and of "femininity" in my critical approach to women's construction of their selves, I concentrate on *a* woman's identity or *a female* subjectivity in order to "articulate the differences of women from Woman, that is to say, the differences among women or, perhaps more exactly, the differences *within women*."[84]

I do not attempt to deny that the social constructions and representations of gender have an influence in the articulation of individual subjectivities; as Althusser reminds us, the subject is "interpellated" or "recruited" by ideology.[85] De Lauretis claims that feminism is the location outside the place of ideology; a location "from where ideology can be seen for what it is."[86] The women autobiographers studied in this book seem to claim a different position as they speak outside feminism, presenting statements that could be labeled as feminist, but at the same time appropriating a place for themselves at a distance from the representations of Woman they have inherited. They create metaphors of their hybrid selves and end up exposing the tensions and anxieties inherent in representing their identities. They set out to revise rules about gender, rules to which their mothers subscribed and by which they have been, are, and will be influenced. In fact, Cialente, Montalcini, and Passerini reveal the acts of mediation necessary to construct disparate genealogies that link the *matroneum* to the public models they embody. Teresa de Lauretis eloquently summarizes the problematic relationships of woman's positions vis-à-vis ideology:

> The discrepancy, the tension, and the constant slippage between Woman as representation, as the object and the very condition of representation, and, on the other hand, women as historical beings, subjects of "real relations," are

motivated and sustained by a logical contradiction in our culture and an irreconcilable one: women are both inside and outside gender, at once within and without representation.[87]

In concentrating on the characteristics of female identities and gendered selves and on the articulation of alternative choices within language to represent women's selves, I will focus on women's positions in the construction of genealogies based on connecting paternal and maternal traces, inside and outside of the historical contexts in which a few women shape their public identities (I stress the plural ending of this noun).

CHAPTER ONE

Camilla Faà Gonzaga

Public and Private in a Woman's Autobiography

Camillae Catharinae Gonzagae Fae Marchionissae
incostanti fato Mantuae ducissae
mox Sanctae Clarae habitu inductae
omnium virtutum exemplum mortalibus
ac demum inter haec moeenia se praebenti
adversamque fortunam pari animo sustinenti.
EPITAPH ON CAMILLA FAÀ GONZAGA'S TOMB

Camilla Faà Gonzaga's *Historia* (1622), as it is called in Fernanda Bonfà's book containing its transcription, is a short memoir that has not interested many literary critics but has inspired the imagination of writers, poets, and playwrights who throughout the centuries have created romanticized versions of her life.[1] Her writing style does not directly inspire such creativity: her goal in writing her life is to create a "historical" account of "facts" that can be considered as a defense against the accusations of the powerful people of the time. She is aware that "the position of women was fundamentally presupposed as one which excluded them from the public sphere of political, juridical and historical action."[2] Her memoir is an act of transgression: a skillful rewriting of the history of Duke Ferdinando Gonzaga's mishandling of his marriage to Camilla, and a way to represent her self, otherwise excluded from the public sphere of the court.[3] In her article "Re-Membering the 'I': Faà Gonzaga's *Storia*

(1622)," Valeria Finucci investigates the genre chosen by Camilla Faà Gonzaga as the literary "space" in which she inscribes her life:

> A memoir is the re-process of a past, which authors summon back more or less chronologically with the intent of authenticating themselves or of correcting negative perceptions of their persons and deeds. Having the format of an apology, of an involuntary and yet necessary self-presentation (or rather, self-restoration), the memoir as literary form naturally appeals to feminine discourse. More than autobiographies, in fact, memoirs match women's desire for reserve and reticence.[4]

To talk, but at the same time, not to say too much, is more than a woman's desire; it expresses the need to create a document that is only indirectly controversial, a work that invades the literary space crowded by metaphors of male selves, but that at the same time negates such an action. Camilla Faà Gonzaga struggles to become visible in and with her text while, at the same time, she constructs a superficial invisibility of her "feminine" literary effort in a world of "major" literary works.

Franco Fido, in his article subtitled "The *Topoi* of the Self," argues that a unitary autobiographical tradition has its roots in the eighteenth and nineteenth centuries. His notion of such a tradition, however, appears to be codified primarily through an analysis of male autobiographies.[5] He states that "the period of legitimation and codification of the autobiographical genre opens around 1720–30, and comes to a close around 1820–40, with a climax ... between Rousseau's *Confessions* and the French revolution."[6] In this chapter, I shift critical attention to a fringe of autobiographical writing that predates the birth of the genre as it is described by Fido. Camilla Faà Gonzaga wrote her memoir about a century before the "birth of a unitarian tradition."[7] In my study of her autobiographical text, I intend to problematize the definition of a unitary tradition. I am neither attempting to establish a female tradition separate from the male autobiographical writings nor searching for a fictional creation in autobiography of a universal female identity that has its roots in this first autobiography. I will stress, however, that even in this first work, a woman is attempting to rewrite both the private and the public spheres with which she has come in contact. Camilla Faà Gonzaga, like many later women autobiographers, aims to create a fictional self that is allowed to occupy a "space" in both spheres, a space different from that constructed by men in power. My decision to privilege this autobiographical narrative was prompted by reading the 1986 volume of *Annali d'Italianistica* dedicated to autobiography, in which Fido's article appears. The preponderant absence of articles on Italian women's autobiographies is striking (the only article on a woman writer is devoted to Sibilla Aleramo)[8] and reveals the need to focus on the scattered traces of autobiographical writings that are not included in the official construction of a unitary tradition.

Camilla Faà Gonzaga supplies a document that acquires a disruptive function in the linear construction of the dominant discourse on history. In her book *Revising Memory,* Faith Beasley investigates women's attempts to rewrite history by transforming it into "herstory."[9] Writing about a seventeenth-century woman writer, Montpensier, Beasley argues: "In the process of transcribing her experience, she [Montpensier] revises both the content and the form of history, weaving her political and personal achievements into an account that both celebrates the inscription of women into history and changes the very fabric of history itself."[10] Like Montpensier, Camilla Faà Gonzaga translates her experience into a written document that revises historical accounts and also creates a transgressive version of her life. Her parallel story, however, was never allowed to reach the public sphere, remaining hidden within the walls of a cloister. Only through today's discussion of her work can her text reveal its potentially disruptive function and become a means to "change the very fabric of history itself."

Faà Gonzaga's memoir can be easily summarized. It contains the story of the destruction of a sixteen-year-old's belief in fairy tales. The text of Camilla's adventurous life consists of a sixteen-page narrative, which has been treated as historical documentation rather than as fictional creation, or as the metaphor of a self. Camilla Faà Gonzaga, in fact, structures the narrative as a historical treatise in which facts are narrated in chronological sequence. She writes about her betrothal to a nobleman, Ottavio Valenti Cavaggioli. This marriage never takes place, because Ferdinando Gonzaga, the duke of Mantua himself, decides to marry Camilla. The wedding with the duke is performed privately by a bishop, who is later among the first to pronounce the marriage invalid.[11] Ferdinando, in fact, needs to create a new alliance with his powerful neighbors and therefore wants to marry Caterina de' Medici. Camilla is exiled, and the new wedding is celebrated. She, on the other hand, refuses to remarry and repeatedly states the validity of her marriage vows to Ferdinando, a marriage never officially annulled by the church. Camilla must accept, however, the only alternative to remarrying: she retires to a convent in Ferrara and thus leaves her son with Ferdinando and his new wife. From her cloistered dwellings she witnesses the deaths of her husband and her son, and the end of the Italian branch of the Gonzaga dynasty.

In her writing, Camilla Faà Gonzaga struggles to create an identity that deviates from the portrayal of the secondary role of women in history presented by biographers and writers. She does not hide her subjectivity in a narrative centered on the public figure of the duke; rather, she constructs her character as protagonist of a story that recounts her private life, the role of the duke in it, and her attempt to enter the public sphere in her rightful position as duchess. However, at the beginning of her life story, Camilla Faà Gonzaga portrays herself as a young girl obediently following her father's wish to marry her to a peer nobleman. Her mother is never mentioned, as later Camilla's role as a mother is treated as only another component of the contentions with the duke. In covering her transformation from private woman to semipublic duchess, Camilla's descriptions of the spaces she inhabits do not include the familial sphere. Her father and brothers are not often her supporters: they comply with the ruler's design over Camilla's life and only pose nominal resistance to Ferdinando's manipulations. Her first person narrative reveals the constant presence of Man, who plays the part of a *deus ex machina* in the construction of her destiny: whether of the father, who controls his acquiescent daughter, or of the duke, who manipulates her personal life, she is the object exchanged from the *padre* to the *padrone*. Ferdinando, in fact, does not allow Camilla to marry her betrothed and proposes to her.

Faà soon destroys the initial portrayal of herself as a complacent victim of male desire and replaces her "objective" description of facts with direct quotations of her replies to the duke's proposal:

> I laughed, thinking that for sure he was saying these things jokingly and in order to find out whether I could be easily duped. Therefore, I answered: "Sir, it would be a great favor for me simply to serve Your Highness's wife. I take your words as being said to while away this hour of dance because, thank God, I have brain enough to know I have no such merits to raise myself to those high ranks." He replied with many other things and the dance ended.[12]

She represents a man's whim and a woman's rationality in an oppositional structure in which Camilla appears superior to the capricious duke. In the construction of her subjectivity, the writer is rethinking and rewriting her role; it is a fictional creation that allows the writer to reinvent her relationship with the duke and transform her self into the protagonist of "her own story." Camilla, a very young lady-in-waiting, is officially employed by the Gonzaga family as lady companion for the duchess, a role rewarded with a monthly wage of "lire 20."[13] The death of Mantua's fifth duke, Francesco Gonzaga, deprives her of the position. Subsequently, Ferdinando, Francesco's brother, leaves his position as a cardinal to become the new duke. He rehires the ladies-in-waiting who had left to follow the ex-duchess. The setting seems ready for the performance of a fairy tale, which is disrupted by the *raison d'état*. The description of Ferdinando's courtship to Camilla marks the turning point of this narrative: Ferdinando, the public man and powerful duke, transforms the ballroom into a privileged space in which Camilla's private and public roles can be reshaped in order to fulfill the duke's desires. Whether or not Ferdinando proposed during a dance, Faà chooses the ballroom as the place where Ferdinando declares his desire to marry Camilla. The choice of such a place is emblematic—the metaphor of Camilla's role in the court. Her subsequent hybrid role as unofficial wife of the duke is already reflected in the semiprivate and semipublic ballroom where her private and public identities are being reshaped. In fact, after their secret marriage, Camilla finds herself in a new semiofficial status created by the duke, trapped in an intermediate sphere in which she defines herself as "treated very differently from all other court ladies."[14] She becomes a mother in the private sphere and an unacceptable guest in the public realm, because her son is not intended to become Ferdinando's successor. In Camilla Faà Gonzaga's memoir, the tension between characters who represent public and private becomes the real protagonist of her retrospective narrative. She insists in clearly defining her roles in the private and public spheres in order to present "her" version of her "life" in relation to the historical events of the time. At the same time, she also supplies a personal rereading of a public man, the duke, and of his control of the space that she inhabits.

Ferdinando, in fact, often changes his mind. He even tries to withdraw his proposal because he wants to have her "as his lover rather than his wife" and Camilla responds:

> When I realized this, I defended myself and said words full of resentment. He answered that he did not want to die because of me. . . . Also I had to remember that I was in his house, and I should not disparage his sense of decency (moderation) because were he to fancy otherwise, he would change his way of acting toward me as well. . . .
> I replied: "Sir, Your Highness should believe me when I say that no man ever died for love, and you will not either."[15]

She must remember that she is not only in his employment but also in his *domus,* his home, his land. Both in his public and private domains, Camilla can only be an honorary guest. The duke alternates terms of endearment with threats until he, as a public man, is certain that he has discovered the correct reason for Camilla's constant rejections. Her reluctance to become his mistress appears to him motivated by a woman's awareness of her sec-

ondary role in a family. Therefore, he understands that Camilla will not dare
to bring disgrace to her father's name. In her narrative, Camilla strives to destroy the duke's character in his role of epistemological hero. Woman is, for
Ferdinando, a predictable text that he can easily read. Camilla's words, however, disrupt his interpretation and unsettle the discourse on women's behavior constructed by the duke. She refuses the subordinate role, as daughter of a respectable man, in which the duke has placed her identity and her
desires, and she worries "only about *my* soul and my reputation" (emphasis
added).[16] Her transgressions, however, are only temporary. The sixteen-year-
old girl is aware that, as she is being denied the possibility of marriage, the
alternative left between *maritar o monacar* is to become a nun, although, she
argues, "to that I had never been inclined."[17]

Fernanda Sorbelli Bonfà, in her 1918 book, comments on Camilla's role in
history: "Her name recurs in almost all the stories that narrate the events in
the dukedoms of Mantua and Monferrato. . . . Another book about her
would seem useless; moreover, she has left a short autobiographical tale of
her pitiful circumstances, pages that are devoid of any artistic quality, but
they are rather moving."[18] Camilla's memoir, labeled as aesthetically deficient,
is, according to Bonfà, a moving female story of private unhappiness. While
describing Faà's memoir as an inferior literary work, most critics have ignored the innovative structure of her autobiographical text as a retrospective narrative in prose, the fictional creation of a metaphor of self and of history. Until now, Beasley writes, "the relationship between women writers
and . . . [their] works at the intersection of history and fiction has remained
obscure."[19] At this "intersection," Camilla Faà Gonzaga's memoir represents
the first attempt in prose to make a woman's life and "herstory" visible
through the discrepancies that separate it from the official chronicles of the
time. In this context, the title of her memoir, "Historia della Sig.ra Donna
Camilla Faà Gonzaga," becomes emblematic both of her revision of history
and of the assumption of her "self" as subject of her narrative.

This short autobiographical work contains an explicit description of a
woman's journey through different roles, totally controlled by the Public
Man, or *Padrone* (Lord and Master), as she calls the duke. Ferdinando, in
fact, changes his mind again and decides to marry Camilla to prevent her
from entering the convent. She, however, becomes his wife in the private
sphere only; the duke states that he cannot "pubblicarla per moglie" (make
her public as his wife).[20] In his conversation with Camilla's father in which
he refuses to "make his wife public," the duke stresses the power that he has
over the malleable public and private identity of his "unpublished" wife.

Woman is, for Ferdinando, an owned text, kept in an enclosed space, to which only he has access. She must, therefore, remain an "unpublished" text, preserved on an "island" in the private sphere that is totally "his-land." Camilla is a private text, a text not to be published because it is designed to satisfy the needs of the duke, needs that have no space for fulfillment in the public sphere of the court. Camilla becomes, in fact, the receptacle that receives Ferdinando's poor poetic efforts, his letters of eternal devotion—in short, his dream of a life separated from his political/public duties and his role as duke. Ferdinando's bride, however, refuses to become the main object in his overcodified text of her life and becomes a reader of it. By rereading and revising the identity created for her by Ferdinando, Camilla can attempt to create a new text, which allows her to survive as subject in a narrative, that is, to "make herself public" and to have her life published.

With the expression "to make a wife public," Ferdinando reveals his decision to create rigid boundaries to the spheres to which Camilla can gain access. Faà frequently describes Camilla's isolation in a limited domain: "I asked him permission to go to Monferrato, to my brothers' house. I obtained it with great difficulty. . . . I stayed there for a few weeks . . . a courier arrived, sent by His Highness . . . he wrote in his hand that I had to leave immediately for Casale. . . . The time came to give birth, and Don Giacinto was born."[21] Camilla is not allowed any influence in the construction of her roles even in the limited corner of the domestic realm. The duke creates a vacuum around her in order to control her potentially disruptive existence, which could endanger the status quo. She gives birth while she is "exiled" from the court and lives at a location chosen by Ferdinando. In this context, the unofficial duchess has no control of her role as mother. In fact, the duke further limits her "space" in the private sphere by depriving Camilla of her son and by enclosing her in a convent. Even while describing her short stay at the court of Mantova, Faà underscores her carefully designed role in the court by affirming: "I was not in the position of a duchess."[22] Before June, 1616, Ferdinando had given her the Marchesato del Mombaruzzo as a present, but she was never allowed publicly to become a Marchioness nor to exercise her power as such. Ferdinando is adamant in keeping Camilla in her unofficial role; in fact while seriously ill and considering himself close to death, he states to a few faithful friends: "This woman should be recognized as my wife by all of you. However, do not refer to the matter openly, because I do not want it publicized."[23] Ferdinando recovers and proceeds with his plans to marry Caterina de' Medici.

If the term matroneum signifies a limited space within the private sphere where women are enclosed and controlled, Camilla seems to inhabit an empty *matroneum*. Faà portrays Camilla as a woman isolated from any community of women and deprived of any influence over her life. Without naming it a *matroneum*, Diane Bornstein supplies a parallel definition of the female sphere of influence in the private realm: "This sphere of influence, or space, was defined so as to maintain the patriarchal family structure, with all the power in the hands of the men, but with women acting as useful servants within that structure."[24] Bornstein also defines the difference between male and female roles in the private sphere(s): while women may have "influence" in the *matroneum*, men have the monopoly of power. A woman's private domain is paradoxically not private as it can be directly manipulated from the outside, and women's influence cannot change the boundaries of their limited sphere within a sphere. Such boundaries are indeed flexible; changes in society modify the "shape" of the *matroneum*. It is not, however, women's changing needs that can alter the relationship between *matroneum*, private, and public spheres. In her article "Some Thoughts on Public and Private Spheres," Gaye Tuchman states:

> Today when over a third of women with pre-school children and over fifty-seven percent of all American women work for pay outside the home, it seems foolish to identify women with the domestic sphere. Rather, they are people with two jobs, people who moonlight at housework even as they claim to seek pay to buy necessities which the family prefers to identify as luxuries. (Asked why they work, most women reply that their husband's income supports the family and they are providing income for luxuries or to send their children to a better school).[25]

Tuchman's observations allow us to wonder whether those women are really occupying a role in the public sphere or rather whether they are still entrapped in a *matroneum* whose boundaries have been extended beyond the private sphere but are still controlled by patriarchy. A woman's work in the public sphere is acceptable provided that it is defined as expendable. Consequently, women become "honorary" but temporary guests in the public sphere. Camilla's short appearance in the public world of the court is similarly reenacted but in a different socioeconomic context. Camilla Faà Gonzaga's experience of entrapment echoes throughout the centuries and appears reelaborated in later women's autobiographies.

Faà narrates her gradual entrapment in different domains, which brings her to a *mise en abîme* of progressively more confining roles and enclosed spaces. At the beginning of the narrative, she defines herself as the daughter of a count and as a lady-in-waiting at the Mantua court. Her double role

becomes more codified once she becomes the wife of the duke, who transforms her into the silent victim of his political plans. The boundaries of the
locus that she inhabits rapidly change in order to increase her "degree of
invisibility" in the public sphere. Camilla must leave the court and abandon
her status as "unofficial" duchess in order to adopt, for a short time, the private role of mother. In 1617, only one year after his wedding with Camilla,
Ferdinando marries Caterina and orders Camilla to return to Mantua, where
he will find a new husband for her. She is adamant in her refusal to remarry
and in her belief in the validity of her vows to the duke. She is also aware of
his power over her person and obeys, while eloquently voicing her disagree-
ment: "No matter what I said or did, however, I had to go, thus ordered with
private letters, as I said, by all the masters [and lords]."[26] To speak and to act
from within the isolated *matroneum,* in which she has been exiled, has no
effect against the orders from the public sphere. Once again, Camilla must
decide between *maritar o monacar,* and she chooses the latter.

It is from the confining room in the convent that Camilla Faà Gonzaga
attempts to break the silence with her autobiographical act.[27] The narrative
is structured as an official document that reflects "strong historical truths."
Camilla Faà Gonzaga mimics the way official history is constructed, yet she
scatters her gathering of facts with historical "mistakes." Historians such as
Fernanda Sorbelli Bonfà have dedicated most of their work to bringing to
light Camilla Faà Gonzaga's imprecise narration of historical facts.[28] However, the narrative of her metaphor of truth is interesting because of, rather
than in spite of, these moments of "rupture," of historical untruthfulness: the
author rearranges dates and facts and changes the names of people who witnessed her secret wedding.

She mimics the dominant portrayal of history in her attempt to keep her
historical narrative plausible, while rearranging the chronological and factual order of herstory. The author is deliberately purloining history and her
private story in an autobiographical document created to take the place of
another official paper of which she has been deprived.[29] Ferdinando had, in
fact, written a declaration in which he pronounced Camilla his rightful wife:

> His Highness went to Florence and those very serene people entreated him to
> recover from me the marriage pact mentioned above. However, either because
> he did not know how to get it back from me or because he did not want to
> upset me further, he neither wrote about it nor had others mention it to me. I
> heard that, in order to achieve his purpose, he made a similar one and presented
> it there, swearing that it was the one recovered from me. He then married
> Madama Caterina de Medici and brought her to Mantua.[30]

Camilla is purloining what, she says, the duke has already purloined. If the official documents are false, then the representation of her "self" in the public sphere is also "false": "I heard that they sent a document to Rome with my signature. It must be counterfeited, since I never undersigned any document."[31] The obsessive repetition of "sottoscrissi" (subscribe/undersign), "sotto-scrizione" (subscription/undersigning), "scrittura" (written text/document) creates the image of "writing" as an act of forgery defined by the adjective *falsa* (false/counterfeited). Camilla Faà Gonzaga appropriates history and exposes the fallacy of historical truth in order to recreate her story and attempt to render ineffectual the official historical discourse on her identity and roles. She wants to prove that both the new marriage with Caterina de' Medici, officially accepted in the public sphere, and the future of the Gonzaga family are based on a forged document. Whether it was really forged or Camilla pretends that it was is less important than the fact that the autobiographer constructs a gendered practice of historiography in which patriarchal history is portrayed as an entity signified by the plausible lies that men have created.

Writing her life and constructing her fictional identity are acts of transgression of the duke's orders. Such transgression becomes evident if seen in light of the description of women's worth in another sixteenth-century female text. In one of the letters, entitled "Del nascimento delle donne" (About the Birth of Women), Isabella Canali Andreini describes the epitome of femininity engendered by patriarchy:

> The patient women are content with living under that subjection, a subjection under which they are born to lead a modest and orderly life. They are content with having the narrow confines of the house as their sweet prison; they enjoy the continuous servitude. It is not a burden for them to be subjected to the severe will of others. They do not mind always being fearful. And when the knowledge of human things is granted to them by the passing years, just like women who have felt modest and respectful since their birth, they do not dare to turn their eyes on anything until they have permission from those who take care of them.[32]

This ironical praise of women stresses their imprisonment by creating the oxymoronic sweet prisons and the enjoyable servitude. It also supplies the definition of Camilla's transgression, which lies in her act of "turning her eyes" on history, without the duke's permission, in order to transform it into a different story. She substitutes a female gaze for the male gaze, which has monopolized the translation of the public sphere into official documentation. Ferdinando, instead, wanted her to remarry, to enclose Camilla in the *matroneum* of a private sphere that another man could totally control. It is after unsuccessfully attempting to disobey orders that Camilla breaks the silence and reflects her "self" in the distorting mirror of her memoir.

Natalia Costa Zalessow idealizes Camilla's life in the convent by constructing a new version of her decision to write her life story.[33] According to Costa Zalessow, the Mother Superior of the convent of Corpus Domini in Ferrara encouraged Camilla in her literary effort. Ideal as it might seem, such friendship is hard to prove. In her autobiographical text, Camilla Faà Gonzaga does not narrate her life in the convent; the story is interrupted with the description of her entrance into the Order. Other women, however, are mentioned as key characters in the construction of her life. The ever powerful Madama di Ferrara, Ferdinando's aunt, the queen of France, and Caterina de' Medici represent threatening figures of women in the public sphere who are accomplices in the male plot to isolate and to silence Camilla's voice. Her description of such women in the public realm creates a dichotomous construction of womanhood: on one end, woman as prisoner and victim and, on the other, woman as perpetrator of patriarchal oppression. In fact, Caterina de' Medici Gonzaga complains about Camilla's "evil nature" and her constant requests for money.[34]

A monthly sum is granted to her by the duke. Such a sum allows her to acquire a privileged position among the nuns. The humble tone of the letters in which she thanks both the duke and his wife is very different from the proud statements about the "truth" that are found in her memoir. In a letter dated June 16, 1622, she thanks the duke for his protection and assures him that she is praying for him and that "she will not forget to do so while she is alive."[35] She is thanking him for allowing her to see her son, who arrived at the cloister carrying a present from the duke. Only three years later, she will be allowed to see her son again. In 1626, the thirty-nine-year-old Ferdinando dies. In 1630, Giacinto, Camilla's son, dies during a plague epidemic. Camilla is left destitute and begins writing letters asking for money: a sum is granted by the duke of Nevers, but is later suspended. She resigns herself to living as a nun in the cloister and abandons even her letter writing many years before her death in 1662.

Ferdinando's two wives acquire very different roles after his death: Camilla is forgotten in the cloister and Caterina becomes the ruler of Siena. However, Camilla supplies the final twist to both their life stories: she seems determined not to accept her destiny as just another woman forced to take vows.[36] She renames herself in the convent and becomes "Suor Caterina Camilla." She adopts Ferdinando's second wife's name and publicly becomes

Caterina (Camilla Faà) Gonzaga, a mirror image of the "other" wife, and therefore proclaims her identity as Ferdinando's wife, as the rightful duchess.[37] She creates her final identity, her renamed body, as a segue to the text of her life, which ends with the description of her isolation within the silencing walls of the convent.[38] In her article entitled "What's in a Name? Self-Naming and Renaissance Women Poets," Fiora Bassanese begins her argument by stating that "in the Judeo-Christian tradition, the act of naming has always carried implications of power. To name is to master."[39] By renaming herself, Faà once more mocks imposed rules and, even in her defeat, attempts to be self-affirming and to challenge the duke's power. In this case, the conventual life requires the sacrifice of her worldly (and even "wordly") identity, which must be replaced by a religious name signifying her resignation to her new life. Camilla, instead, links herself very firmly to her past by strengthening through her new name her relationship to the duke. At the same time, she confirms that convents are far from being "havens from the world."[40] She conveys an example of what Elissa Weaver calls "the abiding attachment of convent women of the 16th to 18th centuries precisely to the secular world."[41]

By breaking the silence, Camilla Faà Gonzaga attempted to gain "authority" in the dominant discourse on History. She is again easily silenced, because her writings composed in the enclosed walls of the convent had no echo in the public sphere. Her memoir was published for the first time in the nineteenth century and again in 1918. Faà's transgressive voice is made weaker in the construction of a historical narrative, in which voices that are parallel but different from the dominant discourse become marginalized. Camilla Faà Gonzaga is aware of the "weakness" of her voice in relation to the "strong narratives" that men can create. She even justifies her decision to write her own life by apologizing for her "disruptive act":

> This is the tale of my unhappy tragedy. I beg to be forgiven for my mistakes
> and failings and please understand my desire to obey those who can order me.
> I beseech also to consent graciously that this writing not be shown, because
> it deals with known people and truth often generates hate. Moreover I would
> not want my ignorance to be mocked.[42]

She ironically labels her narrative a stereotypical "feminine" narrative dominated by "mistakes" that a weak female intellect cannot avoid, while at the same time she repeatedly declares the power of her words. After proclaiming throughout the autobiographical act her identity as the real duchess, Camilla Faà Gonzaga concludes her memoir by hiding behind the screen of her "readiness to obey." Her show of modesty, by contrast, has the effect of attracting the reader's attention to the shift between her proud statements and the rapid apologetic ending. The author is aware of the potentially powerful impact that her words could have outside the private sphere. Her consciousness of the power of both the written word and the tale of her life is translated in her memoir, but it is hidden behind the humble assertion of her ignorance and of her work's literary limitations. These rhetorical moves are not at all unique to her auto-biographical text. Franco Fido reminds us that the "topos of modesty" commonly recurs in the official autobiographical tradition:

> We have the introductory, or meta-autobiographical *topos*, which consists in justifying the very decision of writing one's life in order to avoid accusations of presumption and vanity. Roughly outlined, the author's reasoning unfolds as follows: If some day someone were to write my life, would it not be preferable to have this life's account written by myself?[43]

Camilla Faà Gonzaga's justification of her writing, however, differs slightly from the *topos* described by Fido. Her presumption is reflected in her attempt to construct a female self who becomes the subject of her story and of public history. Roughly outlined, the woman's reasoning unfolds as follows: If someday someone were to write my life, it would only be in order to create a secondary character in a historical narrative dominated by the public figure of the duke. Furthermore, this someone would be a man in search of "strong" truths, a realm to which a woman's voice does not belong. Would it not be interesting to have this account of a "weaker" truth, a woman's truth, and a potentially disruptive truth?

Faà concludes her memoir with an apology for her daring act. Her literary voice is not heard again, as her life story is her only contribution to the world of letters. The importance of her work lies in her attempt to rethink and disrupt, by rewriting, the rigid structures of the two spheres in which she had marginal roles. This first autobiographical text in prose also poses important questions about the relationship between female independent selves and feminine roles defined by the patriarchy. Some of the questions asked by Camilla Faà Gonzaga are also present in another testimony written in the seventeenth century, by Cecilia Ferrazzi, whose autobiographical text has been recently published with the title *Autobiografia di una santa mancata* (Autobiography of a Failed Saint).[44] Ferrazzi's work is complementary in many ways to Camilla Faà Gonzaga's memoir and offers another example of a seventeenth-century woman's attempt to invade the public sphere by establishing a transgressing role for herself. Since she is forced into the convent, Camilla is prevented from acquiring an active role in the public realm. Cecilia Ferrazzi succeeds in becoming an active and "undesirable" member of a male public sphere while attempting to modify it. My brief discussion of Ferrazzi's defense of her self cannot do justice to her work, but I want to illustrate another attempt to create female roles as alternatives to both convent and married life.

Ferrazzi begins to write her life in 1664 while she is on trial, accused of "simulation of sanctity." The Venetian inquisition, however, allows her to hire a man who can transcribe her story, because she cannot write. Cecilia Ferrazzi, for "pretending to be a saint," is finally sentenced to seven years in prison. Like Faà's memoir, Ferrazzi's autobiography is written as a document for a reading public who, in this case, are the judges and the inquisitors. Consequently, Ferrazzi structures the construction of her self as an apparently humble defense in which Cecilia justifies her life. She is a very religious woman who, faced with the choice between *maritar o monacar*, refuses both to marry and to become a nun.[45] In her autobiography, Ferrazzi creates a fictional female identity that escapes from the limitations imposed on women by the public religious institutions of the time. Cecilia, in fact, construes a direct relationship with God, the Virgin Mary, and the saints who appear in her visions. She also rejects the status quo in which men have the absolute power to define and reward sanctity.

Her greatest fault is, therefore, her refusal to belong to the controllable institutions constructed by men and designed for women. Cecilia Ferrazzi not only does not need a man's mediation to create a relationship with the divinity, but she also formulates an alternative to the dichotomy in women's choices, limited to marriage or to the convent. Ferrazzi founds a house for women, whom she calls *putte pericolanti* (girls in danger), a place otherwise identified as a *seminario delle vergini di Venezia* (seminary of the virgins of Venice). Such an independent initiative was designed to supply women with a temporary alternative to *maritar, monacar,* or even prostitution.[46] Elissa Weaver argues that "women's religious houses thus provided the important social service of protecting the honor of marriageable girls, educating them to some extent."[47] Ferrazzi threatens the regular convents' monopoly over the souls and the bodies of young women, refusing any interference from external controlling agents.

Ferrazzi's tale of her life, which constantly reveals her faith in God, also allows the reader to understand Cecilia's faith in her right to modify what men have created in the name of God. In relating the visions that she had as a child, Ferrazzi states: "I heard a voice from within myself that spoke to me:

'Cecilia, you were born to obey and trust in God's will, but it is up to you to dictate to my dear Son.'"[48] To obey, but at the same time to make others obey, is the message that Cecilia receives from the Virgin Mary, who is frequently heard as a guiding voice "from within." What Ferrazzi is attempting to establish is a dialogue between "women" that connects the Virgin Mary, herself, and the women who live in her "seminary." A discourse such as this, which turns Cecilia into the "executor" of a Woman's words and orders, creates a female hierarchical (gynealogical, in a transcendental sort of way) structure that opposes the traditional religious orders and male spheres of influence. The Virgin, in fact, prevents Cecilia from cutting her hair and from joining a convent, that is, an environment for women, controlled and regulated by men's laws. It is again the Virgin who gives Cecilia gold jewelry to wear when the father confessor preaches humiliation of the (female) flesh and condemns women's care for their bodies.[49] The apparitions described by Cecilia Ferrazzi reveal the Madonna as a woman who prevents another woman from isolating herself within the confining walls of a convent and from negating her femininity. The Virgin's maternal order to obey and to create a law to be obeyed by others (i.e., men), is carried out by Cecilia, who struggles to construct a female space which Man's "law" can barely reach. In fact, she often replaces the father confessors, who are disappointing and petty individuals, searching for power within her domain.[50]

Cecilia Ferrazzi's humble tone in the construction of her life only superficially hides her awareness of the value of her achievements. Camilla Faà Gonzaga's and Cecilia Ferrazzi's "meek" voices create female identities who do not appear to constitute a threat to the powerful male voice that can allow and forbid. However, their humble tone also allows them to create a space within literature where their voices are not destroyed, but rather are preserved as "modest" and "inferior" examples of women's literary efforts. For both Ferrazzi and Faà, to inhabit the space of marginality means to experiment with the "topos of modesty" used as a malleable signifier that hides a contrasting signified.

Whereas Camilla unsuccessfully strives to enter the public sphere, Cecilia is punished for constructing an independent identity within the public realm of religious institutions. It comes as no surprise that this autobiography did not help Cecilia Ferrazzi's cause in front of the inquisition; in fact, she was sentenced to seven years in prison. This sentence was, however, revoked in the appeal trial in Rome where, thanks to the intervention of the Venetian *doge*, Cecilia was set free in 1669. The document of her life remains Cecilia

Ferrazzi's only contribution to the world of letters; between 1669 and 1684, the year of her death, Cecilia lived in silence and isolation.

Both Camilla Faà Gonzaga's and Cecilia Ferrazzi's autobiographical acts are distorted mirrors of women's identities, and are followed by silence. Their voices disappear as they are suffocated by the socioeconomic and political context of their century. In their narratives, both Faà and Ferrazzi search, in different ways, for new identities by evading the assigned feminine roles: Ferrazzi can translate her transgression into practice, while Faà can only escape into her autobiographical writing. To leave the private behind and to become visible in the male public realm is their agenda. This one-way movement from the private to the public becomes problematic, however, because it inevitably reinforces the portrayal of the superiority of roles in the public. Such an approach to "spheres" represents the male public realm as the dimension to which one must aspire and in which women must adapt. These writers' attempts to define the positions they want to acquire in the public is not accompanied by a reinterpretation of the private. What is missing in this context is an attempt to construct a "dialectic" of private and public involving a destruction of the dichotomized portrayal of the two realms. Faà's and Ferrazzi's experimentation with an intermediate and hybrid "space of literature," intended as the realm where a woman can write private stories and rewrite public history, merely suggests the beginning of an alternative approach to both spheres. The problem for a woman writer, however, is how to construct a dialectic of public and private in texts and how to shape the "space of literature" as a realm in which public history and autobiographical stories can meet as equals. Such questions, which cannot have a simple or unitary solution, are resolved in fragmented answers within different women's autobiographical acts in the twentieth century.

CHAPTER TWO

Speaking through Her Body

The Futurist Seduction of a Woman's Voice[1]

Hysteria is no longer a question of the wandering womb;
it is a question of the wandering story, and whether that story belongs
to the hysteric, the doctor, the historian or the critic.
ELAINE SHOWALTER[2]

Camilla Faà Gonzaga's and Cecilia Ferrazzi's autobiographical acts contain isolated testimonies of female identities, framed by silence. Their strategies of self-representation have to come to terms with the fact that the surfacing of female voices remains, in their time, an exception. In the context of Italian feminist theory, Adriana Cavarero grounds her work on women's past on an exploration of individual figures that emerged as authoritative identities in philosophy and literary imagination. It is an attempt not to trace women's history of self-representation but to interpret Penelope, Demeter, and Diotima "in spite of Plato"—a strategy that she turns into the title of her book: *Nonostante Platone* (In Spite of Plato) (1990). Plato's interest in the possible participation of women in the symposium can be useful in introducing this chapter devoted to the discussion of an individual female voice within a literary movement: futurism. In his *Laws*, Plato discusses women's absence from the symposium; he concludes that it would require an act of force to make them take food in public because they are "habituated in a retired, indoor way of life."[3] Furthermore, women "wouldn't tolerate the utterance of the correct argument without much screaming."[4] This movement from isolation to participation in a male public discussion seems to transform women from verbal to nonverbal entities who cannot voice their opinions but, on the contrary, can only scream. "Her voice is pure *phone*, not speech," writes Silvia Vigetti Finzi in her discussion of Plato's shrieking women.[5] These hysterical voices of women who emerge from the private are related to the disease that "strikes the lady of the *oikos* [domestic sphere]: hysteria."[6] At the beginning of this century, women appear as uninvited guests in the public sphere of a literary movement that presents itself as an avant-garde artistic current. They strive to be part of, and actively contribute to, the transgressive agendas of futurism, but often find themselves trapped in a male symposium of futurist experimentation in which their creative voices are labeled hysterical, that is, guided by an "excess of . . . feminine desire to reproduce": to be biological mothers, to create themselves as writers, and, within an autobiographical context, to give birth to themselves as subjects and objects of their literary production.[7]

Enif Robert's *A Woman's Womb: A Surgical Novel* (1919) is the biography of a hysterical womb and is the locus of a woman's linguistic experimentations guided by the leader of the movement, Filippo Tommaso Marinetti, who coauthors Robert's autobiographical text.[8] I am interested in investigating the relationship between the two narrating "I's" in this autobiographical text and in attempting to define how Robert's first person narrative is influenced by the coauthor's voice and to what extent her voice submits to his control. I will also discuss Enif Robert's literary creation as an internalization of "the scream," which is transformed into the hysterical womb, contaminated by the degenerative presence of cancer. Robert's invasion of the futurist literary movement originates in an attempt to argue for a different "female sexuality and textuality" in order to "defy the inherited frame of an essentialized [female] embodiment."[9] She constructs, instead, the fragmented story of a de-generation: a narrative in which a woman reveals her inner corrupted core, her sterility, and, consequently, her inability to give birth to herself as writer. The female body is at the center of the narrative and becomes the object of contention between Robert and Marinetti, whose futurist normative writings create the theoretical framework of Robert's self-definition. However, says Judith Butler, "bodies never quite comply with the norms by which their materialization is impelled."[10] Enif's doubly "im-penned" body becomes an elusive entity that transgresses Marinetti's rules and careful shaping guidance.

Robert's futurist agenda is to acquire a new "tongue," Marinetti's *parole in libertà*. She adopts this product of an avant-garde movement in order to transform it into a personal language in which she can inscribe her own life. She also strives to secure her position as a futurist by transforming the narrative of her life into a female futurist manifesto. Robert articulates both theory and practice by introducing her work with the manifesto "CORAGGIO + VERITÀ" (COURAGE + TRUTH), followed by her autobiographical text. She reveals her desire to define women's futurism as complementary to male futurist ideologies. In fact, her manifesto is not an independent document. It is countersigned by Marinetti, who writes: "Approvo incondizionatamente" (I approve unconditionally)(xiv). Enif Robert becomes, therefore, the heroine of a tautology, a literary transgression that is controlled and approved by the Master.

The narrative begins with the description of Enif's desire to break away from the suffocating oppression of society's rules. A widow who refuses to remarry, she is determined to construct a self independent from the gendered identity created by society. Robert states: "Love is not enough for me. In this moment, I really feel little like a woman" (4). Her quest for an independent self is clearly stated, but soon is seduced and controlled by Marinetti's "pen" in his creative contribution to the book and to the construction of a futurist female subjectivity. I would like to stress the use of adjectives such as *futurist* and *female* in this discussion of a woman's subjectivity, which is always related to futurism so that Enif's identity formation is enclosed within specific parameters. "To claim that the subject," Butler argues, "is itself produced in and as a gendered matrix of relations is not to do away with the subject, but only to ask after the conditions of its emergence and operation."[11] Butler's assertion helps me to justify this analysis of a futurist woman's autobiographical narrative in which I focus on the "matrix of relations" within futurism and on the emergence of a woman's voice that operates only in close relation with a man's creativity. If Marinetti cannot do away with the female subject in this narrative, he certainly strives to collapse the separation between *mater*, matrix, and womb in order to allow only the emergence of a heavily "operated upon" (in every sense) female subject. In fact, Enif's search is complicated by physical illness, by disturbances of the womb that are preceded by moments of "terribile noia" (terrible boredom) and melancholia (16). She is partly awakened from her sleepy, still decadent life by the irresistible futurist man Biego Fortis. The thematic core of the narrative is soon displaced from a woman's quest for her identity to a woman's relationship with the futurist superman. When Fortis leaves for the war, the woman's body slowly loses its individuality to become a reflection of the violent experience that men are facing on the front. Her diseased womb needs surgical intervention, and Enif's story "becomes" the story of her womb, of her open wound of femininity.

In "Death Sentences: Writing Couples and Ideology," Alice Jardine speculates on "the question of writing couples, of what it means to 'write couples,' to write-in-couples with/as/through ideology."[12] Ideology is understood by her in an Althusserian sense as "the 'representation' of the Imaginary relationship of individuals to the real conditions of existence."[13] In their relationship as writing couple, Robert and Marinetti are ideologically framed by Marinetti's "representation of the Imaginary relationship to his movement." The roles of this temporary literary couple are clearly defined: Marinetti is the intellectual father and potential lover who represents the essence of the futurist superhero and the logos of futurism itself. Robert's role is to collaborate in Marinetti's obsession by saying everything about women and to create the text of a woman's life as a verbal tomb for Enif's womb.

Marinetti becomes a character in Robert's narrative and replaces Biego Fortis by establishing an epistolary relationship with Enif. Besides approving her manifesto by imposing his signature, Marinetti as a presence in the narrative is not easy to trace and define. He is visible as a character within Robert's life story through the letters that he sends to her from the front. Otherwise, it is difficult to measure the extent of Marinetti's intervention in this autobiography. I have adopted the technique of using the first name of the author to indicate the protagonist of each autobiographical text discussed in this book. In Marinetti's case, such a strategy seems inadequate. Marinetti remains Marinetti: the leader of the literary movement who guides Robert's narrative from a distance. His letters from the front fulfill a double function: they shape Robert's approach to *parole in libertà* and supply futurist/surgical/wartime techniques that can cure Enif's body. Marinetti acquires the role of hermeneutical hero who can perfectly interpret the woman's illness as a sign and supplies a verbal cure that has the power to lead Enif toward a new futurist health. To transform the body into a futurist sign means to draw attention to a discourse and to abandon the tangible body itself with its suffering womb—an uncomfortable presence, which, no matter how hard Marinetti tries, cannot be totally defaced in this doubly voiced, doubly embodied narrative.

Marinetti's cure is initially a transfusion of futurist energy, but is subsequently transformed into Robert's conversion to futurism. Enif Robert's appropriation of futurist linguistic experimentations does not allow her to create an independent portrait of her self, because she becomes trapped in a signifying system that she is unable to modify. Marinetti, in fact, supplies meaning to the episodes narrated by offering a cure for Enif's emptied body, which is surgically deprived of sexual organs. In the end, it is Marinetti who provides the futurist meaning, male signifieds to a woman's empty bodily signifier. In Robert's attempt to personify the new futurist woman, this insistance on the body confirms Sidonie Smith's assertion that the body "functions as a sorting mechanism whereby the culturally dominant and culturally marginalized are assigned the 'proper' places in the body politic."[14] Futurism is an avant-garde movement that attempts to revolutionize artistic expression in order to influence even the minimal details of daily existence and modify both private and public lives. Within the body politic of futurism, Robert's work is marginalized, and her public identity is assigned its proper place as Enif becomes the personification of the futurist woman and (this is not an idle play on words) the embodiment of disembodiment.

In her introductory manifesto, Robert attempts to define both what a futurist woman is and how her literary production can transform her from being a mother and a widow and elevate her to becoming a member of the futurist movement.[15] "We have not understood yet," writes Robert, "what the meaning of 'FUTURIST WOMAN' is" (xi-xii). Robert articulates her search for a definition of woman as a collective female quest. Her choice of the plural subject "we" allows, however, some ambiguity, as the manifesto is also signed by Marinetti. Robert's practice, instead, (i.e., her autobiographical act that follows the theoretical introduction) is written in the first person.[16] A plurality of voices appears, therefore, but never develops a dialogue, since Robert's voice is often reduced to mimicking Marinetti's theories on transgression and femininity. In addition, the relationship between theory and practice, intended as complementary, is further complicated by Robert's attempt to contribute to the futurist male discussion on the definition of woman and female and consequently on woman as a futurist intellectual.

The separation between *femmina* (female) and *donna* (woman) is the starting point for Marinetti and Fillia, another futurist writer, in their search for essentialist definitions that can allow them to locate the entity "woman." While the biological female is the acceptable sexual receptacle for man's natural needs and for reproductive purposes, the gendered "woman" is "a degeneration of man, spiritual weakness, passivity."[17] The traditionally gendered woman is, therefore, an invented entity that needs to be eliminated, because she is "an exploitation of feminine substance imagined by males during times of deep moral decadence."[18] This malleable "feminine substance" can be reconstructed (i.e., regendered) according to futurist ideologies. The binary opposition between the traditionally gendered woman and the biological female—which appears to be clearly defined from a theoretical point of view—is complicated by futurist practice. Marinetti negates this separation in *Mafarka*, a novel in which the goal of the *Uebermensch* is to appropriate woman's reproductive abilities in order to become the father of the futurist son: the airplane.[19] Even in one of Vasari's plays, *L'angoscia delle macchine* (The Anguish of Machines, 1925), woman is defined as a "useless sex" that must be marginalized and "banished to the old continent."[20] The contradictory elements in this male construction of "femininity" transform the entity "woman" into a *problema femminile* (and in Italian *femminile* means both female and feminine) which needs to be resolved.

Marinetti's metaphor of woman as a "tunnel" is the key to reconciling some of the contradictory elements created by Marinetti and his followers.[21] This fragmentation of the female body and subsequent focus on her sexual organs creates a portrayal of women as "positioned peripherally to the dominant group," and, consequently, futurist women "find themselves partitioned in their bodies and culturally embodied."[22] The oversimplified *reductio ad unum* of woman as a symbolic tunnel provides futurist writers the opportunity to consider woman as a receptacle for essentialist definitions.[23] This metaphorically and physically penetrable tunnel, as presented by Marinetti in *Come si seducono le donne* (How to Seduce Women, 1916), awaits the signification necessary to create a futurist woman complementary to and controllable by man.

Enif Robert contributes to the tour de force in search of a solution to the *problema femminile*. In her manifesto, she supplies a detailed portrait of what a futurist woman writer must reject in order to be part of the futurist elite. Becoming a futurist woman involves a total rejection of whatever women have previously written—their symbols, metaphors, style. Robert states that the futurist woman writer has no intellectual mothers, but only literary fathers, to imitate and emulate. In her manifesto, Robert asserts: "I find a formidable logical connection between my very languid friend, afflicted with a rectal tumor, and sentimental women writers. And I am convinced that one main reason for her pitiful plastic poses is found in the literary genre that she prefers" (xiv). Robert's words contain the latent threat that the old models of femininity are corrupting and destroying the core of the being. Robert sees the effects on mind and body as the same, since what corrupts a woman's mind also corrupts her body. In this futurist equation, a woman's mind is her body. Woman is, therefore, only the biological female whose body visibly manifests the consequences of her literary efforts. Her physical and mental health lie, therefore, in her intellectual choices.

Futurism is presented by Robert as a cure, described as "a vigorous cure of COURAGE + TRUTH" (xi). It is a cure that empties women of any previous intellectual influence and gives them, as a temporary loan, a literary soul. What is taken for granted is that Woman is ill and needs to be gendered according to the "hygienic" values of the futurist *Uebermensch*. In return, women become priestesses of the new (futurist) cult by spreading "the word." In a section of her manifesto, Robert comments: "We attempt to change direction and persuade by narrating, from now on, our real lives, interwoven with realities that are not always pleasing; realities that we will NEVER AGAIN have to dilute with dreams" (xv). In this conversion to futurism, Robert's "realities" are never defined other than as opposites of the despised "diluting dreams." This women's manifesto proposes an equation to define how to write a woman's life, an equation that could be expressed as: unappealing realities + (COURAGE + TRUTH) = real life. The courageous truth about real life attracts a reader's attention to the concept of "truth" presented here, but never defined. It leads us to assume the existence of a futurist theory of an absolute truth about women to which Enif's narration of her life must conform.

A definition of courage never appears in her work, which, however, welcomes an external, intertextual definition supplied by Marinetti in his book *How to Seduce Women*, in the chapter entitled "La donna e il coraggio" (Women and Courage):

> It is certain that women who are really women, that is, women rich with animality, love danger and love those who have the habit of living dangerously. I do not want to praise my courage here. I am a real Italian futurist, and that is enough. (102)

> In the most sophisticated women, their core as cerebralized beasts continually searches for and uses danger as an effective aphrodisiac. (104)

Women's courage appears here as a reflection of (futurist) male courage. "Women who are really women," says Marinetti, only fulfill the function of mirrors for men's self-admiration. The essentialized woman becomes the prize for the brave futurist man whose courage seduces the body and mind of the female *belva cerebralizzata* (cerebralized beast). To create intertextual links between Robert's and Marinetti's literary works is necessary in order to acquire some definitions of the elusive terminology that constructs the ideological core of Robert's manifesto. Her text constantly leads to other futurist works and specifically to Marinetti's manual of seduction, which has the role of powerful pre-text that guides the encoding of gender in Enif's body.[24] Woman is, for Marinetti, a particular kind of sign in his discourse. One of the main characteristics of woman as futurist sign is her total malleability. Woman, for Marinetti, is "an ideal starting-point," what Corra and Settimelli called in their introduction to his book "a very important thing which is not, however, essential and superior to all others" (24). She is, therefore, a "useful" but, at the same time, expendable sign. Marinetti adopts and elaborates on Corra and Settimelli's statement, "I love you because you are the ideal starting-point of my *discourse*. I love your friend because what she loves in you is that you are the starting-point and the eloquent force of my discourse" (162). Woman is "a unique perfect woman, wonderful, divine, a woman made for me, exclusively for me" (162). His *How to Seduce Women* is both a guide for the subject, the futurist man, and the object, the aspiring futurist woman. Marinetti's rules revolve around the concept of seduction, of *se-ducere*, of leading a woman's self toward a male "self," of appropriating a woman's identity. The Latin verb *seducere* signifies both "to separate" and "to corrupt." In *A Woman's Womb*, Marinetti's verbal seduction aims to interrupt woman's creativity and to construct an irreconcilable division between her theoretical agenda and her autobiographical practice. In this case, a "seduced" woman abandons her identity in order to be led by the superior futurist man.[25] Such a seduction also involves a hierarchical construction in the definition of the concept of the futurist "Man" and of the marginal futurist woman. To become a member of the movement, a woman is required to become the object of a seduction. Her self is displaced, and its empty shell, the female signifier, her body, is abducted into a male discourse. In this displacement and seduction, women's otherness is signified through their bodies. In Robert's autobiographical text, "others are their [corrupting] bodies, while the masculine 'I' is the noncorporeal soul" embodied in Marinetti's futurist words in freedom.[26]

Marinetti's sexual and intellectual seduction is criticized by futurist women who publicly comment on the idea of seduction in the journal *Italia Futurista* (Futurist Italy) (October 7, 1917). Robert's criticism of Marinetti's manual reveals her attempt to reappropriate Marinetti's "feminine sign" in order to construct the personality of an unseducible woman. In her "Lettera aperta a F. T. Marinetti" (Open Letter to F. T. Marinetti) published in the 1918 edition of Marinetti's manual of seduction, Enif Robert states:

> The verb "to seduce" has long lost any meaning . . . let's forcefully devalue
> that obsession with weakness, fragility, with woman as prey, [models] which
> are willingly accepted by a smaller and smaller number of women; women

who are not yet set on achieving the victorious ownership of their own well-defined and confident identities. (iv)

Robert's article is a revealing pre-text to her autobiographical act in which she attempts to create a female character, a fictional self, who strives to abandon her weakness and fragility in order to acquire "a well-defined and confident" identity as a futurist writer. However, this attempt to define women's total independence is modified into a more conservative portrayal of femininity that reintroduces Man as model for the futurist woman. The previously rejected seduction is accepted in the same document that was initially intended as a criticism of Marinetti's manual. In fact, in the same 1918 edition of *How to Seduce Women,* Enif Robert comments: "There are women whose perfect reciprocity, a perfect unity, of soul and senses, defines them as charming when they give of themselves in rooms filled with perfume and shadows. But those women know at the right time how to be alive, courageous, strong, VIRILE, INTELLIGENT, side by side with their men" (207). Marinetti's seduction is here reconstructed in a parallel concept of women's admiration of Man as model of a new futurist femininity, which relegates women to the inferior role of imitators. Robert's article "Sedurre o essere sedotto" (To Seduce or to Be Seduced) contains the same contrasting statements as in her later manifesto and autobiography. On one hand, Enif Robert attempts to decodify Marinetti's overcodified discourse on women to create an independent "unseduced" self; on the other, she modifies her polemical attitude to be accepted within Marinetti's movement and finally rephrases and reaccepts the futurist "seduction." Robert aims to transgress and, at the same time, to negate her transgression. Such a paradox is evident in the final statements in one of her letters to Marinetti: "But smiling, women, in their fertile silence, sharpen their minds in order to deprive short-sighted men—who knows—even . . . of the monopoly of intelligence."[27] This pseudorevolutionary agenda leads women back to silence, which, even if it is defined as a "fertile silence," signifies marginality and isolation and defies Robert's utopian plan to conquer and monopolize male rationality. After breaking her "fertile silence" to write her autobiography, Robert becomes entrapped in the same system that she tried to negate.

The text of Robert's life begins with the portrait of herself as a twenty-five-year-old widow who resists pressure from her family and refuses to remarry. The first few pages are structured as a diary; the first entry, which follows her programmatic manifesto, is dated June 11, 1915. Enif is described as adamant in her decision to transgress society's rules, and, instead of marrying, she acquires a lover, Giulio. However, her isolated transgression does not satisfy her. "I am bored," writes Robert (4). Boredom is transformed into a quest to change her life and her identity: "I certainly have some intelligence. While looking through this window that absorbs the whole odorous, hot, and blinding Bay of Naples, I think that if I had been born a man I would have been a bit of a poet and a bit of a painter. Love is not enough for me. In this moment, I really feel little like a woman"(4). Enif reveals her need to escape from the suffocating familial sphere and from a limited identity. Her need to open figuratively her life to a different future is reflected in the open window that connects the limited space of her room to the unlimited space of the outside world. She transforms her desire to expand her horizons into a quest that can lead her to modify her identity as object in her love relationships. The limitations in her desire for change are, however, drawn by her biological destiny: she is not a poet or a painter because she is not a man. In addition, Enif feels "little like a woman," and woman is here identified as the opposite of the creative man.

By searching for "another man without a body or a voice, an abstract type," Enif wants to engender her self.[28] The journey in search of the perfect male model is initiated by Enif's description of her superiority to other women. She wants, somehow, to appear as an intermediate "being," separated from the rest of womankind and close to the creative man. It is, in this context, also a separation between the socially inferior women and the superior upper middle class that allows Enif, who can dispense with women's everyday concerns and concentrate on her intellectual development, to construct a more virile identity. While speculating on her difference from "natural" women, Enif chooses a voluntary exile from the rest of womankind: "Nothing in common between myself and those flabby, enormous Neapolitan matrons wearing bathing suits. They are black, slimy lying like seals on sand, surrounded by their offspring who dart and sweat all around them" (4). Enif talks about her own motherhood, but at the same time attempts to break the mirror image of other women as mothers at whom she looks in horror, repelled by the affinities that link her to those animal-like women. Her own son is mentioned only to define him as a potentially virile man, because, even as a little child, he chases little girls and therefore proves his manly power. Within these definitions of difference, however, she cannot completely negate sameness: "I remember the happiness," reveals Robert, "the deeply carnal happiness that I felt eight days after giving birth" (4). To become like a man seems here to imply the necessary rejection of one's own biological identity in order to privilege an idea of rationality that only "a man without a body" can master. The dichotomy between womanhood (body) and manhood (mind) is here reintroduced and underlines the need to acquire a voice by transcending the body and by renouncing one's self as procreator. Yet, by attempting to displace the reader's attention from body to mind, Robert is in a double bind: by negating her insistence, she ends up insisting on the body itself.

The image of woman as an entity close to nature is rejected in the narrative, and Enif's quest for a new identity begins with an affair with Biego Fortis, the futurist "priest" of "tomorrow's new religion" (11). This love affair initiates Enif to a new approach to the representation of reality. The inferior nature, previously identified with woman, acquires a different, superior signification as it becomes gendered as male. Robert describes the new landscape: "Now, there is the sun, the absolute *Lord,* obstinate, solemn, stubborn. It strokes and grasps all the curves, penetrates into all the mouths of the lascivious coast that is possessed and finds pleasure in being imbued by him" (22). In this hierarchical construction of nature, the manly sun acquires positive connotations and creates what Alice Yaeger Kaplan calls "a supernatural landscape in which power and nature are equivalent."[29] In Robert's discourse, womanhood and motherhood become secondary to the privileged male "penetration," which appears as the real creator of life in an act that forces the inferior (female) nature into submission. In her attempt to separate woman from the essentialist definition of mother, Robert proclaims the natural superiority of whatever is male. Man, therefore, can dominate nature through an act of seduction/possession that reintroduces the image of nature as a passive, and therefore negative within the dynamic futurist movement, feminine entity. A priori, the "real futurist" could never be personified by a woman: Marinetti had already embodied Mafarka with the characteristics of the supernatural hero. "Mafarka," describes Kaplan, "is portrayed both as the aesthetic interpreter of nature's powers and as a natural power in his own right."[30]

If both nature and its interpretation are encoded in Marinetti's discourse, Robert can only create an act of literary compliance with Marinetti's carefully defined approach to nature. However, her work does contain "shy" acts of resistance against Marinetti's overpowering demagoguery. In fact, while on one hand, male symbols come to dominate Robert's construction of her self, on the other, the author attempts to resist such an invasion by surrounding herself with women friends who represent different models of womanhood. When Enif is in the hospital where the operation on her uterus is to be performed, she is visited by a friend:

She is a friend from boarding school. A distant memory of an erotic adolescence. A long lasting embrace, very affectionate. A moment filled with Sapphic
memories. (36)

Young nuns. One is very beautiful: lively eyes and mouth, strange woman. She
is taking care of me. That reassures me and makes my first night at the hospital
less dismal. (37)

To total possession by a man, Enif opposes the more tender memories of
sapphic love and reassuring female care, translated into Enif's trust in the
nun's attentions. However, by describing her company of women, Robert
does not negate her previous denigrating statements about "other women."

In "Stabat Mater," Julia Kristeva discusses "the question of hostility between mother[s] and daughter[s]."[31] Kristeva's interpretation of such a question is also an invitation to "reformulate . . . representations of love and
hate . . . in order to deal with the relationship of one woman to another."[32] It
is by looking at motherhood that Kristeva offers an explanation for the
hate/love relationships that seem to permeate even Enif's nonlinear search
for a hybrid, more male than female, identity:

A woman rarely, I do not say never, experiences passion—love or hate—for
another woman, without at some point taking the place of her own mother—
without becoming a mother herself and more importantly, without under-
going the lengthy process of learning to differentiate herself from her own
daughter, her simulacrum, whose presence she is forced to confront.[33]

Enif's attraction/repulsion for other women locates her often in the position
of dependent daughter, but also of severe mother to the flaccid natural
women. The tension created in this double role validates Kristeva's statement; however, the presence of the male model as mirror and arbiter of the
futurist woman further complicates Robert's distorted gynealogical construction by attempting to isolate one "bad" daughter from womankind.

Even Luisa Muraro discusses the concept of women's misogyny intended
as different from the reflection of "male misogyny in a woman's mind."[34] A
special kind of women's hatred for other women is provoked, Muraro asserts, by feminism itself because through feminism "conventional distances
[among women] have become shorter and real differences have become
more evident."[35] Consequently, if a "practice of difference" is not developed,
distance becomes more evident and turns into hatred.[36] In short, Muraro
concludes, "The object of women's misogyny . . . seems to be that woman
who, either deliberately or unconsciously, identifies her gender with inevitable defeat, as disadvantaged and justified in her human littleness."[37]

This definition of women's misogyny, which Muraro creates to analyze Patricia Highsmith's misogynous tales, helps only partially in defining Robert's disgust for other women who represent passivity and defeated "romantic" souls. Muraro also articulates the framework of male misogyny, which, she states, is based on a separation of the female gender into two groups, that is, women and one woman: women as a mass, and woman as the odd exception that Carolyn Heilbrun would call the "honorary man." This essentialization, disturbed only by some deviant but controlled elements, is completed by another ingredient that fuels male misogyny: "Men see in human beings, who are not male, an ugly duplicate of themselves and they hate them because these duplicates prevent them from identifying with God or with whatever they put in the place of God."[38] I do not want to elaborate here on the validity of Muraro's assumptions, but I want to stress how Muraro's definition of women as distorted images of maleness fits Robert's description of herself in relation to other women. It seems that by seeing her self in other women, who reflect that kind of femininity she cannot eradicate from herself, Robert feels weighed down and unable to create herself as the mirror image of the entity she has placed in the God-like position: the futurist superman.

As a reaction, she assembles an elite of friends; they are women of ethereal beauty and superior sensitivity and are members of the privileged upper middle class. Robert writes:

> The professor does not show his face. He knows that [Eleonora] Duse is with me. He hates and despises all female refinements; he avoids the room in which the smell of perfume is too strong and offends his ripping misanthropy that smells blood. (48)

Eleonora Duse's presence has the power to keep Enif safe from male violence. This female magic shield creates an illusion of protection that Enif attempts to preserve in order to resurrect it when the actress is not present. She asks Duse for her picture, which Enif wants to keep by her bedside. After her operation, Enif wants to surface to consciousness and see the effigy of another woman. ("I send a letter to Duse . . . and ask for a picture of her so that I can see her when I come to, *in case . . .*") (52). Duse, the well-known actress, brings books and spends some time discussing with Enif the texts that other people have brought. Futurist books, religious books, and Duse's present, a book by Emerson, lie side by side on the hospital table and supply a plurality of voices, which are later silenced by the overpowering intervention of the futurist voice. Eleonora Duse, however, leaves, breaking the fragile balance of that perfect but temporary mirror of femininity that Enif has created around herself. After the actress's departure, Enif is left with reflecting fragments in which Enif's image reveals new details. Perfection is substituted by imperfection as Enif finds her name reflected in another woman. Enif Robert's full name is Enif Robert Angelini, a name that does not appear on the cover of the book. In the narrative Robert constructs the character of an ugly nurse and names her Angelinin. Robert's negative alter ego, "the semideformed" woman, creates a "rupture" in the chorus of homogeneous female perfection with which Enif has surrounded herself (49). Robert states: "I demand to be alone with little Angelinin . . . my good Angelinin, ignorant and docile. . . . I am leaving for Naples. My good Angelinin has tears in her eyes" (52, 105). Both repulsion and attraction are part of the relationship between Enif and Angelinin, whom Enif cannot as easily separate from herself as she did the inferior women that she had watched from afar, afraid of discovering similarities between herself and the other women.

Enif's Dora-like apparent sexual confusion, which is presented together with women, not Marinetti, as a source of strength, interrupts a potentially coherent discourse on male strength and female weakness. "As a projected phenomenon," comments Judith Butler, "the body is not merely a source from which projection issues, but is also always a phenomenon in the world, an estrangement from the very 'I' who claims it."[39] In Robert's narrative, the body of the narrating "I" becomes a stranger to itself. This "I," threatened by Marinetti's intrusive voice, is also weakened because the body and Enif's transgressive desire conspire to undermine Robert's agenda, which is to prove her control over her unruly body. If, on one hand, Robert's complicity to Marinetti's theoretical agenda is clearly articulated, on the other, Enif's body proves to be for Marinetti the frustrating locus in which his coherent discourse is sabotaged and female disobedience takes shape.

Robert's unique contribution to Marinetti's movement lies in her attempt to expose the problems and contradictions inherent in her translation of her ideological manifesto into literary practice. The relationship between her theory and practice is, in this narrative, the relationship between the theoretical and the personal; in fact, the only practice to follow her manifesto is autobiographical. In her book *Getting Personal: Feminist Occasions and Other Autobiographical Acts*, Nancy Miller argues that "eighties feminism has made it possible to see that the personal is also the theoretical: the personal is part of theory's material."[40] Already at the beginning of the century, Robert experiments with the definitions of both the theoretical and the personal in order to translate them into an autobiographical act. She aims to construct a "space" in literature, identified as an elastic realm that can contain, but not entrap, the changing dimensions of the public and the private. The public theory, her manifesto, is translated directly into the private autobiographical description of a woman's search for a different identity. Robert creates her programmatic document to inscribe it into the story of a woman's life, which soon becomes the story of her body. This narrative also becomes a practice that contains Enif's struggle to gain control over her body and her sexuality. In fact, before her operation, Enif attempts to influence the decisions made by the doctor and the surgeon who have total control over her body:

> —Professor . . . since I *have* to be operated on, since it is necessary, urgent, I would like, at least, to be sure of avoiding any other pregnancy.
> The voice that cuts answers me:
> —It is my duty, madam, to leave any *good part* and to remove what is not healthy anymore. (53)

Enif, who is already a mother, is denied the right to choose a new role and is compelled to accept the dictum of a patriarchal system. However, Robert continues to talk about her body, by pretending to talk about something else, in an attempt to regain control of her signifying system.

A passage from Cixous's "Laugh of the Medusa" can help to investigate Robert's writing about and through her body:

> Listen to a woman speak at a public gathering. . . . She doesn't "speak," she throws her trembling body forward; she lets go of herself, she flies; all of her passes into her voice, and it's with her body that she vitally supports the "logic" of her speech. Her flesh speaks true. She lays herself bare. In fact, she physically materializes what she's thinking; she signifies it with her body. In a certain way she *inscribes* what she's saying, because she doesn't deny her drives the intractable and impassioned part they have in speaking. Her speech, even when "theoretical" or political, is never simple or linear or "objective," generalized: she draws her story into history.[41]

In this attempt to draw "her story into history," or her body into a futurist story, Robert "throws her trembling body forward" and is pushed back by the corpus of Marinetti's rhetoric. In her *Reproductions of Banality*, Kaplan underlines Marinetti's "supplemental erotic pleasures of literary conquest" and cites his definition of "the spirit of men" as "an untrained ovary" that futurist men "fertilize."[42] Therefore, even Robert's process of thinking through her trembling naked body contributes to encoding the seminal influence of Marinetti's virile words disseminated throughout Robert's path for the construction of the body of/in her text.

If Robert's voice is suffocated in this autobiography, this work can be defined as an *autobiografia mancata* (failed autobiography). It is the Italian term *mancata* that doubly defines Robert's work; *mancare* signifies both "to fail" and "to lack." Robert's narrating "I" that constructs the practice of her theoretical manifesto becomes silenced at the end of her autobiography, where the first person is replaced by a third person narrative and where Enif's story becomes another woman's struggle with a parallel disease. Her voice fades into another narrative, which ends the autobiographical act and interrupts Enif's story. It is an *autobiografia mancata*, therefore, as the "auto," the self-narration, the construction of a self, is suddenly severed. In addition, the already "lacking" woman becomes the epitome of a "more lacking" entity, as her body is deprived of her sexual organs and becomes the realm of decay and putrefaction. Enif is in fact confronted with the separation of her castrated body from what she is lacking: "A nurse shows me two dark masses in a glass jar, they are as big as fists. They are my anatomical pieces" (73). The empty body becomes a foreign entity for Enif, an entity that she needs to reappropriate somehow. In fact, Robert argues that she becomes visible only as a fragmented anatomical specimen, cut and separated by male hands:

> At last I will be able to *see* my belly/womb! . . . I see the expression in my doctor's eyes. It is not reassuring. As soon as he looks at my wound, the professor slightly turns and demands:
> —A scalpel.
> . . . I scream:
> —No, not when I am conscious! . . . Murderers! Butchers! Not when I am conscious! My flesh is mine! . . . I am in charge! I have the right! . . .
> They have a hard time keeping me still. I feel the cold blade that plunges into my flaccid skin. . . . I feel a spurt of warm pus on my ice-cold belly! . . . The professor's hands squeeze the abscess. Passively, I let them do it, voicing a soft cry of pain.
> —Let's hope that all the bad stuff comes out!—says a cold voice. (82)

Enif cannot see or touch her body; everything is done from a male point of view and by a male hand against which she initially rebels, but which she later passively accepts. Woman is here filled with "bad stuff," the *cattiveria* that the powerful hand of the surgeon must violently remove. Enif strongly voices her rebellion but is soon silenced. Her refusal to "be opened" is ignored, and, consequently, while her wound is emptied, her voice disappears. This act of emptying the already castrated woman who was already a lacking entity creates a *mise en abîme* in the construction of a woman's identity, a construction that is an attempt to reduce both *donna* and *femmina* to a vacuum.

The empty shell of Enif's body cannot heal even after the doctors' manipulation. She needs a new diagnosis and a new cure in which the attention becomes displaced from her symptomatic womb to her "brain [that is] too virile in a body that is too feminine" (97). The doctors decide that there is something wrong with Enif, because she cannot respond to the cure. The surgeon hints that the doctors' failure is due to women's inability to adapt to the valid cure that men of medicine supply. Enif rebels against such an idea, but nevertheless adopts the surgeon's conclusion by displacing her attention to her complex psyche, which the doctor cannot read and interpret. She decides to leave the hospital after a final discussion with the surgeon:

> I am ironic, cutting, bad. I look like I could send him to hell! He notices it and rails at women:
> —After four years in surgery . . . we realize more and more that women are *a total mess!*
> —Please! Doctors may know, perhaps I say, the functioning of a woman's uterus, but they miss completely a woman's psychological problem, which, I think, is important for her physical well being. Therefore, we are not a mess, on the contrary, it is you who are unable to explain. (104)

After discovering the surgeon's inability to treat her, Enif searches for a new doctor, a hermeneutical and epistemological hero who can cure her body and value her virile mind. Her initial search for an independent self is displaced into the quest for a hero who can construct a new identity for her and cure her diseased tunnel of femininity.

Enif returns to Naples, where her desire to become "whole" again leads her to turn to futurism in order to write about her surgical experience. The writing practice aims to cure her diseased *hystera*, the Greek name for womb. Her "intelligence that influences the blood" transforms Enif's cancer of the uterus into a psychosomatic illness and turns Enif into an hysterical wom(b)an (38). On this subject Mary Ann Doane writes: "The nineteenth century defined this disease [hysteria] quite specifically as a disturbance of the womb—the woman's betrayal by her own reproductive organs."[43] This hysterical woman needs more than the intervention of the surgical knife as she is reduced to becoming her womb. Enif, in fact, defines herself: "How disgusting to be a suffering womb while men are fighting" (25). While attempting to make herself "visible," Robert tells the story of the destruction of her body and of the final *reductio ad unum* of her identity, which becomes enclosed in her open wound that sadly mirrors Marinetti's tunnel. "My wound," writes Robert, "is certainly more eloquent than my mouth" (147).

In describing the etiology of her disorderly uterus, Robert creates a narrative that summarizes the theories on female hysteria. She is the woman whose hysteria is closely linked to disturbances of the womb, to an "erratic" womb as described by Aretaeus, the Cappadocian, in the second century.[44] The wandering uterus is an unpredictable entity, and it was even thought to be the cause of suffocation. The characteristics of the hysterical womb according to Araeteus are fitting in the context of Robert's narrative, in which a woman's mobility from the private to the public sphere is translated into the disease of her wandering womb that neutralizes her role within futurism and suffocates her creativity. A contemporary of Aretaeus, Galen, believed that "this disease mostly affects widows" and was caused by abnormal sexual functioning; the cure could be supplied by physicians or by restoring a healthy sexual life.[45] Enif appears to be a confirmation of Galen's theory: she is a widow. Widows are considered women who have more freedom than others: they have acquired some kind of financial independence and are, potentially, individuals who could escape male control. To diagnose that abnormal sexual functioning causes their disease means that a new normality must be achieved by establishing relationships with men: sexual partners or physicians. Enif, the widow, finds in Marinetti the therapeutic authority she needs to cure her womb, whose pathological wanderings have interrupted her experimental sexual relationships with the futurist men. Marinetti assumes the role of an alternative surgeon whose "cutting" words can cure a woman's diseased body. "Marinetti," affirm Corra and Settimelli in the introduction to *How to Seduce Women,* "is a great speaker whose voice is cutting and whose gestures are energetic and sharp" (15). The "word" becomes a metaphorical knife, able to modify form and content; it restores Enif's biological identity and imposes a futurist male perspective in Robert's articulation of a woman's subjectivity.

Robert's narrative also contains a Freudian approach to hysteria, which is treated by adopting a talking cure that Marinetti author(ize)s. Marinetti's correspondence to Enif, included in the autobiography, adds to the role of Marinetti the surgeon by creating Marinetti the psychoanalyst.[46] This double probing, both physical and psychological, of the futurist woman gives a new meaning to the statement "anatomy is destiny," because sex, sexuality, and gender collapse here into one: the newly created futurist wom(b)an. Marinetti's cure is divided into theory and practice. In one of his letters to Enif, quoted within the narrative of *A Woman's Womb,* Marinetti writes:

> I am convinced that if I were close to you I could cure you. This is not a lark. I have a sure method. Listen:
>
> *Theory*
> Health is the sum of all our desire-strength which keep us tied to life. In all

serious illness what happens is a laceration or a softening of these knots.
We live because we have many reasons to stay alive. We die because little by
little we lose the reasons to live.
It is necessary, therefore, to create new relationships with life in order to
recover.

Practice
Every day think of something pleasant which you have seen or dreamed of
and that you would like to see, touch, eat, drink, hold, possess.
Dream of a bloodless isle of Capri. . . .
Dream of writing a poem, as the high expression of all your soul. . . .
Dream of multiplying with a gesture of love the artistic acts or the genius of a
beloved man. . . .
Dream of the ideal toilette for your grace. . . .
After a month of this cure, you will feel an enormous strength tumultuously
move in order to break, at any cost, the infamous net of the disease. (121,
122–123)

The initial statements portray a woman's body as a rag doll that is coming
apart at the seams. What she needs is simple, says Marinetti—she needs reasons to be alive and this dreamlike rest cure.[47] Those reasons are not to be
found in herself, but are bestowed on her by Marinetti because Enif can only
dream of curing herself without the concrete help of Marinetti's therapeutic
authority. She can also only dream of being creative, of writing her own poem.
His practice guides Enif's thoughts, feelings, and her body, which must be
healthy as it must be given away to the beloved man, the creative authority.
Even the *toilettite*, the excessive care of a woman's body, harshly criticized by
Marinetti, becomes acceptable if it is part of his discourse. *Toilettite* can be
part of the cure because its dosage is regulated by Marinetti, the doctor, the
psychoanalyst.

In analyzing the case of Freud's patient Dora, Philip Rieff underlines the
psychoanalyst's attempt to "change the patient's mind" and to impose his
reading of her life over her own interpretation.[48] Elaine Showalter stresses
Freud's "role of domination over the patient," which Marinetti seems to fulfill
without any indecision.[49] An explanation of Marinetti's insistence on repro-
gramming Enif is supplied by Showalter, who analyzes several occurrences
of hysteria in men. Showalter creates a connection not so much between
hysteria and the womb but between hysteria and history or "hystory," as she
terms it.[50] During the Great War, soldiers seemed to suffer from hysterical
episodes. It was, writes Showalter, a "great epidemic of hysteria among men."[51]
The diffusion of such a female neurosis among men carried the threat of effemination which explains the overemphasized statement of Marinetti (who

is a soldier in the Great War) of his own curative powers in *How to Seduce Women* (1916). Marinetti had, in fact, tested on himself the power of his talking cure against the latent threat of effemination when he spent time in a military hospital. Such a threat appears physically tangible as, wounded in the groin (eleven wounds to his groin and legs), Marinetti writes his manual of seduction to remedy his powerlessness and his fear of castration.[52] In a chapter entitled "Donne, Preferite i Gloriosi Mutilati" (Women, Prefer the Glorious Mutilated Men), Marinetti transforms the futurist man into a new *Uebermensch* whose physical deficiency is transformed into a sign of extraordinary virility. This superman is paradoxically enriched by a loss. According to Marinetti, "Nothing [is] more beautiful than an empty sleeve that heaves and surges on his chest, because the gesture that orders to launch an attack jumps out of it" (173). Marinetti succeeds in acquiring an alternative member from the mutilation of a metaphorical arm. Woman is, consequently, brought back to a position of inferiority because of her incompleteness in comparison to the soldier, who acquires rank in virility through a verbal manipulation of his lack, the empty sleeve, which is transformed into a futurist erection.

Another feminizing threat appears in Marinetti's texts and influences the coauthoring of Robert's autobiographical narrative: women's changing roles during the economic emergency of the Great War. Marinetti superficially seems to accept women's new positions and invites them to fight in the trenches with men: "Let's balance in this way the strength of the two sexes! All the responsibilities to you, too, Italian women, if you want to be worthy of loving the glorious mutilated men" (175). Women are placed on such a level of inferiority that they have to prove not to be deserving of men's love, but to be good enough to love Marinetti's lacking heroes. He constructs the superiority of the lacking man over the lacking woman. The woman who is "as a man" becomes a threat, and Marinetti reveals his preoccupation. Marinetti speculates that "as a consequence of the war, the large participation of women in the national work force has created a typically grotesque marriage" (60). In fact, the unemployed veteran "concentrates his activities on absurd housewife-like preoccupations" (60). The issue of control becomes central for Marinetti and his followers—control over their public roles and their symbolic virility and, consequently, over female roles and feminine identities. In fact, Marinetti's desire for control leads him to theorize, in his *Mafarka*, the possibility of engendering maleness into the body of a machine. His son, Gazoumarah, is (pro)created beyond nature in an act of illusory absolute power.

Marinetti and the futurists are preoccupied with what they perceive as women's search for power. Another futurist, VOLT (Vincenzo Fani Ciotti), succinctly elaborates male fears: "Deep down . . . [women] only demand one thing: to subjugate men. . . . And women behave this way because they cannot act in any other way."[53] If women are already "instinctively" a threat to men, they appear even more menacing in their public discussion, to which Robert contributes. Men's uneasiness with changes in women's literary identities is verbalized by Settimelli in an article published in *Italia Futurista*, March 4, 1917. In "Maria Ginanni Prima Grande Scrittrice Italiana" (Maria Ginanni, The First Great Italian Woman Writer), Settimelli reviews Ginanni's latest book of poetry. He underlines her "full, impetuous strength, which does not lose the charm of the most subtle femininity," but, at the same time, he must approach the topic of the independence of Ginanni's creativity from the futurist movement. Settimelli describes Maria Ginanni as "irreconcilably distant from some of our [futurist] convictions" and proceeds with a revealing statement: "Her [Ginanni's] criticism is so sharp and so deeply sincere that we cannot refrain from respecting and accepting it so that it cannot succeed in modifying us." The woman writer becomes a potentially contaminating entity who threatens to modify the male discourse.[54] Woman—her body and her discourse—must, therefore, be seduced to prevent a potential female seduction of the male discourse. On the subject of seduction, Jean Baudrillard adds:

> Seduction continues to appear to all orthodoxies as . . . a conspiracy of signs. This is why all disciplines, which have as an axiom the coherence and finality of their discourse, must try to exorcise it. This is where seduction and femininity are confounded, indeed confused. Masculinity has always been haunted by this sudden reversibility within the feminine. Seduction and femininity are ineluctable as the reverse side of sex, meaning and power.[55]

The growing cancer of an independent female seductive discourse must therefore be trapped, controlled, and cured within the system that it is threatening to modify and effeminate.

Aretaeus called the wandering uterus "the womb [which] is like an animal within an animal."[56] He presented one of the first portrayals of the wom(b)an as a degeneration of the natural female, who, from passive animal, becomes an uncontrollable entity. Similarly, woman becomes for Marinetti a hyena who feeds on men's cadavers (i.e., eats their genitals) and consequently castrates them. Such a metaphor is not Marinetti's original creation. The leader of the futurist movement proves himself a dutiful disciple of Nietzsche, appearing to share the German philosopher's opinion of sickness and female disease. In *The Genealogy of Morals,* Nietzsche writes: "Is there any place today where the sick do not wish to exhibit some sort of superiority and to exercise their tyranny over the strong? Especially the sick females, who have unrivaled resources for dominating, oppressing, tyrannizing. The sick woman spares nothing dead or alive: she digs up long buried things."[57] In *How to Seduce Women,* Marinetti states: "There are women who love invalid, defeated, and disappointed men. I have said to each one of them; 'Do you smell a cadaver in me? . . . It is not ready, yet! Please come back in twenty years, hyena!'" (137). If woman begins to dig into male discourse, she can weaken the superiority of a male signifying system. She becomes a sick monster, a hyena, a new incarnation of the Medusa.[58]

In *Decadent Genealogies: The Rhetoric of Sickness from Baudelaire to D'Annunzio,* Barbara Spackman argues that "the sight of woman's wound is the sight of the Medusa."[59] In *A Woman's Womb,* the relationship between Marinetti and Enif is carefully carried out at a distance, mediated by language that protects Marinetti from "seeing" Enif, her wound, and her diseased body. Language is a shield that can easily silence woman. Robert attempts to steal Marinetti's language in order to express her "SURGICAL SENSATIONS" in *parole in libertà* (134). She wants to become what Claudine Hermann calls a *voleuse de langue,* by appropriating Marinetti's experimental language, but succeeds only in borrowing a signifying system that she cannot modify.[60] The verb *voler* means both to steal and to fly, but Robert's appropriation of the language does not allow her to "fly on it," to create an independent narrative of her life. The hysterical Robert is very different from Anna O., Freud's patient who is able to invent her own language as a mixture of English, Italian, and French. Robert creates an autobiographical act of ventriloquism. Her attempts to theorize through and about her body are controlled by Marinetti's direct and indirect interference in the text, by his linguistic seduction of a woman's voice. In this textual reflecting shield, Enif sees the never ending destruction of her body, her irreversible castration. Language becomes part of the destructive cure that Marinetti, *arbiter linguae,* bestows on her. In a letter to Marinetti, Robert thanks her master:

> But your magnificent vehemence wipes away every slow objection from a decadent philosophy. It also urges me away from the ponderous reflection of logic. . . . I will not split hairs in a depressing and lame analysis, and gratefully accept the new word. I make it mine and I will mold, as a skillful author, the pliability of desire which must be transformed into *health.* . . . I send to you, wonderful exciter and perceiver of latent strength, my first vibrating greeting

after my healthy awakening, and I, serene, shake your hand with grateful faith. (128–29)

Robert limits her role of "translator" into practice of Marinetti's theories and proclaims her eternal debt to Marinetti, who has awakened her to the revelation of his linguistic cure. She regresses from "tongue snatcher" to a passive sleeping beauty, from subject of her narrative to object in a plot secondary to Marinetti's agenda. Consequently, Robert mails her linguistic experimentations to Marinetti, the soldier, who approves and interprets her work.[61]

In *Speculum of the Other Woman*, Luce Irigaray writes: "She [the girl] borrows signifiers but cannot make her mark, or re-mark upon them, which all surely keeps her deficient, empty, lacking, in a way that could be labelled 'psychotic': a latent but not actual psychosis, for want of a practical signifying system."[62] Robert's active role in searching for a new identity and in constructing a female subject turns into the more passive role of mimic. Her preoccupation with her diseased womb is again replaced by her mimetic narration of the male fear of castration, which appears in her writing as female fear: "Oh, my God! How horrible! Here is a very handsome *alpino* [soldier in the Alpine troops] who is obscenely castrated! I thought that women in Vienna compete with Ethiopian women and devour the sex of Italian prisoners" (169). The doubly lacking woman paradoxically fears man's castration: Robert renounces her female identity, becomes Marinetti, and cannot "make her mark" on a futurist discourse. However, defeated in her "excessive desire to reproduce," she can still expose Marinetti's anxieties of castration.

In *How to Seduce Women*, Marinetti's woman is "an unloaded gun" in need of the war, which "gives mountains, rivers, and woods their real beauty" (63). Woman and nature both need a "violent act" to complete their lacking entities. In fact, "a beautiful woman," writes Marinetti, "can have no other lover than a soldier armed in every way, who comes from the front and is ready to leave" (63). Robert adds to this metaphor by describing the "completing" sexual act as the act of violence needed by her scarred womb. The overpowering futurist "sun" becomes the agent of Marinetti's violence over a woman's body, an act of rape over the acquiescent Enif. Robert describes the sexual act between Enif's womb and the "sun":

> Naked in my open robe, I lie down on a deck-chair and I offer my belly/womb to the sun. . . . The incandescent star shows right away its wonderful uncivilized brutality by hurling itself upon my wound in savage frenzy and undiplomati-

cally. . . . Rush of hot flames that want to penetrate deeply there, in a sweet and
yet painful, slow, yet very fast savagery. It is an all-encompassing embrace and
a laceration at the same time. (145–46)

Enif, the protagonist, loses control of her body as Robert, the narrator, loses
control of the narrative, which is transformed into a dialogue between the
sun and the womb. It is a dialogue outside the female body between two
male terms (IL SOLE, IL VENTRE) (THE SUN, THE WOMB), and it becomes an
added praise of violence over an "inside-out" woman.

> THE WOMB [to the Sun]
> Forgive me. I am yours. Do with me whatever you want. . . . Cut! Wound! Tear!
> Lacerate! Spread [me] open! I will be yours in pieces. Yours! Run me through!
> Or crush me! Turn me into ashes! Like this! Again! Again! (149)

The "voice" of the exposed womb is male and is separated from the woman's
voice which comments on this superimposed dialogue. Enif reacts as a spectator to the violent act between her virilized womb and the futurist God. "I
am tired," states Robert, "of listening to the long-lasting dialogues between
the sun and my womb" (151). Robert ends up thinking and speaking "without" her body and therefore fails in her initial attempt to create a practice
that could link the "theoretical" and the "personal," her body, in her autobiographical act.

Juliet Mitchell calls hysteria "the daughter's disease" and interprets it as
a woman's rebellious act against the Father.[63] In *The Newly Born Woman*
(1986), Cixous describes hysterics as women who demonstrated their "power
to protest."[64] The interpretation of hysteria as a feminist act flourished in the
sixties and seventies. More recently, in *La posizione isterica e la necessità della
mediazione* (The Hysterical Position and the Necessity of Mediation) (1993),
Luisa Muraro has argued that the incomprehensible language of the hysteric
and the connection between hysteria and the diseased womb—women and
their uncontrollable bodies—contribute to the articulation of a symbolic
order of the mother.[65] Robert does not see hysteria as such a liberating act
even if she is, in often contradictory ways, a daughter attempting to rebel
against her literary father. After describing Enif's wandering, diseased womb,
she attempts to prove that other women suffer with the disease and displaces
the reader's attention to hysteria as a punishment to nonfuturist women.
The ideal woman is represented by a beautiful woman, "Donna da preda e
da assalto" (A woman to be preyed upon and to be assaulted), whose body
invites violence (156). This perfect futurist female is surrounded by other
women who Robert invites to despise. While the woman as prey is a passive

object to be conquered, the "others" are active women whose lives, bodies, and minds are ridiculed:

> An English woman. . . . A woman of incredible ugliness. A bizarre type, always dressed in an impossible fashion. A pedantic intellectual. . . . Getting close to her, one discovers that she is an interesting neuropath. She is obsessed with probing and appropriating everything that is knowable. She is weighed down by big words that astound. . . . Luckily, a learned man . . . assured me that she was talking, with total ease, nonsense. . . . Her hysterical womb, with its incontrollable starts, is straight, flat, dark, and is defended by a fake romantic shell. (202)

The woman's ugliness is directly linked to her identity as an intellectual whose search for knowledge is neutralized by ridicule and by disease.[66] It is, however, a revealing portrait constructed by Robert, the intellectual, about another woman who directly mirrors Robert's own initial search through futurism for a transgressive role as a futurist writer. The English woman is here corrected by the learned man, who exposes a woman's ignorance and reassures Enif of the unimportance of a woman's speech. The learned man's control over the woman echoes Marinetti's direct control over Robert's voice and her intellectual development as a futurist. It is not surprising, therefore, that Enif's hysterical womb becomes displaced onto the new figure of an intellectual woman, whose identity is presented as an involuntary mirror image and is led back to coincide with her disabled matrix: the punishment for suffering from "an excess of desire to reproduce."

In conclusion, I propose that *How to Seduce Women* and *A Woman's Womb* are different in one important way: the threats of castration and mutilation are treated with humor in the narrative of Marinetti's manual, which turns to an excess of seduction and to ridiculing women. Humor is absent from Robert's text, in which a woman's double castration is dissected and clinically observed. I would like to suggest that through the creation of the proliferation of diseased wombs, Marinetti wants to define the female body as the "real" place of hysteria, which spreads, almost like an epidemic, to many women, futurists and not. Marinetti reenacts exclusively in women the symptomatic hysterical wombs to distance himself from the possibility of becoming a hysterical man, as was the case for many soldiers in the war and, consequently, from the possibility of being feminized. Accepting that war, so often praised by Marinetti in his work as the virile triumph of the futurist man, could be the source of trauma that does not transform men into superheroes, but rather downsizes them into hysterical women, would undermine futurist ideology as such. In a sense, Marinetti rejects the trauma theory by concentrating on women spreading hysteria, which suggests a potential contamination of the male body. In locating hysteria only within the female body, Marinetti pathologizes femininity. Such a move justifies Mafarka's articulation of his identity as the man who can couple/copulate with himself in a homoerotic act of procreation and give birth to a male son. Such a move also motivates Marinetti's insistence on cleansing and curing the female body by dispensing with its sexual organs in an act of effacement of the other. As a result of the process of women's defacement and subsequent total control on Marinetti's part, women can be gendered as futurists.

Marinetti's creation of the pathology of femininity also involves the articulation of female autobiography as pathological, because it becomes the projection of the diseased female body, which further explains his definition of autobiographical writing as *the* female mode of expression.[67] His collaboration to Robert's autobiographical act transforms a woman's attempt to translate her theoretical manifesto into the story of her body into *his* manifesto, which proclaims that a woman's narration of her self can only be the narrative of her (diseased) body. The pathology of femininity is therefore expressed in what Robin Pickering-Iazzi calls "the pathology of autobiography," in which the translation of theory into the practice of narrating the body in the text can only be an act of regression and self-annihilation.[68]

The *mise en abîme* of women's hysterical wombs continues in the final chapter of *A Woman's Womb*. At this point in Robert's autobiographical act, the narrating "I" disappears and is replaced by a third person narrative that tells the story of another woman. The protagonist is the princess de Ruderis who is confined in bed by her diseased womb, which the doctors call a "foul pipe" (213). The remedy, suggested by the specialists who attempt to cure her, is described in detail: "The body is afflicted by unusual retention of pus. . . . The colleagues agree in recognizing that . . . washing only cleans, clears, and deterges only the final part of the cesspool. . . . The problem we are facing is how to clean completely" (213). What is needed is a more violent cure to clean her infected body, which traditional medicine cannot heal. It is the princess who invokes the radical action of the surgical knife (i.e., Marinetti's cure): "If you do not want to operate on me, I will operate on myself, ripping my womb with my nails" (216). The cure comes, once more, from a futurist, who kills the princess's husband and eradicates the rotting decadence of the institutions that the prince represents. Once more, the woman's body comes to acquire a secondary role as a useful but, at the same time, expendable sign in the futurist ideology. Charged by the strength and violence of the futurist act, the princess is cured of her "toilettite," her romantic and rotting core. She is now ready for the "Lotta di ventri femminili"

(Fight between Female Wombs)—the title of one of the final chapters of *A Woman's Womb*. Pulled by futurist *Ueber*mannish strength, Princess de Ruderis rises from bed and, to celebrate her husband's death, offers herself naked at the window.

The book concludes with the description of a woman's body exposed, offered to public interpretation:

> The princess went out onto the balcony and leaned out screaming:
> —I am ready! Operate on me!
> And the soldiers, forgetting both the killer and the victim, frenetically applauded *without any surprise*, at that however strange apparition of the wonderful naked woman. (217–18)

She is ecstatic in this moment of *jouissance* that only the futurist man can give. The woman responds to violence by calling for more violence over her body. Robert's autobiographical narrative is concluded by another woman's story and by images that belong, once more, to Marinetti's fantasy. In "Contro il lusso femminile" (Against Women's Luxury)(March 11, 1920), Marinetti writes: "*Toilettite* unusually favors the development of homosexuality. We will soon have the need to adopt the hygienic remedy used by a Venetian Doge who made it compulsory for beautiful Venetian women to expose their naked breast at a window, between two candles, to lead men onto the straight path."[69] Again, the source of the disease, *toilettite* in this case, can be neutralized only if adopted within a discourse that transforms her body and her femininity into a usable sign. She is used to warn men of the dangers of effemination—of the dangers of becoming like a woman. In Robert's autobiographical work, the naked body invites men to experiment violently on her female identity to reshape it through a futurist act of surgical rape.

After attempting to speak through her body, Robert creates a discourse about a female body, which is suffocated, because "the technological man," writes Kaplan, and the futurist man, I might add, "must oppress [suppress, in this case] someone in order to exist."[70] This is indeed a failed autobiographical act; the woman's voice and the narrating "I" drown into silence, disappearing from the narrative and from the literary scene. However, it would be misleading to emphasize only a woman's loss of a voice and of her body in the narrative. Robert is one of the first women who attempts to create her own testimony of women's hysteria, which is often narrated by men. In addition, Marinetti's ideological discourse on women also fails in this autobiography: the woman's womb is never healed within this narrative. The book ends with a multiplication of diseased wombs that become mere accessories once the reader's attention shifts to the futurist man and his violent act. The scarred wombs are pushed into the background and reduced to becoming a secondary plot, but they remain unsettling images that defy the construction of woman and female as essentialized entities. The futurist *Uebermensch* fails in his role as doctor and psychoanalyst, since he can only partially control (i.e., seduce) and certainly cannot cure a woman's hysteria.[71] Robert's work, in the end, interrupts and disturbs Marinetti's coherent and linear discourse on the relationship between word and body, cure and disease. The successful talking cure with which Marinetti experimented on himself cannot reach a point of closure once it is translated onto the still elusive female body. It becomes, in the end, a failed seduction.

CHAPTER THREE

From Genealogy to Gynealogy and Beyond

Fausta Cialente's *Le quattro ragazze Wieselberger*

I am annoyed that we lack a history of fatherhood.

THOMAS LAQUEUR[1]

But the official history cannot conceal the fact that,
as Gertrude Stein remarked, "fathers are depressing."

SARA RUDDICK[2]

Alice Jardine defines *gynesis* as the "putting into discourse of 'woman.'" It is also a process in which "the object produced . . . is neither a person nor a thing, but a horizon, that toward which the process is tending: a *gynema*. This gynema is a reading effect, a woman-in-effect that is never stable and has no identity."[3] Jardine focuses her attention on processes of gynesis in texts by male theorists, since they were and are the intellectual fathers of many feminists. My approach to Fausta Cialente's autobiographical text, *Le quattro ragazze Wieselberger* (The Four Wieselberger Girls) (1976), is grounded in Jardine's definition of a "woman effect"; I do not use this concept of gynesis here in the construction of a reading practice of male texts, but rather I apply it to articulate Cialente's gynectic construction of her gynealogy and, subsequently, of her disparate genealogy.[4] She creates her life and her identity-in-effect through an enunciation of her relationship with the women in her family and of her search for the "location" of her cultural subjectivity.

Her decision to exile herself from Italy, to write and publish in her native language while living in Egypt and, later, England, reveals Cialente's interpretation of Jardine's female "horizon" as a never stable entity that attempts to explore the interstices between cultures.

An opposition between male identity and an unidentified female plurality is the starting point for Fausta Cialente's construction of a self in this autobiographical work which is a fragmented interweaving of official history and personal "life/lines."[5] *The Four Wieselberger Girls* contains autobiographies of both the mother and the daughter.[6] In the first section of her narrative, Cialente attempts to write another person's autobiography: this is not a contradiction in terms but rather an attempt to write one's own life starting from another woman's life story.[7] The second part of *The Four Wieselberger Girls* is the narration of Fausta's own life, starting from the first memories of childhood to the years after World War II. Together, the first and second sections of Cialente's autobiographical text attempt to construct both a portrait of familial and public spaces and a concept of women's subjectivities that take into account past and present: the identity of mothers and daughters throughout most of the twentieth century.

The reader is, in fact, immediately confronted within the title of this autobiographical narrative by a binary opposition that introduces the female characters—the four sisters—identified by the name of the father, Wieselberger. The male characters dominate the beginning of the book, and the female characters represent the unimportant and plural female presence ("the girls") within the household. The narrator looks back on her family's past, the bourgeois life of the four sisters and her ancestors, and on official history, that is, the "irresponsible" *irredentismo* of Trieste's middle class (irredentists advocated the incorporation of Trieste into Italy). Cialente brings the private story of her family into the public sphere and, in a reverse movement, public history is reflected within the nuclear familial sphere. From the initial discourse of oppositions in the autobiography, the author's text creates a unity between Memory, that is, official history, and personal memories, where the fragmented inheritance from the father and the mother can coexist. In fact, Cialente's text does not contain what Butler defines as "an effort to identify the enemy as singular in form," because that would "mimic the strategy of the oppressor instead of offering a different set of terms."[8]

The term *genealogy* does not accurately describe the imagined "new" past in Cialente's work. The use of *gynealogy* more precisely describes this matrilinear personal history. Such a gynealogy is not only a transition toward the construction of a heterogeneous and hybrid genealogy. Gynealogical techniques create the necessary framework in which disparate genealogies develop. Their role as transition and mediation is not an expendable one: even within braided genealogies, the female identities of the mother(s) are not destined to disappear, but remain loosely connected with the acts of gynealogical mediation that have made the construction of hybrid genealogy possible. I want to suggest that tracing the process of gynesis within this autobiographical act involves an analysis of the self-representation on the part of a woman who aims to articulate her maternal and paternal inheritance and to redefine it at the same time. In this case, Cialente's narrative adds to Jardine's concept of gynesis and becomes the location of gynealogical techniques that, as I will describe, tend to create nonessentialized female identities articulated in western and nonwestern cultural contexts. In Cialente's text, the gynectic putting into discourse of woman becomes a process in which redefinitions of daughterhood and motherhood are also grounded in a daughter's attempt to come to terms with patrimony, the paternal inheritance. What is created is an interweaving of paternal and maternal traces that frame a daughter's attempt to discuss female sameness and difference.

In the first part of the autobiography, Fausta Cialente, as narrator, has the role of reader and writer of her mother's life. She describes the entrapment of Elsa, Fausta's mother, in a marriage portrayed as an institutionalized prison where woman's creativity is silenced. When talking about her own marriage, Fausta takes refuge in silence: she creates a narrative void. The mother's life can fill such a void if we consider her experience as complementary to the daughter's failed marriage. Elsa leaves her husband late in life, and Fausta's marriage soon fails. The latter, however, does not write about her marriage as if her "self" is already hiding in the character of her mother. What is created is Elsa/Fausta's "autobiographical biography," which plays an important role in the construction of matrilinearism within Cialente's autobiography.

Elsa exists only as a character in metonymic relation to her sisters: Alice, Alba, and Adele. The Wieselbergers are a "sensible, wealthy family" living in the still-Austrian Trieste toward the end of the nineteenth century (19). The father's presence is accompanied by a female plurality, a generic entity that includes the sisters and the mother. He is a well-known composer, while the mother and the daughters fulfill their duties in the familial sphere. The relationship among the sisters is already implicit in their names; the father has decided to give them all names beginning with the same vowel. Only the youngest escapes that fate, because he chooses instead the name of an opera heroine he liked, Elsa. The process of "naming" is repeatedly presented as the act of limiting a woman's identity: all of the women in the house are nicknamed *babe,* by the father. In a private sphere inhabited by the generic identity of *babe,* the paternal creativity is a familial priority. In fact, his orchestra rehearsals totally disrupt the domestic life:

> Those evenings when the orchestra came to play in the house, the family had to dine rather earlier than usual so that the lady and girls . . . had enough time to clear the table in the dining room . . , the large glass door that separated the dining room from the house entrance had to remain open. Instead, all the doors leading to the kitchen and the "service" areas had to be kept closed because the father did not want to hear, during the performance, the noise of the washing up and the chatter, the *ciacole,* of the women servants. (15)

The two doors, one open and one closed, represent the difference between the two spheres: one inhabited by the Father and the other by the *babe.* The open door through which music, that is, male creativity, penetrates is the passage to the outside world. It is the public door that connects the paternal authoritative identity as a musician to the male *logos* of creativity, which can be disturbed by the nonsensical *ciacole* of women. The closed door between the rehearsal and the domestic activities defines the private world of the *babe* as the sphere that disturbs man's creativity. Some of the women are allowed to listen to the music, and they contribute to it in a rather bizarre way. The two oldest sisters, Alice and Alba, sit in front of the brass section of the orchestra and eat lemons so that the players salivate more and perform better. This funny anecdote, however, underlines the fact that the daughters can acquire only a marginal role in relation to the father's art. They are never isolated behind the closed door, but neither are they allowed to play in the father's beloved orchestra. Their education is carried out within the private sphere, and only Elsa will have the opportunity to pass through the open door toward a public, creative role. Named after an opera heroine, Elsa becomes an opera singer; but her stay in the public realm will not last long.

The sisters are both "same and different," and the relationship among them is expressed through their silence as women and as characters in the narrative; together they absorb the father's inheritance, his love for music, and their mother's passive acceptance of the father's will. The mother has a heart condition; she desires only tranquillity and is disturbed by the daughters' talk, which she calls *sempieze,* nonsense. The maternal passivity helps to create a quiet familial environment that complies with a "patrilinear [and patronymic] project."[9] The connotative value of two words, *ciacole* and *sempieze,* shows the real nature of the relationship between Gustavo Adolfo Wieselberger and his meek wife. The peaceful atmosphere in the house is the result of the absolute compliance with the demands of the patriarch. Linguistically, the mother's definition of women's talk, *sempieze,* is a direct echo of the husband's derogatory approach to the female voices, *ciacole* (chatter), in the house. The mother, who mirrors the father's tongue and has no independent voice, makes no demands beyond the limits established for a middle-class wife. The boundaries of the private sphere are explored only by the daughters; however, to leave the private and enter the public realm is, for them, impossible.

The "girls" become characters who represent the transition between their mother's total acceptance of her role and the granddaughter's, Fausta's, pioneering role in the public sphere. The character who best symbolizes this transition is Adele, the "girl" who dies young:

> A few faded pictures of her remain; in them, she wears a dress for a ball, and she really looks like a fairy. However, the corners of her mouth are bitterly bent downward in a sorrowful expression, as if she knew that she had to die when she was about twenty-seven years old of a disease at that time mysterious. (23)

Adele is better known in the family as *la bella* (the beautiful one), who has had an incredible number of suitors. Yet, what is left for posterity is a picture of her as a mysterious woman with a bitter expression. Adele loves to recite poetry, yet never seems to write it: she reads it in many languages as if she has stepped into a world of creativity, but she cannot be a part of it; she can only echo the poetry that she admires. *La bella* refuses marriage and dies at an age when women were already considered spinsters. She refuses to be enclosed within the *matroneum* of wifehood and maternity, but remains suspended in a "no-man's-land" where, if no man can penetrate, she cannot acquire a creative role other than the mythical Echo's relationship to language. She is also unable to establish a personal signifying system through which she can survive and seems, in fact, to fade away because of her inability to articulate her potential creativity. Her bitter expression in the portrait is both the sign of her knowledge that she is going to die and the mirror of the other girls' future unhappiness. Alba remains throughout her life the keeper of her sister's memory by transforming her into a mythical woman. Adele and Alba have shared a common refusal of marriage. However, Alba becomes identified with stereotypical negative connotations of spinsterhood: she is aggressive and moody. If Adele escapes through death and acquires a new dimension in memories, Alba is still enclosed, trapped within the private sphere. After the first few pages of the text, no character seems to remember that Alba was considered the "intellectual" and not just the introverted and lonely spinster who becomes the father's faithful companion and nurse.

The father's law conditions the daughters' approach to reality and reveals an embedded sense of social class and of the position created for them by the patriarchal order. The static atmosphere that characterizes this middle-class family is described by the narrator as a protective environment that secludes the sisters and gives them the illusion of living in a personal golden age, of being part of an elite, which has the holy historical role of uniting Trieste to the Italian kingdom. The Trieste of the time is an international city where several nationalities coexist. However, the "girls" belong to that social caste of people who blindly consider themselves superior to the large population of Slovenians. Even if, in their personal relationship with the Slovenian care-takers at the Wieselbergers' summer house, they succeed in overcoming their racism, they have "the despicable habit of calling them in dialect *s'ciavi* ["Slovenians," but also "slaves"] or even better 'these damn *s'ciavi*'" (48). From their golden peaceful cage the sisters are able to look at reality only through the eyes of the father. Cialente calls the Wieselberger women "authentic bourgeois women" (68), who, from the privileged position assigned to them by the name of the father, distance themselves from other women and be-come honorary members of the patriarchy through their silent acceptance of the unwritten rules of domination. As Wieselbergers, daughters of the father, they look at other women without being able to read a different story from the one they have been told. In their everyday life, the "girls," the *babe*, meet the *venderigole*, women who work at the market, or see the *sessalote*, who stand for hours while they wait to be hired but do not develop any class consciousness. The "girls" witness the hard life of such women working at the market who, after hours in the cold, can only face more hours in such weather after drinking the local alcoholic beverages. Like well-instructed schoolgirls, the Wieselbergers superciliously disapprove: "Those drunkards— the sisters disdainfully used to say" (21).

The narrator's intervention in the text supplies comments on the com-fortable life the Wieselbergers have in Trieste and also stresses the short-sightedness of the father's and, consequently, the girls' vision of history: "Already a reactionary and greedy bourgeoisie was fattening itself up; a mid-dle class that he, ingenuous musician, was not able to judge and even less condemn. All the more so, as from its heterogeneous ranks came the castes that filled theaters, concert halls, and the beloved Philharmonic" (32). The concept of liberation from the Austrians, still portrayed in today's history books as the "natural" desire of all the *Triestini* to join their blood brothers, is rejected by Cialente as historical fallacy. She stresses the presence of a large number of *Triestini* still faithful to the Austrian empire and, above all, the existence in the city of a large number of Slovenians—who occupied key positions in public offices, because the *Triestini* often refused to learn German. Cialente describes a society and its racism such that "it was with scornful envy that the irredentists could even cry out: These peasants! Who become lawyers, doctors, and managers!—as if the fact that they had the right to study and improve themselves was unacceptable. They did not even realize how racist their contempt was" (49). The nationalistic fanaticism of the *irredentisti,* which the father expresses with goliardic eloquence by farting at the name of the emperor every time he reads it in a newspaper, is exposed by Cialente as a mixture of bigotry, racism, and historical short-sightedness.

The first part of the autobiographical narrative strives to introduce other-ness as the main subject of the discourse: it is the otherness both of the mother, described only as an extension of the collective feminine in the house, and of the Slovenians, who are seen as victims of history and blind nationalism. Public history and the personal, familial story are intertwined in Cialente's articulation of multiple concepts of difference. Elsa's mother, Fausta's grand-mother, is described as a polyvalent character: she is a woman and therefore other, but also a complacent victim, an accomplice of the establishment and, more specifically, of Gustavo Adolfo Wieselberger's *irredentismo.* On her way to construct a new genealogy, Cialente rejects the mother figures in her fam-ily in order subsequently to redefine and reclaim the maternal message for which she is searching. Elsa, Fausta's acquiescent mother, embodies the "alliance to the law she herself appear[ed] to have violated."[10] Elsa has also presented her daughter with "the riddle of daughterhood, a figurative empty pack."[11] In Cialente's "revisionary daughter text,"[12] this "empty pack," which Lynda Boose identifies with the "lack," the identity of the lacking woman, is being subverted in the act of revising the patrilinear and patronymic histor-ical and familial projects.[13]

The *irredentisti* look at the Slovenians as inferior, as intruders in a territory that they have arbitrarily claimed as their own. The outcome of such fanati-cism is World War I, which, as catalyst, helps Fausta, the daughter, to acquire a clear perspective on the bigotry involved in the family's *irredentismo.* Elsa, instead, is blind to the common characteristics that link her to the oppressed Slovenians. The narrator needs to articulate her political stance by rejecting the maternal compliance:

> The war I witnessed had not only disgusted me, but had kindled in me a hatred
> which I felt could not be healed: it was hatred against any form of nationalism
> and racism ("these damn slovenians/slaves, these Austrian sympathizers, these

damn Jews"), therefore, against any abuse. Furthermore, I had already learned that the first to be penalized and crushed are always the poor. (208)

When the narrator's "I" becomes the subject of the autobiography, Elsa's oppression is voiced through Cialente's analysis of all oppressions with which Elsa and her sisters came in contact but never attempted to understand. Unveiling reality through the eyes of the daughter becomes the strategy that allows the narrator to change the mother's approach to reality. It is a dialectical creation of matrilinearism, which does not rely on a diachronic structure. The chronological progression from the grandmother to Elsa and finally to Fausta does not reflect a progressive inheritance of female wisdom. A mythical woman is not portrayed in this autobiography: knowledge is acquired by gradually transgressing those rules accepted by the Wieselberger women. Fausta acquires a female identity that is not inherited from the mothers but is obtained by disobeying the rigid impositions to which the grandmother had completely acquiesced and which Elsa had timidly challenged before accepting a traditional role as wife and mother.

Alice marries a rich Jew in 1886 and becomes an unhappy wife and mother. Elsa's fate seems different from her sister's. She acquires independence from the family, beginning her career as an opera singer in Bologna and having considerable success, which is interrupted by her engagement and then by marriage. However, the handsome young officer who falls in love with the gifted singer has the power to disrupt, to forbid, to separate his acquired wife from her comfortable relationship with her sisters. The collective maternal image for Cialente is further weakened by the male intervention that suffocates the creative component of this close *quartetto* of sisters. The death of creativity is symbolically represented in the text by the disappearance of the most beautiful among the sisters. She is described in the narration as the "poet" whose death is negated by the survival of the "word" in the hands of another woman, the writer and narrator whose sameness and, at the same time, otherness from the dead ancestor creates a connection between the two main parts of the book. Man has, in *The Four Wieselberger Girls*, the power to silence women's independent creativity, but his ability to interrupt a female discourse is only temporary. The silenced poet, Adele, and the silenced singer, Elsa, are a rediscovered text for Fausta.

Elsa and Alice share a common destiny, but once they belong to a husband, they appear unable to confess their unhappiness to each other. Within the narrative, they scrutinize their changed life by looking at pictures from the family album:

[Alice] is a matronly lady in her light long dress . . . in a picture, certainly taken at home, she wears a gloomy dark dress. An enormous threatening hat is on top of her blond hair. She leans against a three-legged table with a little statue on top of it . . . it seems to forebode some unhappiness to the still lady who is haughty and sad: it is her destiny, perhaps. (65–66)

Alice is weighed down by the heavy dress and the "enormous" hat, and seems to need the support of the table to stand still, to face her overdetermined fate. Her life is described through objects, her future unhappiness is reflected in a lifeless statue, as if it were Alice's mirrored image. Signification is displaced in the narrative from language to objects—the pictures and the still life surrounding Alice's portrait. She is the epitome of female silence. For Elsa, instead, there is a short interlude with art that allows her to travel in Italy accompanied by Alba. In a photo of the time, "they both stare into nothingness; their eyes wide open, they even look scared" (68). The narrator interprets their expression as an indication of the girls' awareness of their precious independence and fear of the risks they will encounter. She is searching for the voice of maternal creativity, which is suffocated by what Cialente calls a "banal" matrimony. In the picture, the mother's voice has not been silenced yet, and Elsa and Alice can be read as pioneers of women's future freedom: "They want to show their contemporaries that they are beginning a new era—which they timidly but bravely represent" (68).

However, indifference and acceptance, not transgression, are in store for Elsa, whose creativity is neutralized by a marriage that "seems to have canceled from her own and her family's memory the events and hopes of those years dedicated to studying and to a career which, very soon, incredibly soon, drowns and disappears within the mist of a strange indifference and acceptance" (63). The sisters' married lives are filled with humiliation and betrayal: Alice's husband can afford to pay for a mistress; Elsa's husband chooses from among the servants who, at least, wash themselves. For years the two sisters remain passive and silent. By their silence, they, in turn, educate their daughters to silence: "They are two cautious bourgeois ladies who accept the rules and limitations of their class and, even after their sad experiences, are ready to educate their children—the little girls in particular—to hardship and sacrifices" (73). In "Maternity and Rememory," Marianne Hirsch sees the "mother as doubly 'subjected': she is 'subjected to' the institutions of family and maternity . . . , and those institutions in turn 'subject' her to the needs, demands, and desires both of the culture itself and of the child whom she rears to become subject to that culture in his or her own right."[14] The doubly subjected mother in Cialente's narrative rears her children not to become subjects in a culture, but rather to perpetuate the passivity of subjection by turning them into future maternal mirror models of herself. Fausta distances herself from the maternal reproduction of oppression and strives to create a female subject. She is able to articulate the tension between subjectivity and subjection, present in her mothers, which allows her to attempt a redefinition of practices of motherhood and daughterhood.

The constant intervention of the narrator in the text reminds the reader of the narrating subject's presence, of a woman who describes her maternal origins as the beginning of a female bildungsroman that incorporates the grandmother's, the mother's, and, later, Fausta's experiences. Memory and imagination are one in this fictive representation of the mother. Imagination plays an important role in writing another's autobiography: it is a somebody recognized as the same because she is "mother," and a somebody at the same time recognized as other. Reading the mother as a text in order to write the revisionary text of the daughter's life creates a distance between the maternal character and the protagonist of the autobiography. The task of the narrator, who is fulfilling the dual role of writer and reader, is to incorporate the idea of mother as an open text from which to separate herself.

Choosing to begin an autobiography with the life of another has been considered a common pattern in women's autobiography. Such an assertion contains a universalizing effect of the description of women's autobiographical texts, which has been opposed by many critics who, like Nancy Miller in "Autobiographical Deaths," have uncovered the same techniques in men's autobiographical acts.[15] However, in this context and without any essentializing goal, Cialente's narrative reveals itself as a text in which "the self-discovery of female identity seems to acknowledge the real presence and recognition of another consciousness, and the disclosure of female self is linked to the identification of some 'other.'"[16] The other for Cialente is not, however, only a man, as is the case in many of the autobiographies analyzed by Mason, but is the mother, or mothers, who represent the female identities through which Fausta can construct her "self." Engendering herself through the mother and through the "female" elements in the narrative, Fausta attempts to embody a different woman personified within public and private spheres.

In the description of her life, Fausta, as protagonist of the autobiography, is very distant from the passive maternal woman. In fact, she acquires the ability both to be part of and to act forcefully in order to modify the patriarchal discourse in which she once felt trapped. Her resistance to becoming a maternal mirror image is inherent in her attempt to oppose the paternal power and its embodiment in the complacent women of her familial sphere.

Both as an intellectual and as an antifascist, Fausta temporarily acquires power and an authoritative position, defined by Carolyn Heilbrun as "the ability to take one's place in whatever discourse is essential to action and the right to have one's part matter."[17] The newly constructed concept of female identity is created by looking at the mother as both same and different in order to create a third term, the adult Fausta, "as *two* women, defining each other as both like and unlike, thanks to a third 'body' that both by common consent wish to be female."[18] This new "female body," defined by Irigaray, is represented not only by the woman that Fausta becomes but also by the resulting triangular structure in which mother, daughter, and the construction of a woman's transgressive identity can be found. The idea of a woman's self thus created by the dialectical relationship between mother and daughter not only constructs the future adult character of Fausta, but also modifies the rigid structures of the past and totally changes the mother's traditional acquiescence to her husband's will. In fact, later in life Elsa leaves her husband, who cannot understand why "his wife would not put an end to her comedy of separation" (227).

Together, creativity and memory acquire a special meaning, since it is within the fictive elaboration of the daughter character that the memory of the mothers, the Wieselberger women, is articulated. The daughter's creativity, therefore, is already the elusive center of the first section of Cialente's autobiography. The imaginary world of someone else's biography, as created by the narrator, brings to surface the tension between "historical truthfulness and aesthetic design in autobiography."[19] The need for a wider definition of personal memory is the core of Cialente's construction of hybrid genealogy. Fausta is positioned within and without the female community in order to weaken the dichotomous definition of spheres within the familial households. Cialente's discourse on the female past goes beyond an analysis of women's oppression: she underscores their marginal transgressions and literally dissects the male characters from her past to fragment their identities and unsettle their privileged position. Only as a result of such fragmentation can father figures be rewritten and their positions of power and authority be redefined.

Fausta's mothers embody the negation of women/mothers as subjects. The representation of Alba, however, interrupts this repeated and homogeneous subjugation. She rebels, but her rebellion is mute; she refuses marriage but remains trapped within the familial boundaries and spends her life caring for an aging father. She then becomes an odd spinster, defeated in her struggle against the brothers-in-law whom she publicly accuses of infidelity and neglect. Fausta Cialente writes: "None of the sisters has learned how to float more freely, not even Alba, and that would have been logical and possible even at that time, if they had originated from a different stock. The four Wieselberger girls therefore seem to be still and forever four, even if one of them has disappeared" (22). The metaphors of drowning, of the girls' inability to float, of their loss of self, and of the mysterious fog are repeatedly presented in the description of the sisters' lives. They remain girls, unable to construct an identity as women; they are unable to detach themselves from a fictitious peaceful "golden age" in which they lived; they are unable to float, because they are weighed down by an overdetermined idea of motherhood, wifehood, and femininity as constructed by patriarchy. The end of *The Four Wieselberger Girls* is instead dominated by the "surfacing" of a female identity partly inherited from the mother and passed on to the daughter and the daughter's daughters. This newly created chain is visually represented as walking along the shore: they move in an orderly line, from Fausta to the grandchildren. They walk along the beach, where water and earth come together; it is a no-man's-land appropriated by woman in order to construct her identity in time and space. In this new narrative context, women's "life/lines" cannot be "washed out" anymore by a patriarchal *telos* that drowned into nothingness Fausta's female ancestors.[20] The sisters' private tragedy is reflected by their mother's death. Her awkward big and heavy body, her straight hair, her resigned expression "seem to say that they have already given up on everything" (66). This is the picture that the three daughters keep to remember their mother, as if their lives were doomed to become like hers, and, as Cialente says, they thus forget even that their mother had once been as young as they. The picture of the old mother on her deathbed is discarded by the grandchildren, who choose to remember her as portrayed in the picture of the younger and less defeated grandmother. A different female story is ready to be told; it is a narrative in which the representation of woman is signified neither by passivity and silence nor by disappearance.

The portrait of the mother closes the circular narration emblematized by the father's picture on the cover of the book. The father is portrayed as a young composer sitting at a piano, holding a sheet of paper symbolizing his creativity. In the background is the open landscape of the Adriatic Sea with a promontory of Trieste's coast. The choice of such a cover for the Mondadori edition of the book, fortuitous as it might be, renders visually explicit the unbalanced portrayal of the father and the mother in the four sisters' memory.[21] The old, dying mother and the eternally young, creative, and active father help to reconstruct the traditional binary opposition between male and female characteristics.

The author's memories of childhood begin with an image of a perennial uncomfortable winter: "It was almost always winter" (79). She recalls the feeling of being an outsider in different places where the family had no roots. Cialente adds that "of those places I remember only the names, the cold, the storms, as if they did not have other milder seasons" (79) and portrays herself as a stranger to these unfriendly lands. This description of an initial feeling of unhappiness is complementary to a long passage from Scipio Slataper's *Il mio Carso* (My Carso), quoted at the beginning of one of Cialente's chapters. In Slataper's book, another stranger is portrayed: it is the *s'ciavo* (slave/Slovenian), who, in this context, is allowed to reacquire the dignity of which the racism of the Triestini had deprived him (78). Fausta's autobiography, therefore, reintroduces the problematic definition of otherness that was a thematic core in the narrative of her mother's life.

Within gynealogy, the silent subjects of alterity are also engendered by both children. Fausta and Renato share a common plot, reflected also in their feelings toward the mother and the father. Renato is just a few years older than his sister, and they share fantasies and experiences: "Even if we used to insult and beat each other like all siblings in this world, we were above all accomplices, probably without even realizing it" (95). Marianne Hirsch, in *The Mother/Daughter Plot*, introduces the idea of the representation of the brother as a maternal substitute.[22] She uses the term "fraternal plot" to refer to a fictional dimension in which the brother becomes "the man who would understand."[23] Fraternal traces are scattered in Cialente's construction of the past, and they form a plot that begins with the silence of both siblings ("Who ever dared to say anything? We, Renato and I, had already learned to keep silent; we were a good pair of hypocrites"; 80) and ends with the public recognition of their creativity. The narrative contains the story of the discovery of a shared language and the development of creative expression. Hirsch describes the "brother's tongue" as "a tender form of discourse which revises both the coldness of paternal authority and the rage or anxiety underlying maternal silence."[24] Thanks to the brother's tongue, Fausta can enter and mimic the language of patriarchy and acquire the power to develop her own creativity.

Fausta and Renato are often temporary guests in their grandfather's house, where they feel uncomfortable as they do not share the language and the political ideas of the Wieselbergers. Their reaction to the foreign atmosphere is similar to their mother's: their "feminine" silence brings them together, isolates and protects them from Gustavo Wieselberger's patriarchal authority:

I think that Renato felt less troubled than I did, and he asked me not to *bazilare* [to worry], a term that we used by adapting it to the first conjugation: "io bazilo, tu bazili." Sometimes the fear that by talking with our cousins we would give away what we were not supposed to say [i.e., the father's antimilitarist, antimonarchical, anti-Italian ideas] made us go off by ourselves. What happened was that we ended up playing together as if we were in Italy and not guests in the villa on via dell'Istria. (108)

When together, Fausta and Renato can move from silence into linguistic experimentation, which develops into what they call "the game of words" (108). For their games they choose a forbidden location, a place at the margins of the grandfather's land: a pond nearby, considered a dangerous place for children. They disobey orders and sit near the water, allowing themselves to transgress the limitations of their everyday language. The game starts with one of the children saying "Would you eat . . . ?"; anything disgusting could be the answer to such an introduction:

I was faster in making up combinations, and Renato used to look at me with some suspicion, behaving as if he believed that I had practiced before the game; and that was probably not true. Once I managed to combine something in which I had included also roach pulp and galleyworm legs. Renato, overwhelmed by disgust, but nonetheless showing something I am not sure was surprise or envy, exclaimed: "Well, today you win!" (109)

The brother's tongue is, in this context, a language that can be defeated by the sister's ability at "the game of words"; Fausta's consciousness of her creative ability is born and is accepted by her brother. Both children are, however, expelled from the place of discovery that has allowed them to create a common linguistic plot. The momentary sanctuary near the pond has permitted them to step aside from silencing rules. This symbolic place, once abandoned, becomes an untouchable locus of creativity that develops in different ways for Fausta, the future writer, and Renato, the famous actor.

Silence is, nevertheless, Fausta and Renato's answer to the father for whom Fausta feels an "unconfessed terror" that is accompanied by an "unconfessed pity for the mother" (95). The acute sense of separation from both parental figures slowly changes as, in the narrative of her childhood, Fausta gradually attempts to uncover this mysterious entity called "femininity" and a new relationship to the women of the family. The regular visits to the children's house made by other officers' wives (Fausta's father is an officer in the Italian army) bring the children in touch with the overcodified concept of femininity that is so important in the "caste" in which she belongs (87). The wives are divided according to degrees of respectability. Among them is a group of women Fausta is ordered to ignore, as if they did not exist; they are, of course, the ones the child prefers to all others. Fausta constructs concepts of female subjectivity as a result of her curious exploration of real and imaginary territories that are officially forbidden to her. The initial transgressive sympathy for the "fallen wives" of the officers is the prelude to an episode that constitutes a rite of passage for the young girl: the discovery of prostitution. The exploration of a faraway area of the city is initiated by Renato, who is older than Fausta and who leads her to an unknown neighborhood. Renato's behavior and statements determine the hidden significance of this place where women publicly sit on doorsteps or are seen through windows. As he tells her who they are, his voice soft and low, he holds his sister's arm "as if he wanted to run from that place and those," and he says: "Do you see them! They are whores" (126). By transgressing the father's restrictions and by moving beyond the borders of the space assigned to her, Fausta learns of a hidden world of otherness, considered as a signifier to which Fausta supplies, later in her life, signifieds that connect the oppressed—the *s'ciavi*, the Wieselberger girls, the "fallen" wives, and the prostitutes.

The narrator's search for the meaning of alterity is carried out by stressing the constant discrepancies in the golden cage of the grandfather's bourgeois life. An alternative paternal literary voice appears in Fausta Cialente's text to comment upon and contrast Gustavo Wieselberger's racist ideology. The narrator quotes from Scipio Slataper: "*S'ciavo*, do you want to come with me? I will turn you into the master of these large fields by the sea. . . . You came from lands nobody wanted to inhabit, and you cultivated them. . . . For long years, they have spit your own slavery on your face, but now your time has come. It is time for you to become the master" (77). The Slovenians, seen by the *irredentisti* as the unwelcome barbarians on Italian soil, can acquire in this fictional context a new meaning as suggested by Scipio Slataper's words. To speak of "otherness" in this context means to reflect on the voices that are able to uncover the forgotten history of minorities. Breaking the silence and disturbing the dominant historical discourse is expressed on various levels in the narrative. The concepts of "slave" and "slavery," which could be interpreted either as the oppressive enclosure of women within the private sphere or as the open racism against the *s'ciavi*, is also personified in a third element, the character Alì (42-43). The Wieselberger girls refer to a turning point around which many of their memories are constructed: it is the time when Alì was the young, black servant in the neighbors' house. A rebellious boy brought back from a trip to Africa, he could only communicate in *triestino* and was thus compelled to speak a language that was not his own. Alba attempted to teach him Italian with little success. Soon Alì disappeared, and a stray dog was adopted in the house and named after the black boy. The silenced Alì, whose name is a floating signifier that can signify a human being or a dog, brings to the surface the role of language as a means to negate and to oppress. Alba felt that it was her duty to "teach" him another language of white patriarchy without recognizing the role of Alì as mirror of her own oppression. She is, along with her sisters, silenced by the same rules that she cannot defeat by disappearing, like Alì, into a different "original" land. It is only Fausta who, at the end of her construction of her disparate genealogy, finds a new locus of creativity in her voluntary exile in Alì's land.

Fausta's search for the hidden meaning of otherness in the private sphere is echoed by the silence of the mother. This silence is broken infrequently by moments when Elsa becomes again the artist she was and successfully sings for a few friends:

> Strangely, that applause made her turn pale rather than blushing, and we felt that she felt troubled as if she could not get any pleasure from her singing, which sometimes was joyful and in which I felt the glimmer of a mysterious happiness that made me feel light, lighter in a world framed by light and happiness; a world that she had given up to choose a marriage from which we had originated. (90)

The sudden glimpse of her mother's creativity and the hidden message is a prelude to the different woman Elsa will become when, years later, she removes the "yoke" of her marriage and shows the family her strength by rescuing her husband from bankruptcy. Once her family's finances are saved by her creativity, Elsa returns to her music and becomes, as a music teacher, the family's main support. The short moment of closeness and understanding Fausta feels for her mother's hidden richness is destroyed by the implacable laws of gender dictated by patriarchy: as women, everything must be abandoned to become wives and mothers. The pity she felt previously for Elsa is too simple a feeling to express the new relationship that slowly develops between mother and daughter. Elsa's singing hides a maternal message that reaches its climax in the final chapter, where the construction of matrilinearism becomes the necessary transitional structure toward the creation of a woman's future and of the rereading of her past.

Fausta's gynealogical present and braided future identity are grounded in the desire to go beyond the bare analysis and representation of oppression.

In fact, even the relationship between Fausta and her father is subject to profound change. The terror she feels for him is accompanied by the never voiced awareness that her humble mother is culturally superior to the father. The child feels a weak link to her father's family and their past and is instead attracted to the Trieste family. The language of the father, Italian, is, however, the only means Fausta has to communicate with the branch of the family she prefers. She can understand the dialect, but it is a language she cannot speak; speaking a different language signifies the objective separation between her maternal ancestors and the young girl. *Triestino* comes to be associated with *irredentismo;* it becomes the symbol of the structure in which the Wieselberger girls are "linguistically" trapped. In Cialente's literary production, the solution to the problem of acquiring a linguistic and political identity is the choice of a physical and metaphorical exile. The narrator displaces language from its patriarchal cradle into a new social and narrative context. She writes in Italian from Egypt and uses her literary and oratorical skills against the fascist motherland. The image of fascist Italy as motherland accurately describes once more the destruction of both the rigid dichotomy between male and female characteristics, and the representation of the father as Father, as the incarnation of the oppressor. It is, in fact, the mother who profoundly sympathizes with the regime and is, once again, trapped within a repressive structure that she blindly accepts. The paternal heritage slowly surfaces in Fausta Cialente's autobiography. As an adult, Fausta's Weltanschauung is constructed on her father's political ideas, on a complete refusal both of her mother's *irredentismo* and, later, of her blind faith in Mussolini:

> We had always heard our father speak with utmost contempt (he was an odd officer, angrily antimonarchical); whenever he mentioned the king he called him "that evil misshapen fool [*stortignaccolo*] (but never in front of the relatives from Trieste—our mother had begged him not to). Talking about the queen, he used to exclaim ironically: "Oh, yes the one who is the wet nurse to her children, the glory of the nation!" (105)

Her father's demystifying approach to history puts Fausta in touch with a pragmatic antimilitarism and anti-*irredentismo,* which exposes the ideological fanaticism of Fausta's favorite members of the family but also contains the paternal contempt for women.

The father, whom she has previously rejected, now becomes an important component in Cialente's construction of a discourse on her public identity. In fact, the father character is fragmented so that his pacifism and his ideals are appropriated and transformed. The core of the problematic construction of a woman's subjectivity in *The Four Wieselberger Girls* lies in its attempt to create a nonmythical woman who can be the daughter of both the father and the mother. Absorbing the paternal position and point of view within the public sphere, from which the mother is excluded, allows Fausta to acquire a privileged position within the text as "reader of the father." This also allows the protagonist to leap intellectually beyond the father and to understand the limitations of his ideological discourse:

> The anger and the indignation that I had always seen in him came from his contempt for the rulers and for a career to which he never became accustomed and that had undoubtedly made him suffer. However, his rebellion and his criticism were not linked—as I had to realize later—to the reality of social turmoil to which he was foreign and the dawn of which he could not see. (181)

The pity for the mother, which has been such a consistent part of Fausta's approach to the parental figures, is displaced and shifts from the mother to the father, who becomes pathetic in his personal unhappiness, his anti-Semitism, and his only partially enlightened political ideas. This new text that the author constructs is a personal history in which "traces of the father" are an important component.

It is finally the father who, as an ex-officer, starts to understand social problems and becomes, through his pacifism and republican ideals, a weaker power and authority figure. The paternal image is understood by Cialente as being the same as but, at the same time, different from the patriarchal construction of the paterfamilias. It is by privileging that difference that the narrator can construct an inherited "patrimony" acceptable in her creation of a personal memory.[25] If the father is seen as transgressing the rules established by patriarchy, then the paternal character acquires characteristics of alterity that create a link between the female characters and the father. Cialente fragments his life and privileges his antimilitarist and antifascist ideals, which he proclaims even when he is still an officer in the Italian army. This newly created paternal identity is a hybrid character, an image of transition between two binary oppositions. He also becomes a social and ideological *métis*. He retires into a private life of failures, since he is not successful in his attempt to create a career after leaving the army, and his loneliness and marginalization are stressed by the narrator. He is abandoned by his wife, is unable to take care of himself, and needs a female companion as a nurturing substitute for his wife. When he is no more identified by his uniform, his ideological transgression is neutralized by his isolation. Trapped within a domestic sphere, the father as an "old man" becomes an approachable identity that can be manipulated within the structure of an autobiographical act. The genealogical analysis of Fausta's past is therefore structured within a form of textual *métissage* in which maternal and paternal images are closely interwoven to create the braided genealogy of the protagonist.[26] In this context, the act of mirroring is no more centered around the mother-daughter relationship. It is the father who becomes a reflection of the immobile woman trapped in a private sphere from which she was, and now he is, unable to escape. Deprived of his public power, this passive father becomes a feminine paternal figure who is a weaker authoritative figure and haunts the margins of that patriarchal realm he used to embody. This stranger to his own self is adopted in the daughter's text as a means of mediation between past and present.

Cialente locates the common ground shared between the mother's private sphere and the paternal public sphere in Fausta's writing, in her creativity. Creativity is, in *The Four Wieselberger Girls,* always linked to some kind of public performance. The mother proves to be an artist in front of large audiences before her marriage. Later, it is a smaller public of friends that applauds her domestic performances after her marriage. For Fausta's brother, creativity is reflected in his theater performances, through which he acquires national notoriety. While the mother fails to succeed because other priorities are imposed on her life—marriage and maternity—Renato's short but brilliant career as an actor is not impeded by the rules of a fascist society. While still proclaiming the importance of her role as mother in the private sphere, Cialente succeeds in portraying the *matroneum* as a fictive "plastic" space. Her aim is to unsettle the boundaries that limit the traditionally female sphere that had frustrated Elsa's creativity, boundaries that must be expanded in order to redefine what Sandra Gilbert calls the "'empty pack' of daughteronomy" dominated by acquiescence and resignation.[27] As a child, Fausta had, in fact, witnessed her mother's efforts to reach a compromise between creativity and her destiny as wife and mother. Only in the daughter's life can such a "compromise" be found. Without sacrificing the importance of motherhood, the narrator stresses her role as writer, journalist, and antifascist, thus achieving that mobility among spheres for which the mother had searched.

In Cialente's autobiographical biography of the mothers and biographical autobiography of the daughter, Elsa's unhappiness in marriage functions as a mirror for the other female characters, including Fausta, the daughter. The narrator talks about her marriage as "an escape," a way to escape from the patriarchal Italian society and to begin a different life in Alexandria, where her marriage soon fails (216). Yet, the man she marries barely appears as a character in the narrative. He is relegated to the background, and Fausta's marriage is covered by a silence that is broken in a different context, an interview in which Cialente talks about her husband:

> He was the one who allowed me to enter the world of modern music, by which I was strongly fascinated right away. But he has been my master in many other things: in culture and politics, for instance. The balance of my married life is positive, even if at one point I decided to leave Egypt and my husband.[28]

The point of contact between Fausta and her husband lies in creativity and in their involvement in the public sphere. Their relationship within the familial sphere is revealed as secondary within the narrative. The disturbing note in Fausta Cialente's positive portrayal of the man she "had" to leave is the husband's role as teacher in many things, who is appreciated because he supplies the means to enter the public realm, but must be abandoned once the woman acquires the authority to rewrite the silenced images from her maternal past. The separation is thus described: "It was necessary because of the tragic death of my brother, the actor Renato Cialente; my mother had been left alone, I had to devote myself to her."[29] The story of the husband is suffocated by her private story, in which living with the mother and preserving the brother's memory become priorities. The husband is initially silenced as he becomes one with the character of the grandfather. They both love music and educate Fausta to music; however, their creativity is "taught" but not shared. Nevertheless, the husband acquires a "different" voice, because he finds its position in the plot of the "exile," which is an imagined space where woman can acquire an authoritative identity and enter the public sphere represented by the world of literature and politics. The husband's political voice is heard several times in the narrative, and it is in contrast to the racist ideals of his bourgeois family. In his transgression, the husband can become an ally to the woman's antifascist battle and share a common space of resistance.

In her Egyptian exile and its social and cultural environment, Fausta is again faced with an added context of alterity. Egypt reveals itself as another land of the father(s). The original "patriarchal land" reflects itself in the new country, where the separation between the dominators and the dominated is again clearly cut. Cialente writes: "I became attached to the country and the people, an unusual occurrence for me. The affection and the sympathy came, at least partially, from my reaction to the barely hidden racism that Europeans and Levantines alike, including [her husband's] Jewish family, displayed toward the natives" (220). Cialente displaces the act of portraying otherness into a discourse on history and of the protagonists of contempo-

rary historical events, including the blindly racist Jewish members of the
husband's family, who, at a time when Jews are oppressed and murdered
in Europe, perpetuate oppression on others. The natives become the subject
of Cialente's creativity in novels such as *Cortile a Cleopatra* (Courtyard in
Cleopatra; Cleopatra is the name of an area in Alexandria); her writing is
interrupted, however, by the war and her active participation in antifascist
propaganda. She works to broadcast antifascist programs from a radio station
in Cairo. At her father's death, Fausta feels "a deep, definitive laceration" that
initiates a process of separation between Fausta and her father's land (288);
in fact, Cialente writes, "the behavior of Italians is such that I almost always
feel the need to leave" (246). In an interview, Cialente affirmed: "I have never
felt that I am Italian, partly because of my origins and partly because of the
life I have had."[30] The language inherited from the father is separated from
the fatherland, so that even while writing in Italian, Fausta Cialente remains
in voluntary exile from Italy.

Critics such as Paola Malpezzi Price have underlined the autobiographical
nature of Cialente's narratives.[31] In her autobiography, those texts reputed to
be autobiographical are not mentioned, as if the indirectly autobiographical
act cannot be articulated within the narrative of her life story. This tension
between making her life public and silencing within such a narrative the already published texts invites an investigation of the various representations
of the hybrid protagonists in Cialente's works, including her autobiography,
as complementary personifications of the construction of international subjectivities. Fausta's escape from Italy is in part dictated by a rejection of the
anxiety-ridden structures of her family's national and nationalistic ideology
and of Italy's struggle to create an artificial unity, which will develop into a
dictatorial oneness in the name of Mussolini (Cialente moves to Egypt in
1921, after Italy's acquisition of new land that includes Trieste at the end
of World War I and just before the beginning of the fascist dictatorship).
Cialente chooses a "border life" for herself and her characters in order to
explore realms of cultural difference and transgression. Displacing her self
into a different national context means for Cialente to explore the interstices
of in-betweenness, what Bhabha calls "the overlap and displacement of domains of difference."[32] In *Courtyard in Cleopatra*, Marco, the protagonist, is
the son of an Italian man and a Greek woman. His father raises him in Italy;
upon the father's death, Marco returns to Egypt, where he was born and where
his mother still lives. Marco passively witnesses the life in the courtyard,
paralyzed by a sense of the "unhomeliness" in the cross-cultural context in
which he lives.[33] His difference is grounded in his identity both as a racial

métis and as an outsider in the struggle for social mobility that guides the relationships of the dwellers in the courtyard. Once Marco is offered to achieve status within the commercial middle class, he reacts by disappearing from the familial courtyard in an act of further geographical displacement (he moves inland among the natives and away from the western Levantines), which is more acceptable to him than the acquiescence to sameness and homogeneity. In *Ballata levantina* (The Levantines), Daniela, the protagonist, investigates the realms in which she became an adult; her familial sphere is dominated by the grandmother, a prostitute. Marginalized by the hypocrisy of the white colonizers, Daniela finds herself an uninvited guest in a white race that despises her. The sense of "unhomeliness" is pervasive in Daniela's attempt to mediate between her identity as undesirable and the society of which she is supposed to be part because of her racial identity. The grandmother's transgression to the rules of acceptability of the white colonizers translates itself into the character of the granddaughter who inherits a contaminated identity, which is the locus of her difference. Furthermore, Daniela's difference from her grandmother, her separation from the familial house, and her added marginalization within the public sphere of the Levantines' life transform her into the unacceptable hybrid. The war and the subsequent emergencies and tensions, divide the Levantines of Italian origin between antifascists and fascist sympathizers, providing Daniela with the opportunity to assimilate, to become the "same" and to belong to either group. However, sameness is perceived as unacceptable, and, at the moment in which a traditional happy ending threatens to take place, Daniela kills herself in a mysterious way that leaves doubts and blurs the difference between accidental death and deliberate suicide. Even in her death, Daniela chooses to inhabit the space of indeterminacy.

It is such a space that translates into Cialente's autobiography and mirrors her personal choice of voluntary exile, which allows a constant redefinition of the location of her cultural identity. In her introduction to *Women's Writing in Exile*, Angela Ingram writes:

> Voluntary exile, something of a luxury when we consider it closely, constitutes for a number of writers an escape from the entrapping domain of the silenced mother-under-patriarchy, the manifestation of women's internalized exile/estrangement: a "matricidal" intent is writ large through some of the text of exile. Such an escape into the world of the apparently liberating word, the world of culture, of adulthood, though, often means entry into the confines of patriarchal languages and heterosexual and heterosexist imperatives. Enabled, on one hand, to write, to create new worlds and to create what should have been home, many writers find the other hand shackled by the expectations

and rules of the world of words they have chosen to inhabit. For some, however, the ambiguities and paradoxes inherent in finding a place to write are at least partly resolved by finding a "home" in writing itself.[34]

Fausta's voluntary exile is her solution to the "matricidal" tension in the narrative. It is her reaction to the mother's double exile from Trieste, which she leaves to follow her husband into the Italian kingdom, and from creativity. Furthermore, by exiling herself, Cialente creates a mediating condition between matricidal and patricidal tensions by deterritorializing the spheres and by reterritorializing her creative realms of authority. Her choice of voluntary exile becomes a protracted choice of marginality, because a new land to inhabit permanently is never found. Home, then, becomes the fictional context of literature; above all, it is the locus of the construction of a disparate genealogy. It is, however, a realm not recognized by the fatherland of patriarchal language. Fausta Cialente cannot escape connotations of marginality, because in the context of Italian literature she is labeled as a minor female author of the twentieth century. To inhabit the words becomes the only way to construct not a marginalized voice, but rather a disturbing voice at the margins, which aims to destroy the rigid oppositions within patriarchy by creating an intermediate, hybrid place in which to dwell. It is her voluntary exile, as portrayed in the autobiographical text, that is not a completely controllable entity in either the public or the private spheres.

However, creativity for Fausta Cialente partakes of both private and public realms. Her public involvement in propaganda, her political role during World War II, and her fiction writing are presented as important parts of her life. In the final chapter of *The Four Wieselberger Girls,* Cialente returns to the private sphere of family life, where the creation of a different self is successfully carried out. Surrounded by her daughter and granddaughters, Fausta encloses herself in a familial atmosphere and leaves the public struggle behind. She steps out of the political diatribe in the postwar world, where the oppressed sometimes prove that they have learned very little and become the oppressors: "I saw the miserable camps of the refugees from Palestine, those of the first war with Israel; I reacted with indignation, which maybe surprised my travel companions" (250). The concern about the new Jewish state, voiced by Fausta's anti-Zionist husband, as follows, is welcomed with sympathy, albeit detached sympathy, by the narrator:

> To create another nationalism? Are there not enough of them? Have they not brought us enough bad luck? If at least they could found a really democratic and modern state, that is a tolerant state! But they will do exactly the opposite

with the money of the American Jews, the cream among the reactionaries, those who would never dream of moving to Israel, do you want to bet on it? (251)

"I would not have been able to bet anything at all," silently answers Fausta to her husband's rhetorical question while she is already flying to join her daughter. Public thoughts and private choices are intertwined in the text. This rejection of conflicts and violence is the element of transition from her publicly active life and her political visibility in order to reconnect with her daughter. "Although mothers are not intrinsically peaceful," writes Sara Ruddick, "maternal practice is a 'natural resource' for peace politics."[35] In the exact moment when Cialente seems to articulate her rejection of public roles, she supplies the means for a revision of the public itself and a resistance to the violence that she abhors. However, her maternal discourse on peace in matrilinearism is not developed, as her matrilinear practice does not become a theoretical stance. The attraction of a public involvement is surpassed by the desire for a private life with her daughter. Yet, after a short private parenthesis of creative silence, Cialente returns to writing. While choosing a life with the daughter and rejecting a political, public role, she returns to writing to participate from the margins in the cultural life of a country that she can accept only from her voluntary exile. This semipublic, semiprivate realm allows Cialente to construct a self that can be, within the narrative, the daughter of both a public and, simultaneously, a private sphere: she becomes the element of rupture of a rigid oppositional structure.

The final chapter of Fausta Cialente's autobiography contains the cathartic moment of closure in the construction of a woman's self. Fausta joins her daughter in Kuwait. It is after the end of the war, and she feels "tired" and "exhausted"; she wants only to rest and live with her daughter and the grandchildren (255). The new temporary home, only accidently in Kuwait, becomes a female Garden of Eden from which woman cannot be expelled. This no-Man's-land described does not belong to any historic-geographic place; it is an atemporal and mythical location. In the primordial landscape of a deserted beach, the protagonist feels that she is breaking all limitations; she has the feeling of attempting "some steps in the unlimited solitude of a new world that has just surfaced from the ocean" (260). It is in this context that Jardine's gynectic horizon is translated into a geographic maternal landscape. Fausta's footprints on the sand create a new path in the discourse on female identities and daughterhood, but also represent an adult woman's identity, a woman who does not "exist only in relation to her child," because she becomes "a [writing] subject in her own right."[36] Her reconstruction of the past and the construction of an independent identity are merely starting points in the construction of a female future: "These dear figures who walk in front of me are really mine, I thought while tenderly looking at them; they are doubles of myself. . . . The fact that they represented for me the continuity of life could only be a severe awakening to reality" (262). By representing the daughter and the grandchildren simultaneously as same and other, the narrator expresses the possibility of creating a never ending discourse on women's subjectivity that cannot be enclosed within the text of her autobiography.

In this temporal line, which tends toward things to come, the past can find its true place. Fausta interrupts her walk on the beach, and, turning, she sees and hears her dead mother: "I still love you, but leave me in peace now, and think about living by making as few mistakes as possible. We have made so many of them" (263). Her mother's message, delivered against this mythical landscape, between the amniotic fluidity of the ocean and the desolate land, creates the concrete reality of matrilinearity in which the death of the mother can be accepted, because it is not final and is not signified by silence and disappearance. The mother's words, delivered in the plural, include a multiplicity, a collective past of which she only represents the symbolic unity translated in the text, thanks to a *métissage* of traces. Fausta's walk continues into creativity—toward "the open page, that is, this sea and this sky, behind my three distant figures"—and into her text, her autobiographical act, her newly constructed gynealogical techniques and hybrid genealogy (263).

CHAPTER FOUR

Rita Levi Montalcini's Perfect Imperfection

A Woman's Role in the Public Sphere

Il gioco dei bottoni rientrava nella categoria dei giochi infantili . . .
[era] quello di immaginare che cosa il futuro teneva in serbo per ciascuna . . .
"povera, ricca, monaca, sposa."

The game of buttons belongs to the category of children's games . . .
[it was] a game in which we imagined what the future reserved for each one
of us girls . . . "Poor woman, rich woman, nun, wife."

RITA LEVI MONTALCINI[1]

In their article entitled "Conflicts and Tensions in the Feminist Study of Gender and Science," Helen Longino and Evelyn Hammonds approach the subject of women in science by declaring that sciences are still "bastions of masculinity."[2] Longino, a philosopher, and Hammonds, a physicist, set out to investigate feminist theories on gendered sciences and "the reception of feminist critiques of science by practicing women scientists."[3] Their conclusions reveal that women are still not encouraged to develop a "self-critical perspective about their own disciplines" and that the separation between women scientists and women who attempt a feminist critique of women's position in science still must be overcome.[4] Longino and Hammonds bring into evidence women scientists' "little sense of history," since even the strategies employed in facilitating the access of women to a scientific field are

identical to the ones employed before World War II.[5] Sandra Harding's
investigation of both the question of women in science and the question of
science and women scientists within feminism aims to "make the activities
of feminists in science intelligible and legitimate to the administrators who
have power over their projects."[6] This interest in the relationship between
gender and science, gendered science and history, which is developed by
American feminists and theorists, has not been one of the focuses of contemporary Italian feminism. This chapter, devoted to Rita Levi Montalcini
and the story of her life as a scientist, deals with an Italian case that expands
beyond the border of Italy itself. Not a feminist herself, Montalcini introduces and discusses issues that have been the core of the debate of the critics
mentioned above, developed in an American context with which Montalcini
is familiar. Issues of scientific practice and daily action, science and race, and
science and society are some of the focuses in Montalcini's autobiography,
which narrates the life of a woman in science from the twenties to today, from
Italy to the United States and back.

Rita Levi Montalcini's *Elogio dell'imperfezione* (In Praise of Imperfection,
1988) reconstructs a personal and historical "path" that is parallel to Cialente's
life story, narrated through the historical events of the first half of this century.[7] Both Cialente and Montalcini recount their mothers' silence and their
fathers' power to silence female voices. In complementary but separate autobiographical texts, they acquire personal voices that describe a plurality of
women's identities through generations and elaborate on female roles in the
spheres that they inhabit. Montalcini's *In Praise of Imperfection* narrates two
different but not completely distinct female journeys. On one hand, she ret-
rospectively rereads her father in order to construct the paternal inheritance
that has allowed her to enter the public sphere. On the other, the author
constructs a metaphor of her "self" who gains access to the public realm of
scientific research by redefining rules that allow a woman to become part
of a scientific elite: she inscribes maternal traces into her path to success.
Montalcini quotes Yeats in the introduction to her autobiography:

> The intellect of man is forced to choose
> Perfection of the life, or of the work. (7)

She rewrites Yeats's irreconcilable aspirations in order to define her own role
in the public world of science. Consequently, the poet's perfection is transformed into "imperfection of the life and of the work" (11). It is imperfection
that becomes the unifying element between life and work, private and public,
and destroys the dichotomized portrayal of the two spheres. Imperfection

becomes for Montalcini a way to reach "perfection" or, at least, perfection's signifiers, in order to expose the limitations inherent in any discourse that aims to construct the myth of perfection itself; she was awarded the Nobel prize for medicine in 1986. Her success, Montalcini writes, is achieved not through a straight linear progression of smaller achievements, which already signify the final one, but rather through the fragmented, nonlinear progression of failures and successes. Montalcini reconstructs "success" and "perfection" as flawed and only imperfect entities that cannot be receptacles of strong truths but rather of smaller, weaker truths. Her "perfect imperfection," which can be achieved through a nonlinear personal and public journey, could be described as a "zigzag" or, in Montalcini's words, a *processo disarmonico* (dissonant process)(11).

The author begins her autobiography by demonstrating this technique of zigzag. Her introductory chapter is devoted to the delineation of her public role in research and to the description of her methodology, her personal imperfection. However, the subsequent chapter is a reconstruction of the familial realm in the Montalcini household at the beginning of the century. The narrative is characterized by a discordant rhythm that allows the autobiographer to enter and exit the private and public spheres in these initial chapters. While present and past are combined, the dichotomy between the two spheres is also challenged by the author's outline of her roles in the public and private realms. This zigzag, a discontinuous and fragmented movement, allows the protagonist to inhabit both spheres without becoming entrapped in the private realm nor being an honorary guest in the public world.

Montalcini's native Turin is described in the first chapter by Giorgio De Chirico (quoted by the narrator) as the birthplace of Rita's twin sister, Paola. The author adopts a male narrative within her own text to describe the patriarchal city. De Chirico, in fact, privileges the "important" sights in the city and creates a list of masculine glories. The statues of Lagrange, Missori, Garibaldi, Verdi, Victor Emmanuel II, and Emanuele Filiberto signify, according to the famous painter, the city itself:

> One can see Lagrange, the famous scientist, who leans on the robust arm of colonel Missori, who wears his mustache grognard style, and is the man who, in a battle against the Austrians, saved Garibaldi's life. . . . One can see Garibaldi himself, the soldier without fear, the bearded lion . . . listening to Giuseppe Verdi, who is talking to him. . . . One can see King Victor Emmanuel II, all made in bronze, covered with ribbons, cordons and decorations, in bronze as well, who discusses strategy with Emanuele Filiberto of Savoy, who is leaning against the hilt of his long sword. . . . Turin lives under the sign of Taurus. The first inhabitants adopted the bull as their emblem. . . . Paola Levi Montalcini is from

Turin. It is in this monarchic, fluvial, and orderly city that she has lived and worked until today. (17–18)

The male narrative completely replaces the author's words, as if Montalcini can describe with eloquence the patriarchal world in which she was raised only by silencing her own voice. De Chirico creates a city where power is symbolized by the hard effigies of famous men cast in bronze. Such a portrayal of the capital of Piedmont (and once also the capital of Italy) is, however, completed by a description of another side of that city. In De Chirico's concluding statements, Turin appears as a *città fluviale* (fluvial city), a place with a weaker, softer side. By beginning her autobiography with a quotation, Montalcini reveals her agenda in the translation of her life and the construction of her self in a personal narrative. She adopts a male portrayal of the public order in order to modify it and privilege the "marginal" within the male discourse, that is, the city not as a monarchic place that symbolizes male success, but rather as fluvial, and, consequently, she develops from it a different portrayal of a public sphere:

> But it was not necessary to accentuate in an almost grotesque way that mustache in order to remind his subjects of the manly attributes of their first king. . . . They were, if anything, too well known, at least to the inhabitants of Turin at the end of last century, who were proud of his war exploits as much as of his hunting expeditions, occasions in which he had drinking bouts and took liberties with the local beautiful girls. . . . Nevertheless, Victor Emmanuel II had certainly become king after his death, as proven by his haughty expression, that mustache, the ramrod posture, and all those cordons, medals, decorations. That famous mustache, which I stared at from our window, was of such a size that, as my mother used to say, each part could have been used as an armchair for an adult man. (18–19)

The imperfect king becomes very easily the perfect image that official history successfully constructs. What public history does not elaborate remains hidden because it is "imperfect" and, consequently, invisible among the hard statues of official memory. The same official history, celebrated in the open and public spaces of Turin's squares, is replaced by Montalcini with the "minimal" story of a woman who is simultaneously writing her life and exposing the fallacy of public history.

The initial pages of Montalcini's autobiography are crowded by men who describe women. In the introductory chapter, the narrator talks about one of her young research assistants who divides female mice into *madri sozze* (degenerate mothers) or *madri carissime* (very affectionate mothers) according to their attitudes toward the newly born mice (9). Such a dogmatic definition of motherhood is followed, in the first chapter of the book, by De Chirico's description of the hard city to introduce the character of Rita Levi Montalcini's sister. Both men supply an idea of perfection against which women are gendered: it is either a man's discourse on motherhood and an essentialist definition of ideal womanhood or the portrayal of the reassuring symbols of male virility that embody the official history of a city from which women have been excluded. The statues narrate a history that Montalcini modifies by initiating a different discourse on the portrayal of a woman in the retro-spective narrative of her life. She privileges an "imperfect" portrayal of her self and of her journey from childhood to womanhood and from the private to the public sphere.

The starting point in the construction of her "self" lies in the father's def-inition of the young Rita as *la sua sensitiva* (his sensitive one), as the least probable member of the family to abandon the security of the familial status quo to explore a different sphere and construct an independent identity (23). "I think," writes the narrator, "that now [my father] would recognize me as his daughter and not only as 'his sensitive one'" (23). What Montalcini demands is to be identified outside of this opposition between strong male identities and weak female entities; in the construction of her subjectivity, she plans to articulate an idea of female subjectivity that allows her to go beyond dichotomized representations of gender.

In describing her family, however, the narrator adopts the dichotomy cre-ated by De Chirico to develop a discourse on the traditional structure of the familial sphere and on the members of her family. Her father is first intro-duced as the mirror image of Turin's pillars of masculinity. The connection between Rita's father and the public images of patriarchy is symbolized by characteristics shared by both. Victor Emmanuel and Rita's father wear sim-ilarly imposing mustaches, described by the author: "The father's and the son's mustaches [Victor Emmanuel II and his son] had not marked their times less than the hooped petticoats and the ladies' wasp waists. The former and the latter laid emphasis on secondary sexual characteristics in order to explicitly underline the differences in roles" (19). As a reflection of the king, Rita's fa-ther becomes the metaphorical son of the public man par excellence and in-herits the power intrinsic in his superior role. Montalcini depicts the private and public spheres as two separate entities, both of which are dominated by the paternal figure: "Our small family unit offered an exemplary model for the application of these [patriarchal] ideologies" (34). Her father's ability to move from the public into the private sphere is contrasted by her mother's immobility in her role as nurturer and wife. The maternal role in the domestic realm is signified by silence and by the acceptance of her husband's will. As mother, she is enclosed in a *matroneum,* which the husband can enter but which she cannot escape. Both in Cialente's *The Four Wieselberger Girls* and in Montalcini's *In Praise of Imperfection,* womanhood and motherhood are, within the familial sphere, identified with passivity and acquiescence. Both Rita and Fausta, the two daughters who are protagonists of, respectively, Montalcini's and Cialente's narratives, strive to put a distance between their mothers and themselves, between the silence that the daughters would inherit from their mothers and their need to make their voices heard. Rita and Fausta search for a new definition of womanhood and more flexible constructions of female subjectivities that are not signified by silence and oppression. Both Cialente's and Montalcini's autobiographical texts construct spaces of creativity in which they trace the *iter* that brings them to create independent selves. In these spaces appropriated within the literary public sphere, daughters as writers portray the private identities of their silenced mothers, who, in this context, contribute to the construction of the visibility of their own daughters as authors of other women's lives. Such a space contains the description of a journey that begins with their rejection of the traditional paternal and maternal inheritances that perpetuate the oppression of a woman gendered as mother, wife, and daughter.

Rita's fear of her father represents the initial fear of his power. The disgust she feels for his phallic mustache is reflected in the child: Rita refuses to "kiss" the father.[8] She kisses instead the air around his face, but she has no difficulty in kissing her mother. The author defines the separation between her inability to approach her "hard" father and her love for her "soft" mother:

> I had in fact acquired the habit, when moving close to him [the father] in order to wish him "good night," to turn my head before touching his face and to send my kiss into the air. It certainly did not escape an observer like my father that I had no difficulty in kissing my mother. However, in her case, it was not only the strong affection I felt for her, but also the pleasure of brushing against the soft and scented skin of her face, that was reason enough to conquer my natural aversion to physical contact. (19)

Such a division between the opposite male and female characteristics once more mirrors Chirico's portrayal of the city as "hard" on one hand and "fluvial" on the other. Rita reveals her need to keep a distance between her overpowering father and herself, while she is attracted to the "soft," ethereal mother whom she enjoys embracing.

The mother's character is portrayed as a pre-raphaelite woman and as the ideal of feminine perfection as seen through the male gaze. A photograph of

Rita's mother described by the narrator portrays the mother as the epitome of fragility and sweetness:

> Her exceptionally beautiful face, framed by her blond hair gathered up on her nape, has a thoughtful and serious expression and is lowered over the child's head, which is as beautiful as hers. The child . . . stares at his minuscule big toes that are visible from underneath the mother's arm. Her striped blouse that covers the slim body of a twenty-year-old and her upright position against the railing make one think of a figure painted by Dante Gabriel Rossetti. (51)

In this aesthetically refined picture of domestic bliss, the Madonna-like portrait defines woman as an acquiescent figure whose happiness lies in motherhood. This, in turn, defines the limits of the *matroneum* in the Montalcini household. The collapse of any separation and difference between motherhood and womanhood signifies the marginality of Rita's mother in the familial sphere. Even Rita easily discovers, at a young age, the impossibility of her mother acquiring a different role: "It is difficult for me to remember when, early in my childhood, I became aware of the different roles my father and my mother had in the administration of our family and of our father's enormous and never contested prevalence over those small and big decisions that concerned us" (36). The father's voice is privileged in the private sphere just as it is in the public; the paternal "imperiousness of . . . voice" and the maternal *dolcezza* (sweetness) represent the father's active role and the mother's passive silence (37).

Montalcini recounts an anecdote that clearly delineates the paternal power position in the domestic realm; it is a story about her father's love for romantic dramas. One of them, *Il padrone delle ferriere* (The Owner of the Ironworks), contains a few lines that Rita's father loves to repeat. He rehearses in private the relationship between the two characters in the play, in which the man declares to his wife: "You love me, . . . I adore you, . . . but I will break you" (37). Once again a man characterizes woman according to his own ideas on femininity: a woman here is an entity to break, to tame, and to transform into a weak being that is dominated. The opposition between weak and strong, soft and hard, keeps reappearing in Montalcini's narration of her childhood:

> My father shared the general admiration for that great actor's [Zacconi's] power of expression and showed it by repeating the famous sentence in front of my mother, who used to smile, because it seemed to her unthinkable that there could be any allusion to the relationship between her and my father. We used to keep silent, but I remember my profound resentment . . . against Zacconi and my hatred against the owner of the ironworks, who considered himself the owner even of his wife, with the approval of the spectators. (37)

Powerful male expression and female silence are the irreconcilable opposites that embody male and female voices in Rita's family. Her father rehearses in the private sphere his public role as *padrone delle ferriere* (he is, in fact, in charge of an industry) and monopolizes the domestic realm as the place where men "engage in repairs and rehabilitation, chew over performances and think how to improve them, and even rethink the whole play in which [men] are engaged."[9] The familial sphere, in the Montalcini household, dominated by a male voice and a male will, is complemented by a *matroneum* filled by the silence whose echo encompasses the mother and the children.

Marriage is portrayed as an institution that a woman can enter only after abandoning her individual personality. Maternity becomes a woman's biological destiny, transformed in marriage into an additional means to "weaken" a woman's independent identity, because "under patriarchy the mother's life is exchanged for the child's."[10] Rita decides, therefore, to reject marriage and motherhood. Her refusal of a stereotypical female destiny allows her to escape from a traditionally predetermined fate. Carolyn Heilbrun offers the theoretical strategy for reading the tension between woman as defender of patriarchal values and woman as transgressor of male values:

> The real tension . . . between the fleeing woman and those struggling to preserve the family, is the tension between order and change, particularly evident in our society. It is most evident within marriage, where the man desires order and the woman change. If the women are unclear about what change should encompass, they know it begins with their departure.[11]

Rita is determined to reject the traditional male order, where mothering is considered an instinctive and natural side of femininity. After deciding not to become a mother, Rita must restate her refusal to mother even when she has already acquired her public role of scientist. She narrates the story of a colleague who, after becoming alcoholic, is abandoned by his wife, who takes the two daughters with her but leaves him their only son. "I refrained," writes Montalcini, "from visiting him. Despite the affection I felt for both him and P., I did not feel up to fulfilling a maternal role for them. I had never felt any inclination to such a role" (188–89). She cannot be part of the patriarchal plan in which every woman is essentially a mother, ready to perform according to male needs. Man's order, which demands the immobility of the gendered woman as necessary to reach his "perfection of life," is unsettled by Rita both in her construction of an imperfection that transgresses male rules and in her search for mobility between the different roles that she can play in the private and the public spheres. "Imperfection" becomes a "room of her own," but not a sealed room of her own.

In framing the concept of an imperfection of life, Montalcini reveals the need to challenge the traditional dichotomy between masculine and feminine, between strong and weak, between male perfection and female imperfection. To do so she rereads the father as a text that can be fragmented and reinterpreted. She weakens the paternal character by exposing perfection as a fallacy, constructed to establish the unchallengeable myth of male superiority:

> I think that I can state that in scientific research, neither the level of intelligence nor the ability to follow and complete with precision the task undertaken are essential factors to reach success and personal satisfaction. . . . The fact that the profession, carried out in such an imperfect way, has been and is even now a source of inexhaustible joy, makes me think that the imperfection in the execution of the tasks that we have chosen or that have been given to us is more suitable than perfection to human nature, which is so imperfect. (11)

By privileging imperfection as the unifying characteristic among "human beings," Montalcini creates an alternative path to gain access to the public sphere—not as entities gendered by patriarchy, but rather as "beings" who need to be renamed and reinterpreted. Montalcini's interest in the human subject and his or her nonlinear progress toward discovery and self-revelation is grounded in a concept of a public subjectivity that declares and at the same time negates the success achieved. In her *L'azione perfetta* (The Perfect Act, 1993), Chiara Zamboni indirectly comments on and shares Montalcini's theoretical position: "The imperfection of the perfect act is inherent in its existence in reality and in our own human contradictions."[12] These perfectly imperfect human beings become temporary heroes in Montalcini's *processo disarmonico* (dissonant process) and achieve a flawed success. With this process, Montalcini calls into question the value of intelligence as the traditional rational guiding element to achieve complete success in the public field of scientific research where she operates; instead, she describes her success as the result of a process carried out "without having a preestablished plan, but rather guided at times by my inclinations and by chance" (11). She therefore attacks the idea of the perfect agent in scientific research whose linear progression and "objective" analysis are the only guarantees of success. Montalcini's demythologization of science and of its accessibility also articulates Evelyn Fox Keller's idea that "objectivity itself is an ideal that has a long history of identification with masculinity."[13]

The issues that Montalcini develops concern the roles of women who gain access to the public scientific world and who reject the dichotomized vision

of the gendered world of science, what Keller calls the "science-gender system."
Attempting to construct a universal female alternative in order to resolve
such a question would only supply a new term to balance the dichotomized
vision of science. There are, however, individual answers that in this case take
the form of Montalcini's imperfect approach to the public sphere of science.
Keller argues:

> Having divided the world into two parts—the knower (mind) and the knowable
> (nature)—scientific ideology goes on to prescribe a very specific relation between
> the two. It prescribes the interactions which can consummate this union, that
> is, which can lead to knowledge. Not only are mind and nature assigned gender,
> but in characterizing scientific and objective thought as masculine, the very
> activity by which the knower can acquire knowledge is also genderized. . . .
> Masculine here connotes, as it often does, autonomy, separation, and distance;
> it connotes a radical rejection of any commingling of subject and object,
> which are, it now appears, quite consistently identified as male and female.[14]

In the construction of Rita's character, identified as *la sensitiva* (the sensitive
one), Montalcini supplies an alternative identification of the "knower," further elaborated in the definition of the imperfect intelligence of the subjects
involved in scientific research. In the concept of human being as an imperfect scientist, Montalcini fragments the ideal of unitary knowledge that only
the traditional "knower" can achieve. Montalcini's zigzagging path to a multifaceted concept of knowledge problematizes both the linear progression to
success and the relationship between the knower and knowledge. While destroying the myth of the strong knower, who turns nature into a malleable
and totally comprehensible entity, imperfection transforms such conquest
into a "softer" means of investigating nature and thus becomes a receptacle
of weak truths to be imperfectly known, rather than an entity to be tamed
and controlled.

Montalcini's imperfection in the public field comes from her experimental
construction of imperfection in the private sphere, where each member of
the family is fragmented in order to destroy the total oppositions between
masculinity and femininity, between fathers and mothers. Rita's physical re-
semblance to the mother is a signifier accompanied by the contrasting signified of paternal inheritance: her father's love for the sciences.[15] Rita's twin
sister, Paola, resembles the father, but has inherited the maternal creativity
and becomes the famous painter that her mother was never allowed to become. Montalcini constructs a braided genealogy in which male and female
traces cannot be kept separate. In her reconstruction of the past, perfect lin-
earities are fragmented and reveal that even the "perfect" patriarchal character

of the father is, in her retrospective narrative, an imperfect interweaving of traces: "Our father's personality had been shaped in the happy and worry-free life of a large family, in which everyone, since childhood, had a decisive personality, which came more as an inheritance from the mother than from the father" (19). The father of whom Rita is afraid becomes in Montalcini's autobiography the "point" of rupture in a patriarchal chain. He becomes the man who has inherited and privileged maternal traces. Linearity is therefore replaced by a "zigzag" that connects fathers and daughters, mothers and sons. Even the brother, who is an architect and a sculptor, embodies a softer discourse on his identity by facing the dilemma of either embracing the father's "perfect choice" or following a career as a sculptor:

> Gino had in common with Paola a strong artistic personality that made him choose a career as an architect. His exceptional abilities in drawing . . . made him want, once he had completed his studies at the *liceo* with top marks, to dedicate himself to sculpting. Our father, who desired for him a degree in engineering like the one he had, opposed this choice, which did not offer any guarantee for his future, and accepted, a bit reluctantly, his son's preference for architecture intended as a compromise between the profession of sculptor, preferred by Gino, and the profession of engineer, which did not attract him at all. His choice, as Gino later recognized, was a lucky one. (21)

Rita's brother, through his imperfect compromise, bridges the separation between the inheritance from the father and that from the mother, who was a painter before becoming a wife and a mother. Gino also symbolizes the mediation between "the coldness of paternal authority" and the young Rita's struggle to make her voice heard.[16] As in Cialente's autobiographical text, the brother's tongue is what Hirsch calls a "more tender form of discourse," which allows Rita to develop a close relationship with him.[17] He is the destroyer of the perfect paternal dream to create an identical image of the father's self in his only son, and shares with his sister the desire to construct an identity independent from the direct paternal influence.

Initially, however, it is by looking at a father figure that Rita can attempt to construct her independent entrance to the public sphere. "It is the father," writes Keller, "who comes to stand for individuation and differentiation . . . who indeed can represent the 'real' world by virtue of being *in* it."[18] This model, however, needs to be redefined so that the "hard" father can become an approachable entity for the daughter. By weakening the paternal power and by reinventing the father, the author creates a paternal character through whom Rita can enter the public sphere that excludes the mother. Montalcini affirms: "In the last century and in the first two decades of this

century, in the most progressed societies (if one wants to accept the mis-
taken idea of the equation between industrialization and progress), two chro-
mosome Xs represented an insurmountable barrier to gaining access to
higher education and to being allowed to make use of one's talents" (34).
The separation between female and male realms is here tangibly portrayed
by Montalcini as an almost visible barrier. Rita's mother is an ambivalent
character for her daughter. She is the parent that Rita privileges, but she is
also the woman who has accepted the patriarchal teachings and has passively
obeyed the religion inherited from her forefathers and mothers. The mother,
initially portrayed as a mirror image of the daughter, must be rejected as different in order to reread both parents as texts to be written by the daughter.
Montalcini's agenda is to change the meek tone of the maternal voice in
order to overcome the *barriera* that separates the two spheres. Her search
for an imperfect access into the public realm involves an attempt to enter
a male-dominated space without adopting the "imperiosity" of a perfect
"penetration" into an unexplored territory in the public sphere.

   Rita personifies an entity in-between spheres and is able to mediate between oppositional structures by way of constructing a concept of hybrid
genealogy, thanks to the transition created by gynealogical techniques. The
silence of the mother, apparently inherited by the daughter, acquires a different connotation as it is filled with signifieds borrowed from the father.
The "powerful" public man reveals his otherness in his transgressive attitude
toward dogmas and bigotry and a blind acceptance of the family's religious
belief. He defines himself as a "free thinker"; such *forma mentis* isolates him
within the Jewish community because of his outspoken criticism (28). He
acquires characteristics of imperfection as he becomes a model of alterity,
which is expressed in his refusal to accept tradition. He destroys the linearity
of paternal laws transmitted from fathers to sons in order to privilege a disruptive ethic of *liberi pensatori*. His transgressive attitude toward dogmas always creates considerable turmoil within Rita's extended family. The author
quotes the words that Rita's father pronounces during a Jewish religious
celebration: "I do not understand why, almost five thousand years later, we
should feel happy not only for our exodus from Egypt and the end of slavery,
but above all for the fact that the Eternal Father had punished our enemies
by inflicting all these plagues on them." And Montalcini adds: "It was so important for him to warn us against a passive acceptance of the holy scripture,
in particular, and more in general against a passive acceptance of orders
given by authorities, to give up this occasion to make free thinkers out of us."
(26) Rita's father occupies a disruptive and hybrid position as he accepts his

ethnic identity, but refuses the ideological and religious connotations inherent in his "Jewishness." He becomes "other" not only for the dominant racial group, but also within his own community. Therefore, he conveys to the children the importance of independent thought and exposes them to what they sometimes consider an incomprehensible refusal to embody an essentialized identity as part of a homogeneous group:

> Was I Jewish, an Israelite or what the hell else? Since we neither went to church nor to the temple . . . it was never clear to me how I should answer. My mother, when I asked the question, told me that it was better to ask my father. He gently stroked my hair and, in a serious way that impressed me, said: "You," he said, meaning my brother and sister as well, "are free thinkers. When you are twenty-one you will decide if you want to continue this way or, instead, if you want to embrace the Jewish or Catholic faith. But do not worry, if people ask you, you have to answer that you are a free thinker." So I did from that moment on, arousing great perplexity in those who asked me that question, those who had never heard of such a religion. (26)

Rita appropriates her father's ethic of *liberi pensatori* and extends its use to the private sphere by using the paternal philosophy of life in order to weaken his own power. Montalcini consequently translates this "dialogue between opposites" into the public sphere and develops a more general theory of imperfection that even modifies traditional ideas on how to gain access to and succeed in the public realm, because "neither intelligence nor ability . . . are essential factors in success and public satisfaction. In one and the other, total dedication and closing one's eyes in front of difficulties are more important: in this fashion we can face problems that others, who are more critical and acute, would never confront" (11).

The creation of the identity of the "imperfect scientist" derives from a displacement of the familial father-daughter relationship into the public sphere, where Montalcini construes a difficult mediation between what has been considered the figure of the brilliant researcher and that of a more "pedestrian" scientist. Two paths emerge, and Montalcini privileges the silent but productive tenacity that echoes the creativity of the women in her family. However, in her attempt to gain access to a public role, the female inheritance is left in the background to reemerge later in her life. She searches for an alternative to the fear she feels for the paternal power in order to redefine the symbolic order of patrilinearism. She needs male models that embody authority, but not power, because in order to become a public woman in science she has to come to terms with intellectual father figures. Montalcini explains her search, which turns into a shared female experience:

The two of us [my sister and I] have discarded, since our adolescence, the idea of having our own family, because we considered that this commitment was hardly compatible with the full-time dedication to the activities we had chosen. Neither my sister nor I have ever regretted our choice. An incredible similarity has also manifested itself in the relationships that we established with our teachers. The relationship between her and Felice Casorati was almost identical to that between Giuseppe Levi and myself. Hers, just like mine, was characterized by profound admiration and affection, which would not, however, influence the search for our identities. (197)

She insists at the same time on her debt to fathers and on her independent search for a female identity. Both admiration and separation define Rita's relationship to male authoritative models, who are acceptable only after a redefinition process at the center of which a female self is placed. In the case of the paternal philosophy of life, Montalcini performs an act of appropriation and transformation by turning it into a more complex theory of "imperfection." Such a theory privileges otherness and a subjective perspective expressed even in the title chosen by Montalcini for her autobiography. It is a "praise of imperfection" and at the same time it is a praise of the "minus," the lack, which becomes the subject of this autobiography.

Such an ethic is further elaborated in the critical context of another "praise," the postmodern "Elogio del pudore" (In Praise of Reserve), by Pier Aldo Rovatti.[19] I propose to introduce a new dialogue that is parallel to Montalcini's interweaving of opposite traces and that can create an exchange between texts.[20] It is an exchange that elaborates common themes in different genres. In his "Elogio del pudore," Rovatti attempts to construct a theory of ethics within the postmodern *pensiero debole* (weak thought), which has been accused of appropriating feminist theories to develop the notion of *indebolimento del pensiero* (the weakening of thought). Maurizio Viano has affirmed that the philosophy of this branch of Italian postmodernism has borrowed from feminism the lengthy discussion of "otherness" and "difference." Viano has specifically stated:

> Neither *Il pensiero debole* nor other texts contain even a minimal acknowledgment of the role that the carriers of a difference essential to the human species have played in the process of the weakening of thought. Even if it sounds like a formula, there is some truth in saying that thought makes itself weaker when women make themselves stronger. So why don't we own up to them?[21]

If we only admit such an intellectual debt, however, we are confronted once more with opposites: on one hand, feminist thought; on the other, the "weak thought" as an ungrateful son. The alternative is to establish a dialogue between "texts" that allows for the fragmentation of absolute dichotomies. Montalcini's work is an invitation to such a dialogue. In fact, De Chirico's words become part of her narrative, while at the same time her father becomes the way to gain access to the public sphere, where her work is the result of a continuously disruptive dialogue with the scientific world.

Viano has constructed a useful formula—*la donna si fa forza* (women make themselves stronger)—that expresses the new presence of feminist thought within the public sphere and women's appropriation of roles previously considered "male." This new presence succeeds in problematizing the concepts of public realm and of strong rationality that has been weakened by feminist thought. Montalcini tells about her journey from the private to the public sphere and credits this transition to the paternal inheritance. Once in the public realm, her space of practice is translated into her theory of imperfection, which weakens the strong truths that regulate the access to and success in the public realm of scientific research. Montalcini has never publicly recognized herself as a feminist, but her agenda and her weakening practice are complementary to Elisabetta Donini's autobiographical and feminist declaration that her personal approach to science involves the need to "elude the myth of objectivity attributed to scientific knowledge."[22] Montalcini's feminist stance outside feminism occupies a position in-between the two main objects of debate in contemporary feminism: she emphasizes issues both of equality and of sexual difference. She positions her self on the one hand as a woman who has achieved a role equal to and beyond a man's role in science, but she also addresses the relation between gender and science and in particular the need for a woman to distance herself from the inherited ideas of science as an objective truth. Such a concept, which is inherent in creating a praise of scientific imperfection, is made explicit also by Elisabetta Donini: "The issue is no more about claiming that women, just like men, can work in science, but rather about distancing oneself from this concept of science and destructuring the fashionable pretenses of objectivity. This allows us to reveal its gendered components and show how deeply it is marked by maleness."[23]

What Montalcini appears to suggest is a change in the perception of the father as the only means to enter the public sphere in order to privilege other women. Women can create imperfect ways to abandon the limiting roles in the private sphere and acquire different identities outside the *matroneum*. The term of reference shifts for women from the father as the only model of mobility between the two spheres to a new model that can become an alternative mediation between public and private realms. Montalcini's construction of her self within her autobiography performs the symbolic function of guide in the creation of an independent identity. Her autobiographical text also establishes a dialectical relationship with the reader, who can appropriate Montalcini's "path" of imperfection.[24] This "life/line," which connects the text to a public of readers, is a reflection of those threads of Ariadne that create a special relationship between Rita and the other women in the family and have inspired Rita in her choices. "It was a tragic event that supplied me with an Ariadne's thread," writes Montalcini. "The three people that . . . I had considered and loved with immense affection as my guardian angels were my mother, Aunt Anna, and Giovanna" (41). Giovanna, the maid in the Montalcini's household, becomes ill with cancer, and Rita witnesses her suffering. It is by looking at another woman and not at the strong paternal model that Rita decides her future, that is, to study medicine. She also attempts to reassure Giovanna that the thread, the link between them, will be kept alive by the new knowledge that she will acquire. Viano's *la donna si fa forza* in this context means that the Ariadne's threads that connect one woman to another are also the links that empower women and strengthen the relationships among the members, borrowing from Viano's article, of the "weak sex" and their "weak thought."[25]

This suggested dialogue between "weak" and "strong"—perfect and imperfect—creates a discussion in which alterity is deprived of its connotation of inferiority and becomes in Rovatti's "Elogio del pudore" the subject of postmodern ethics: "Ethics is not constituted as a content of wisdom . . . , but rather as the effort and the risk of going back to a stage previous to the already construed light of knowledge, that is, to alterity."[26] Therefore, knowledge is not the result of a linear process that inevitably brings man to the point of a final and absolute discovery. The search for a "weak" knowledge becomes, in Rovatti's words, a *movimento altalenante* (swinging movement), an *oscillazione* (oscillation), and, in Montalcini's words, a *processo disarmonico* (dissonant process).[27] It becomes a zigzag that can lead back to what is "other" and what has been excluded from the traditional unitary idea of truth.

The ethics of alterity consequently becomes the realm of weak (i.e., imperfect) truths where the content of wisdom, that is, traditional strong truths, is no longer privileged. The threads of Ariadne, which connect Rita to the other women in the family, are interwoven with other "threads" that link a woman to men in order to construct the pattern of otherness. The ethics of otherness taught by the father allows Rita to search for a paternal figure behind the figure of the silencing public man. What she uncovers is an imperfect father whose weakened power can be appropriated by the daughter and therefore can provide access to the public sphere. Rita recognizes herself in the father because she has discovered a common ground that represents the apex of a zigzag, a "point" in common in their experience of alterity. Imperfection becomes the locus of alterity. It is the *alter locus*, where a woman can construct a metaphor of self and create a representation of her public and private selves. Regarding difference and identity, Rovatti states: "Each of us could recognize himself no more as a full identity, but rather as a multileveled process with many voices: and furthermore, the search for alterity, differences, internal oppositions in ourselves could be the path to destroy a false recognition."[28] According to Rovatti, identity becomes an entity *in fieri;* he deprives it of immobility in order to open it to the possibility of continuous change. In engendering woman as an immobile inhabitant of the private sphere, patriarchy has supplied a perfect definition of her role as mother, wife, and daughter. Only by emptying her identity can new signifieds be found. It can only be, however, an imperfect signified, which is part of that "process on different levels" that privileges alterity, difference, and mobility.

These layers of identity, which bring to the surface the father's alterity, are investigated by privileging the imperfect internal oppositions in the paternal character. It is in exploring the discordant elements in the father that Montalcini can create an imperfect father who becomes the link between the *matroneum* and the male-dominated public sphere. To construct her imperfect father, the author must "empty," or fragment, the father character. The paterfamilias is transformed from a transparent, legible mirror of patriarchy into a more complex text that can be defined as "opaque," in other words, not so easy to interpret, because he has become a transgressor of patriarchal rules. In his book *La società trasparente* (The Transparent Society, 1989), Gianni Vattimo defines the concept of transparency by applying it to the idea of a transparent society as "self-conscious [and] enlightened," an entity that can be totally known.[29] Vattimo's interest in "weak" as opposed to "strong" truths, and "opaque" society as opposed to "transparent," is present also in Rovatti's "Elogio del pudore." A transparent, modern society is intended by Vattimo as the opposite of his idea of a postmodern contemporary society. The idea of transparency is connected with the inherent possibility within modernity of constructing a "unitary concept of history" and, through a unitary Weltanschauung, of reaching "strong truths" that only belong to the realm of metaphysics. A postmodern society, on the other hand, is intended as "opaque." In *La società trasparente,* Vattimo argues that "the liberation of the multiple cultures and of the multiple Weltanschauungen, made possible by the mass media, has instead belied that ideal of a transparent society."[30] It is this fragmented society that is the realm of "weak truths."

The imperfect father is recognized as "same" by the daughter; he becomes a flawed mirror of alterity. "The recognition through fullness," writes Rovatti, "happens to lose its validity when that through which recognition can take place operates at the level of weakening. The other will be like I am if I recognize in him an analogous movement from transparency to opaqueness of the self, an analogous openness to the alterity in him."[31] Rovatti here constructs an intermediate space between two opposites. Applied to the dichotomy of male and female, such a common ground is created by depriving the gendered male of transparency, of perfect legibility, as a pillar of patriarchy in order to trace the other in him. The result is a possible dialogue between differences and diverse practices of otherness; the newly constructed space is where the "lack" is privileged and where the father can be rewritten as *alter*. Montalcini underscores the imperfect "minus," which Rovatti further investigates: "One must practice the art of *the minus* . . . fight against the 'superfluous eye,' which prevents us from 'seeing' something that manifests itself only through an attenuation, a withdrawal, a withdrawal of the self."[32] Montalcini deprives the paternal character of his "perfect" eye. Her goal is to disrupt the patriarchal gaze that can control the space of the female *matroneum*, where woman is for man a totally known and controllable entity. In Montalcini's scheme, woman becomes opaque: she can no longer be seen as transparent nor be engendered through motherhood and wifehood.

The weakened father and the newly constructed opaque woman inhabit a third intermediate sphere; this sphere is a constructed space of alterity. Thus, linearity is once again subordinated, and an indirect movement of zigzag is privileged. From the private realm and via the intermediate sphere of marginality, Rita enters the public sphere, then completes the zigzag by returning into the private to reread the maternal inheritance and develop a transgressive concept of a woman's identity and a metaphor of (her) self. In her journey to rewrite the father, Montalcini creates a self that becomes mobile and is more able to displace itself from the private to the public sphere and vice versa.

In the public sphere, Rita also searches for female voices, models, and communities. After receiving permission from a less than enthusiastic father to attend medical school, Rita contacts a girl, her cousin, to gain access together to the male world of university studies and of science.[33] An imperfect collective entrance into the public is privileged by a redefinition of a search for success in which the "I" assumes weaker boundaries. It is not the trip of

one personality searching for perfection, but rather it is the journey of two
women who are imperfectly interpreting the male world of science. Eugenia,
Rita's cousin, supplies an eloquent metaphor of imperfection:

> Since she [Eugenia] was a child she had been the victim of their [the brothers']
> jokes and vexations. They had taught her to remove ceremoniously her hat,
> which at the time used to be very large for girls, . . . just like the boys did with
> their little caps, every time they encountered family friends in the street. When
> she was five or six, they also tested her with small mathematical problems about
> the number of chestnuts or candies that they could buy with thirty coins if
> they could buy thirty candies with ten coins. *Un pacchettino* (a small packet)
> was her nonrigorous, but very prompt reply, which became one of the family
> sayings. (45)

The example of Eugenia's approach to mathematics serves two different purposes: on one hand, it portrays a woman ridiculed in her attempt to imitate
men; on the other, it represents a woman ridiculed because she has supplied
an imperfect answer to a question.[34] A woman who mimics men is described
as a comic character who is laughed at because of her transgressive attitude
toward the brothers' teaching of a perfect subject. The episode is narrated by
Montalcini before describing the girls' exams, which they took in order to
enter medical school, and it once more presents the problematic question of
the role of women as members of a male-dominated sphere. The historical
framework of imperfection is eloquently described by Carolyn Heilbrun in
Reinventing Womanhood: "The past is male. But it is all the past we have. We
must use it, in order that the future will speak of womanhood, a condition
full of risk, and variety, and discovery: in short, human."[35] Rita's choice to
become a doctor is prompted by the death of another woman, a servant in
the household. It develops into an attempt to elaborate male past and patriarchal tradition. By entering the medical field, Rita aims to supply a rereading of such a sphere in order to appropriate the male past and use it to formulate her alternative theory of imperfection. In her retrospective narrative in
prose, Montalcini interweaves a multitude of traces (Rita is always searching
for what Montalcini calls "Ariadne's threads") in order to construct a gynealogy and braided genealogical lines in which the past and male and female
traces are used to articulate Rita's independent self (41).

The death of Rita's father plays an important role in Montalcini's braiding
of her past. At the father's deathbed, maternal creativity is mentioned for the
first time. A portrait painted by Rita's mother hangs on the wall over the
father's bed. The painting had been made before the mother's marriage, and
it now represents a woman's sacrifice in order to obey her destiny as acquies-

cent mother and wife. Only when the silencing man is dying can woman's creativity acquire a voice. The death of man signifies the disappearance of the deus ex machina of female destiny, but, at the same time, it allows the daughter to rescue from disappearance the paternal transgressive voice that becomes part of her female retrospective narrative. In the autobiographical narration of past events, the description of the father's death becomes a pause, an interruption in the chronological sequence of facts. The episode takes place after a few years of medical school for Rita, when she is still an apprentice but is almost ready to leap beyond her role as medical student. This pause becomes a new angle, a new vertex of the zigzag, of her nonlinear progression from the private to the public sphere. "In a pause," writes Rovatti, "not only a wait is created, but rather also an inversion: a pause interrupts the movement of a subject who is preparing for the world."[36] This pause becomes the moment when Rita can combine both the father's and the mother's alterity. In fact, the weakened father is now destined to disappear while the daughter confronts the maternal creativity that had been sacrificed on the altar of masculinity. This pause is followed by a swerve, a change in direction that leaves the father and the mother behind. Only their traces are rescued by Rita, who elaborates them and gains entrance to the public sphere as daughter of both the father and the mother.

Montalcini's threads of Ariadne that weave the concept of alterity acquire a more universal symbolic value in the historical context of Italy in the late thirties. Rita, in fact, is publicly named "other" by society because she is an undesirable Jew. After the promulgation of the racial laws, she is compelled to abandon her research at the university, to which the Jewish faculty is denied access. "The seed of anti-Semitism," already present in Italy, manifests itself as an official crusade against those defined as different (83). In Montalcini's autobiography, the construction of her self and of the concepts of otherness coincide at the point in her narrative where Rita finds herself in metonymic relationship with all the victims of racism.

To explore the concept of anti-Semitism, Montalcini elaborates the racist theory and practice in the colonial campaign in Africa: "The colonial undertaking in Ethiopia showed for the first time the country's racist politics, among other things, by establishing a very rigid barrier that separated Italians from natives, which was similar to the so sadly famous separation in South Africa" (83). The defenseless other becomes the protagonist in many pages of Montalcini's autobiography where she once again reinterprets her father's ethic of "free thinking," which needs to be redefined in this new sociohistorical context. Jewishness signified bigotry and an oppressive tradition for the father; in the late thirties and early forties, it becomes the signifier of otherness and therefore becomes acceptable to the daughter. The Jewish identity has, in fact, acquired in the public sphere a general meaning of other as transgressor, and even as subject of resistance against fascism.[37] Rita rescues the term from its denigrated meaning and states: "For the first time I felt the pride of being Jewish and not an Israelite, a term that was used in the liberal climate of our childhood, and even though I remained profoundly nonreligious, I felt a link with those who, like me, were victims of a campaign as ferocious as the one instigated by the fascist press" (84). Rita's identity consists of a *mise en abîme* of different levels of otherness: as a woman, as a Jew, as a Jewish woman, and as an antifascist. Rita's character is reshaped in order to give birth to a female identity that refuses to be identified as a mute victim. Being "proud of being Jewish" acquires a new meaning for Rita, who decides to resist the silencing force of the regime by continuing her research within the very limited and limiting space of the private sphere, the only space left open to her.

Since society has exiled her from her public role, Rita persists in researching in a rudimentary laboratory organized in her bedroom. Her results are published in foreign journals so that her public voice does not disappear. By refusing to interrupt her research, she wants to establish a protest against the use of science on the side of the fascist regime. However, her attempt to weaken "the support the sciences can give to established power, by challenging the hegemony of a privileged world picture" is in turn weakened itself by the isolation in which it is practiced.[38] She is joined in her isolation by an old teacher, Giuseppe Levi, who collaborates with her in her laboratory and her research. They share, for the first time, the common ground of otherness, since both are exiled from the public academic world. In their research, carried out in Rita's apartment, the separation between public and private becomes almost transparent. It is not only a destruction of the separation between the public place of work and that of privacy, but rather the creation of a different relation of equality inevitably established between the two doctors who operate in this semipublic and semiprivate space. This private sphere of public research is, in fact, safeguarded by the continuous attention of Rita's mother, who takes part in preserving Rita's voice from disappearance. "Even my mother," writes Montalcini, "kept watch over it: she used to forbid entrance to curious people by stating that I was busy operating and I could not be disturbed" (96). In this intermediate realm of research, Giuseppe Levi is an honorary guest and temporary contributor to Rita's work. It is "her" space, her (bed)room of her own, what she calls "a miniscule laboratory that resembled a cell in a convent" (97). This compromise of scientific research taking place in "a convent" constructs an innovative idea of science drawn into the traditional female domain of isolation. It is the realm where Rita can modify her involuntary exile into a space of creativity, and of resistance against oppression. It is a place where she can transgress laws and break imposed silence: "What was added to the pleasure that I already felt was the pleasure of carrying out a project in the prohibitive conditions created by the racial laws" (94).

This space also acquires the characteristics of an intermediate sphere where public history and a private story can be reexamined and rewritten. To create a public "space" within the restricted space of the private sphere, where Rita has been exiled, means to create a new *métissage* between public and private, at a time when being a *métis* signified becoming the epitome of inferiority. Montalcini argues:

> In the academic environment, eugenics had become fashionable. Its interest was to promote the improvement of the race. A "genetist," who had signed the racial manifesto, assigned to a student a dissertation topic that dealt with demonstrating the risks in marriages between Aryans and Jews. If, in fact, as the professor had stated, the newborn inherited the robust skeleton of the Aryan father and the weak insides of the Semitic mother, the *métis*, as they used to call children born from mixed marriages, would suffer because of the incongruity of organs unsuitable to such a boneframe. It was even worse when it was the case of Aryan organs compressed into a small Semitic skeleton. (89)

Montalcini proves, on the contrary, the commensurability between two entities, two opposites that can "imperfectly" coexist. Her *métissage*, which brings the large body of public research into a restricted space of the private sphere, inhabited by the exile, the weak other, can create an "offspring" in research that she adopts and develops in the academic world and in her medical research at the end of the war.

After the war, Rita returns to the University of Turin to continue her academic work, but Viktor Hamburger also offers her a temporary position at Washington University in St. Louis; she decides to accept this offer. In 1947, in the company of Renato Dulbecco, Rita travels to the United States and talks with her friend of their future in the new country. Dulbecco hopes to remain in North America for an extended period of time, but Rita foresees the impossibility of spending most of her life in the new land. "Neither my mother nor Paola," states Montalcini, "would have ever taken into consideration the possibility of moving to the United States. I thought that I would move back to Italy at the end of my stay" (123). Italy, in this context, signifies the place where Rita has established a special relationship with the women in her family, a relationship that has created a welcoming female space to which she can always return. The motherland is, therefore, the women's domain that has kept both Rita's research and Paola's creativity alive during the isolation of the war years.[39] Yet, Rita chooses once more a voluntary exile, this time an exile from the motherland, in order to obtain better conditions in which to continue her research. The land she leaves behind is identified with the people that she believes she is abandoning for only a short period of time, six months. Her exile lasts instead many years.

In the United States, Rita is confronted with old images of separation, the traditional dichotomies between male and female roles. The new country is in many aspects similar to the Italy she has left behind:

> The students were organized in a circle around us; they were sitting on the grass. The girls listened while knitting, a habit that underlined in a pleasant way the lack of formality in the American educational system. However, it also underlined the disparity between the sexes, reawakening in me a profound aversion for such a typically feminine activity. (125)

Everything has changed—the land, the university, Rita's role in research—but actually nothing has changed in this new cultural context where having "two chromosomes X," that is, being a woman engendered by patriarchy, is still a disadvantage, just as it was in Italy at the beginning of the century. Such a first impression is confirmed after meeting Viktor Hamburger's wife, Martha, who reveals her frustration with her life as a housewife, having wanted to pursue an academic career as a sociologist. Rita wonders "how much her frustration for the fact that she had not fulfilled her desire contributed to the collapse of her [Martha's] mental balance"; in fact, Martha will later spend a long time in a mental institution (126). Rita is also confronted with the open anti-Semitism of her first host family and with the never hidden fascism of the many Italian Americans she meets. After these descriptions of her initial experiences in the place of voluntary exile, Montalcini structures the autobiographical narrative around Rita's medical experiments. In her multileveled voluntary exile, her work creates a new sphere, separated from the disappointing first encounters with this apparently new, but in fact quite traditional culture. It is the sphere where Rita can acquire a privileged position, since she is aware of her power in reshaping and changing its boundaries.

The subsequent chapters relate Rita's successful, as well as her failed, experiments, but they also describe her collaboration with her colleagues. The scientific world is indeed a sphere mainly inhabited by men; it is, however, also the realm in which Rita succeeds in constructing her identity as a scientist whose role and "space" cannot be modified by male intervention. While she is researching what later will be called NGF (Nerve Growth Factor), Rita is visited by her former teacher from the University of Turin, Giuseppe Levi. Montalcini describes his arrival at the laboratory where Rita works:

> I knew that in a few days he would arrive in the United States, but he had not announced his visit, to surprise me. He could not have found me in a more euphoric state. I informed him right away about the extraordinary phenomenon that I had just discovered, and I begged him to observe through the eyepieces what I had just described to him. He observed in silence, cleaned his fogged-up glasses. He looked again. In the end his anger—an anger that brought me back to the distant years of my internship—exploded. Had I forgotten in such a short time everything I had learned from him? . . . He only hoped that I was not about to make my "discovery" public, which would have irreparably damaged my reputation and, indirectly, also his. I knew, because of a twenty-year experience, how useless it was to try to convince him of the validity of my interpretation. (157)

The paternal figure of the old teacher temporarily invades Rita's space of research and attempts to undermine her confidence in her own conclusions. His disappointment in Rita is expressed through his sudden anger and his dogmatic judgment—both of which prevent dialogue and any further exchange. Levi feels betrayed by Rita's independent conclusions, and he reasserts his right to judge, reshape, and modify her work. She appears in this episode as an ungrateful daughter whose actions are a threat to the superior deductive power of her intellectual father. This voice is an echo from the past and reminds Rita of that "imperiousness of the voice" of her father. However, while the paternal voice could silence the mother, Levi's angry words only increase Rita's determination to prove the imperfection of her mentor's teachings. She has, in her construction of a self and of her identity as a scientist, leaped beyond her natural and intellectual fathers. She is aware of the importance of the paternal transgressive teachings (her father is both a *libero pensatore* in his attitude toward religious dogmas and an antifascist; Giuseppe Levi is an antifascist and adamant in his refusal to lower his voice when he criticizes fascism), but she does not fear their overpowering voices, which can neither interrupt her work nor silence her voice.

Rita's voluntary exile, however, creates a physical distance between her mother, her sister, and herself. The separation slowly isolates Rita from her sister's sphere of creativity. She reveals, therefore, the need to return to a motherland, a female domain where women's public and private roles can find a common ground:

> Every time I returned, I contemplated her [Paola's] compositions created during the long foggy winters in Turin. I was surprised by the incisive strength of her drawings, but Paola used to shake her head at my admiring declarations. Would a permanent return to Italy have allowed me to enjoy her closeness and to communicate with her? Or would she hide behind a "screen," as she had done since childhood? Were we destined to live close to each other, enjoying our affectionate closeness, without my ever being granted access to the world from which she draws her creative ability? With great pleasure, I succeeded in overcoming that barrier when, after the death of our mother, she came to live with me in Rome. (196–97)

This *schermo* (screen) that has come to separate the two sisters becomes the symbol of Rita's unacceptable distant relationship with Paola. While a private affection is a strong link between Rita, Paola, and their mother, Rita wants to create an exchange among their public identities. Her return to Italy allows her to destroy the distance that has kept them separated; indeed, in 1961 Rita decides to return to Rome to organize a research center where she can continue her work. Shortly thereafter, her mother dies. In this autobiographical text, her mother's death becomes part of a narrative in which Montalcini reveals the indestructible link that connects her to both her mother and her sister: "I used to repeat to myself that nothing would succeed, until the end of my life, in destroying the links that connected us since our birth" (20). Such a special preoedipal relationship is kept alive in the tale of a woman's immortality in the matrilinear chain that links mother to daughter.[40] The mother's final wish is an invitation to destroy the *schermo* that separates Rita and Paola: "When you receive the news [of my death], leave on the first train. Not to arrive in time to say goodbye and not to embrace me once more, but rather for Paola who right then will want you close to her" (200). The mother can be kept alive only if a gynealogy, of which she was part, is not destroyed by her disappearance, but rather is preserved in memory and in a new, closer relationship between the sisters. It is in Rita's memory, in the daughter's retrospective narrative, that the maternal character, the silent woman, is not only saved from complete disappearance but also acquires a more public voice. The text of the daughter's life becomes the shell/self in which both public and private can coexist and in which even the mother's voice becomes part of the daughter's act of writing her own life.

This autobiography, which is Montalcini's only work of fiction, contains a plurality of voices and combines disparate influences. In this text, as in

Cialente's *The Four Wieselberger Girls,* different and traditionally oppositional traces can be interwoven. Both Montalcini and Cialente construct semi-public, semiprivate realms that allow them to create a "floating self" as the daughter both of a public and of a private sphere. The mother's death is followed by the death of Giuseppe Levi, the paternal figure who has followed Rita in her career. The inheritances from both of them play important parts in the creation of a fictional self in this autobiography, which Montalcini defines as a "final balance or a statement" (11). The narrator succeeds in constructing the *métissage* that she sets out to create at the beginning of her narrative, that is, to "reconcile two irreconcilable aspirations, according to that great poet Yeats: 'Perfection of the life, or of the work'" (11). Such opposites find a common ground in an imperfect construction of a daughter's self and in the *processo disarmonico* (the dissonant process) that describes a woman's changing roles in her acquired mobility between the private and the public sphere. Montalcini suggests an alternative practice of success, which she describes as a collective effort to which many of her colleagues contributed through the years. After several chapters dedicated to many collaborators, Montalcini portrays the ceremony where she received, together with Stanley Cohen, the Nobel Prize for their research on Nerve Growth Factor, which becomes anthropomorphized in her description:

> On Christmas Eve 1986, NGF appeared again in front of an audience in the spotlight, in the brightness of the large room decorated for the celebration in the presence of the monarchs of Sweden. . . . Wrapped in a black cape, NGF bowed in front of the king and for a moment lowered the screen in front of its face. We recognized each other in those few seconds, when I saw that it was looking for me among the crowd that was cheering it. It lifted its screen and disappeared just like it had appeared. Did it return to the wandering life in the forests populated by the spirits that walk at night over the ice-covered lakes of the North where I spent so many lonely hours in my early youth? Would we see each other again, or right in that moment was my years-long desire to meet it fulfilled and I will lose its tracks? (216)

While Montalcini stresses the collective effort in the years of research, she also describes the final successes as belonging not to herself, the winner of such a prestigious award, but to the "object" that has been discovered. Rita steps back and becomes a spectator who transforms the triumph into a "fabulous" narrative, dominated by the unsettling presence of questions without any answer.

The epilogue of Montalcini's *In Praise of Imperfection* reveals the circular structure of this autobiographical text. The final pages are dedicated to

Primo Levi, whose writings become part of Montalcini's narrative. His texts that narrate his experience as a Jew and his imprisonment in a concentration camp are mentioned in the final paragraphs and are introduced by Levi's own words: "I beg the reader not to look for messages. It is a term that I detest because it puts me in a critical position, because it gives me a role that does not belong to me; a role that belongs to a human type I distrust: the prophet, the bard, the seer. I am none of those" (227). Levi's statement reopens the discussion on Montalcini's imperfect human beings who can only create imperfect messages. Montalcini interrupts her message in order to create an open end for her autobiography, which becomes intertwined with another text—Primo Levi's. This construction of a dialogue between texts offers a continuum between two writers who are both investigating their identity as others. In the opening pages of her autobiography Montalcini reveals her plan to destroy Yeats's oppositions. She concludes her autobiographical act by adopting Levi's ideas on the fallacy of the message as a prophetic perfect and universal truth. By accepting another voice, another message, within her narrative, Montalcini stresses the minimal value of her message as an incomplete and imperfect entity. She therefore (in)completes her retrospective narrative by reopening the discussion on the concept of otherness and allows another voice, Levi's words, to continue such a discussion. Montalcini reveals the impossibility of reaching a definite point of closure in the construction both of her self and of the concept of human being that she wanted to re-gender. By reproblematizing the construction of subjectivities, Montalcini allows the fictional invention of her "floating" self to become an invitation to follow the threads she has created on the path to imperfection.

CHAPTER FIVE

Luisa Passerini's *Autoritratto di gruppo*

Personalizing Theory

La narrazione autobiografica rivaluta . . . tutto quello che nella vita dei gruppi non riguardava direttamente la presa di potere.

The autobiographical narrative reevaluates . . . everything in the life of communities that did not directly concern the acquisition of power.
LUISA PASSERINI[1]

The autobiographical acts analyzed in the previous chapters contain the descriptions of women's journeys from the private to the public sphere. For Camilla Faà Gonzaga and Enif Robert, such a quest ends in silence. The public sphere becomes for Fausta Cialente a realm to inhabit only from the margins, in a voluntary exile that is translated into an involuntary exile by virtue of the marginal role assigned her in the contemporary literary world. From her unquestionably visible role in the public sphere, Montalcini succeeds in weakening the definition both of scientific knowledge and of the traditional male "knower." I suggest, however, that she does not directly confront the old male rhetoric that is still marginally present in her discourse: there is no gender in art, science, or philosophy where gendered identities are replaced by neutrality.[2] Montalcini's successful weaving of male and female voices is concluded by Primo Levi's message that threatens to become a specular image to De Chirico's *auctoritas*, presented in the initial pages of her autobiography. The narrative of Montalcini's life ends, therefore, with a male voice, coherent in the *métissage* of voices that she constructed, but still unsettling in its finality, in its potential role of bringing closure to a woman's discourse of her self.

Luisa Passerini's *Autoritratto di gruppo* (Group Self-Portrait, 1988) reverses the one-way movement from the private to the public by defining a woman's role in the public sphere not as the end of a journey but as the beginning of an alternative path in which the public sphere is not privileged (227). Passerini's visibility in the public sphere as a political militant, as a university professor, and as a public figure is displaced and inscribed into the private. Instead of looking back from her public identity to the private roles left behind, Passerini rereads her public roles in autobiographical pages that investigate the portrayal of a woman's role in the traditional, still male-dominated public sphere. Therefore, her agenda is to translate the public into the private and, at the same time, to analyze the meaning of her role as a private individual, a woman, in the public sphere. In order not to create a dichotomized portrayal of her private and public identities, Passerini constructs an autobiographical hybrid context that destroys the separation between theory as a superior public discourse, and a woman's autobiographical practice as an inferior and marginal act of creativity.

In her translation of theory into practice, Passerini explores her role as subject and object of an autobiographical narrative in which Luisa, the protagonist, is described through the filter of present memories of the past, by quoting passages from an old diary, and through the narration of Luisa's sessions with an analyst. In her fragmented construction of her self and her story, Passerini experiments with creating her identity by accepting contributions from other autobiographical voices, which she translates from private and public oral testimonies of the sixties into her autobiographical text. Passerini's self-portrait becomes, therefore, the elaboration of her theoretical approach to History as developed in her works on oral and collective history, on fascism and feminism. In her historical research, Passerini privileges marginality. In the theory that she personalizes in her autobiographical narrative, history appears without a capital letter; it is a discourse on history that focuses on the fragmented narratives of oral and collective memories. In his book *Theory and Practice*, Jürgen Habermas focuses on the problematic translation of philosophical discourses into praxis within the public sphere. He reminds us, for instance, that "the relation of theory to therapy is as constitutive for Freudian theory as the relation of theory to praxis is for Marxist theory."[3] Passerini positions herself at the periphery of the Habermassian discourse by drawing new elements into her discussion, which focuses on gender, on the intersections of public and private spheres, and on the autobiographical space as an experimental locus with fluid boundaries. The methodology of my approach to her work reflects the process through which I have learned "about" Passerini's theory and practice, from her autobiography to her theoretical publication in a reverse movement that privileges the construction of a woman's self in the literary space of autobiographical narratives. *Group Self-Portrait* becomes a mirror, however deforming, of theory and at the same time a private looking glass that displaces the reader's attention from Passerini as public theorist to her construction of a private self, complementary and not subordinate to her public roles. To theorize about a woman's personalization of theory means to investigate the relationship between the theoretical and the personal and the hybrid structure that is consequently created: a nonlinear narration of public history and private stories.

In *Getting Personal,* Nancy Miller analyzes the possible definitions of "personal criticism" and asserts that "personal criticism entails an explicitly autobiographical performance within the act of criticism."[4] By looking at various articles and texts that experiment with a hybrid autobiographical-critical form, Miller argues that in personal criticism "there is self-narrative woven into critical argument" and adds that "personal criticism may include self-representations as political representativity."[5] Miller's interest is in exploring the shift from the impersonal "we" of the critic, who promises "objectivity," to a more personal critical "I." This "I" inscribed into the space of theory is a gendered identity that becomes subject of a discussion on the definition of the role of women as critics once they translate their female or/and feminist "I's" into a public theoretical text. Miller explains that "personal criticism . . . is often located in a specified body (or voice) marked by gender, color, and national origin: a little like a passport."[6] By weakening the myth of the "impersonal" in theory, Miller concentrates on "theory [that] can be personalized and personal [that can be] theorized."[7] In the context of this book, my interest is also in the opposite of the movement described by Miller. Miller's work revolves around the inscription of the personal into the theoretical, of the private into the public. In Passerini's work the movement is from the theoretical toward the personal within an autobiographical context that privileges the "fictionalization" of the public and the private. Passerini privileges the autobiographical "I" in order to construct a literary space where a woman writer can construct her self as subject of a hybrid narrative.

Passerini supplies the reader with an interpretative key to her auto-biographical act, a key that defines the structural "hybridity" of her narrative. The narrator divides her text into "odd" and "even" chapters and explains: "The odd chapters are a free elaboration of a diary written between 1983 and 1987; the sections in italics make use of two long interviews with me made by Roberta Fossati and Claudio Novaro, and of some previous autobiographical pieces.... The even chapters are constructed from a collection of interviews made in those same years" (227). The people interviewed were members (and some of them leaders) of the student movement in 1968–69. Other interviews are selections of life stories collected during a seminar at the Carceri Nuove (New Prison) in 1986–87. Voices of women terrorists Nadia Mantovani and Susanna Ronconi, for instance, are added to the previous testimonies on the sixties in order to create a fragmented autobiographical "path" from the sixties to the eighties.

The plurality of forms and contents defines this autobiography as a space where Passerini develops other women's experimental works on how to write a woman's life. Adele Cambria defines such a technique as *ibrido formale* (formal hybrid), as "women's new writing style."[8] The term *ibrido formale* signifies for Cambria "writing that is located between essay, autobiography, and novel."[9] This loose definition can certainly include Passerini's literary work, which, however, contains an even more fragmented structure and a deliberate agenda to define a woman's identity within an autobiographical text that is, at the same time, a subjective historical narrative. Passerini's interpretation of *ibrido formale* partakes of the ongoing general discussion on the role of the narrator-historian in the construction of a plurality of representations of history. In "Don Benedetto e l'ego-storia" (Don Benedetto and Ego-History), Passerini discusses Pierre Nora's collection of essays entitled *Essais d'ego-histoire* (Essays on Ego-History, 1987) and states:

> Nora proposed ... to gather an already outlined tradition, mainly in the literary genre of the preface, and to attempt the experience of writing oneself, "investing the present with a historical approach." He suggested writing "neither autobiographies nor confessions and not even professions of faith or psycho-analytic pieces," but rather he suggested that a new genre must begin: we could translate it as ego-history. In this genre the historian deals with himself in the same way as he deals with things in the past.[10]

This experimentation, which allows the historian to become subject and at the same time object of history and of a discourse on history, tends to weaken the traditional linear construction of History by privileging the individual as maker of history. It also weakens the identity of the "knower" of history by allowing the historian to become part of the narrative. However, this new "space" ignores the gendered identity of the "ego" involved and reveals its lack of elasticity by signifying history and "ego-history" as male. In "Don Benedetto e l'ego-storia" (Don Benedetto and Ego-History) Passerini adds:

> On the whole, historiography . . . has expunged women and women's identities, as if they did not have a history. Ego-history, with some hesitation, has done nothing different: here and there, a few mothers appear when their role in the cultural formation of children is mentioned . . . but it is really a short-lived occurrence, as if the universe of written history wanted, again as always, to pretend that history is exclusively male.[11]

Ego-history lacks women's contributions and, Passerini suggests, "pretends" to be male. The choice of such a verb attracts the reader's attention to the construction of history and its male-dominated ideologies. Passerini's *Group Self-Portrait* intervenes in this discussion in order to displace the critical attention from a male ego-history, which only welcomes traditionally gendered women, to a woman's identity as center of a narrative on public and private subjectivities.

Initially, such a shift of attention seems to privilege a woman's public visibility within history, but it is only one of the plots in a narrative that does not relegate the story of the private self to a secondary role. In *Group Self-Portrait,* Passerini first presents her self as the visible, public woman. In the initial chapter entitled "Specchi" (Mirrors), Luisa is portrayed as a university professor whose identity as writer of her autobiography is the mirror image of her public role as historian, as collector of historical memories from the sixties. She moves in a public sphere where, however, she feels uncomfortable because her "self" is a rigid identity defined by her visible, however transgressive, work as a narrator of history. The collective memories that Luisa is gathering are partial reflections "of [her] own past" (9). They are the same and, at the same time, completely different, as Luisa cannot totally recognize them as her own. "The mirror," Passerini argues, "is opaque" (9). This privileging opaqueness links Passerini's text to the discussion on "opaqueness" and "transparency" in the Italian postmodern *pensiero debole.* The narrator identifies Luisa's "illegible" side and her otherness that rejects the totally penetrable (i.e., knowable) identity of a public woman in a totally visible role. The portrayal of the successful woman who has acquired a space in the male-dominated realm of academia is here contrasted by Luisa's repeated need to define her identity as a private woman—an identity connected to the public role that she has successfully played. After mentioning her work in the introductory paragraph of the first chapter, Passerini inserts the description of Luisa's sudden sickness on her birthday. She is defined in the negative as a nonmother, and finally even the failure of her ten-year relationship with a man is mentioned. This opaque image is described as a disturbing reflection: "I lie here defeated under the weight of my own contradictions" (9). Already in the opening paragraphs, Passerini portrays her dichotomized identity, torn between a public role and an unexplored private silence. Passerini, reader and transcriber of other people's lives, faces the difficulty of constructing a literary voice with which to embody her own life. "The confrontation with one's own memory and with the shift from orality to the written text," Passerini adds, "is disheartening" (10). Her theoretical approach to the translation into writing of other people's oral memories must here be redefined and personalized in a narrative where the autobiographical "I" acquires a privileged position.

The autobiographical text is a more private looking glass in which Passerini's public roles become secondary: "The transcriptions of the first interviews seem unusable. They reproduce neither my emotion in seeing myself in a mirror nor the other's emotion in narrating . . . one's experience as a whole" (10). Her quest for the construction of the complexity of her self begins with the search of an analyst in order to attempt the exploration of the "I" and of what Passerini calls the "i.," *l'inconscio* (the unconscious). The use of psychoanalysis to construct a dialectic between conscious and unconscious is theorized by Passerini in her contribution to the concept of the "humanization of history." In her introduction to the collection of essays entitled *Storia orale* (Oral History, 1978), Passerini theorizes an ideological and methodological discourse on oral history and collective stories that reappears in the autobiographical context of her "ego-history." Through a humanization of history, the separation between consumers and producers of history can be, says Passerini, weakened and potentially destroyed:

> One must . . . take into consideration the specific disciplines that have dealt with facts about subjectivity on their own level. The issue is how to apply the acquisitions of psychoanalytic theory in order to take into consideration the individual internal dialectics between conscious and unconscious, between what is natural and what is symbolic. That is indispensable in order to analyze biographies and life stories.[12]

Group Self-Portrait becomes the locus where Passerini's theorization of a new investigation of history can take place. In her personalization of theory, Passerini displaces the attention from a "hu-man-ization" of history to a "woman-ization" of a historical, collective narrative in which the conscious and the unconscious analyzed are female.

At the beginning of this exploration of her-story, Passerini focuses her attention on the unbalanced relationship between her public identity and her neglected private side, which becomes the subject of discussion with Doctor G., the analyst:

> I tell my dreams to Doctor G. I had worried in previous weeks about what kind of future my analysis would have. I was tormented by financial problems, which I felt as shameful: at my age, I could not even pay for my analysis without having problems. That seemed to me a defeat, another sign of my wasteful expenditure of substance and energy. (11)

Luisa is defined by lack and loss: lack of money, which shows her unsatisfactory role in the public sphere, and loss of "substance," loss of self. In this initial session with the therapist, Passerini presents the image of a slightly modified, traditional woman whose gendered identity is accepted in the public realm. Investigating "spaces" becomes the thematic and linguistic core of part of this first chapter, in which a woman's "lack of energy" is transformed into a search for a redefinable "space." The narrator argues: "I slowly acquire the sensation of an inner space. I often dream of the main square of the city where I was born, the square of my childhood and adolescence. There is a difference between the inner square, which I feel 'inside and behind,' and the image of the real square, which I can evoke with my mind's eyes" (12). These remembered spaces are signified by emptiness, by lack of any female presence, as if the loss of a female identity were an act of mutilation. The traditionally lacking woman is here transformed into a woman whose "lack" is signified by the severed thread to the women in her family. The early death of Luisa's mother is in fact defined as a "mutilation," which suggests the irreparable separation between mothers and daughters (13). The therapist contributes to Luisa's story by suggesting the possibility of rereading the separation between Luisa and her mother not as a mutilation, but as an atrophy. He supplies the possibility of a reweaving of severed threads.

The insistence on choral contributions to Luisa's voice is constant in the narrative. The therapist's words create a dialogue that is complemented by other people's testimonies, when interviewed by Passerini, and by Luisa's memories of childhood, when she is interviewed by a colleague. In order to translate her life into this hybrid autobiography, Passerini experiments with her role as subject and object of the story: in her "even chapters," she interviews her coprotagonists in the historical events in which she took part, and becomes the object of interviews that explore her minimal anecdotal recounting of her past. In her book *Storia e soggettività: Le fonti orali, la memoria*

(History and Subjectivity: The Oral Sources and Memory), published in the same year as her autobiography, Passerini theorizes about the importance of "discovering oneself from the outside, through the eyes of the other."[13] In her autobiographical chapter on mirrors, she plays with alternating her position as translator of other people's words into the distorting mirrors of her work, and her position as the "translatee," the object to be modified by another's ideological discourse on history and on the translation of oral stories into history. "External and internal, objective and subjective," writes Passerini in *History and Subjectivity*, "the definitions must be redefined."[14] In this "game of history," however, the autobiographical context maintains the construction of a woman's subjectivity as an important focus in the narrative. By experimenting with roles, the need for a redefinition of female identities emerges; such new constructions cannot be based only on a different positioning of the "subject" and the "object" in history. To allow woman to gain access to the public sphere, to occupy a "space," does not involve an acceptance of a woman's identity into a male-dominated realm. In her autobiography, Passerini attempts to inscribe her private identity within the public realm of her work in order to be not only a private individual in the academic world, but a private woman whose traditionally gendered identity is questioned and refigured. The delineation of her access to and of her role in the public sphere is based on collective orality and memories, on the dialectic relationship between passive and active roles as object and subject. Passerini's ideological framework weakens the act of "entrance" into a new identity; such a movement is not an act of penetration, but a more gentle form of discourse that aims to unsettle the rigid boundaries between dichotomies.

In her role as object of an interview, Passerini allows memories to surface, "evoking images from the lost, very far away part that had ended in the past: that happy part . . . before separations and losses" (13). In this interview, transcribed in italics into the text, Luisa remembers the father(s) and the mother(s) of a world where "women did everything" (14). Women's "space" is defined by their influence in a corner of the private sphere, but also by their lack of real power. The father is portrayed as a mythical figure, a professional soccer player, defined by his mobility, his freedom to "wander," which creates an evident contrast to the women's "immobility" in their *matroneum*. In the interview, Luisa recalls:

> As a child I had the impression from those tales that it was men's destiny
> to wander away and disappear. Women stayed, they survived, became harder
> under the weight of responsibilities. My family was made of hard, intelligent,
> capable Piedmontese women; women who were used to giving orders, to

taking risks, to holding the financial power in their hands. They were women who passed on a message: any link with men is ill-omened. In the end even the best thing that came out of such a connection, children, was better to do without. (14)

Women's power is here channeled to maintain the status quo, their "hardness" and "intelligence" are used to restrict the boundaries of their selves. Women are destined to personify the survival of the family structure by taking care of "others" while men are allowed to expand the space of their "ego." To wander and to leave the family behind becomes the symbol of a male journey, which consequently signifies abandonment and isolation for women. Their responsibilities and the apparent power gained weigh women down and define the boundaries of the *matroneum* that they are destined to inhabit.

Within Passerini's *ego-storia,* the narrative of the mothers' lives creates a contrast with Luisa's journey, her independent quest. Luisa's symbolic voyage is translated into concrete images in her dreams, and into her life as she leaves home to perform her interviews. Mental journeys, dreamed journeys, real journeys—all lead to the past when in Milan, Luisa sees one of the ex-leaders of the student movement, Mario Capanna. He is to speak in the largest square in Milan. His journey in politics has led him to acquire a public space, a voice to be heard by many in Piazza del Duomo (Cathedral Square). Luisa is confronted with the separation between her experience and a man's experience, even in their shared activity as political activists. Separation and difference are still signified by connotations of inferiority if experienced by a woman:

> Some friends who had moved to the States came to see me. My old friend and comrade in political activism is annoyed by the news that I am in analysis: "But you did not need it." I have betrayed my identity as a comrade with whom he can share his superiority. He is riding the waves of success: he has a woman who is twenty years younger than he; he travels, writes, lives energetically. I have, instead, to sink to the bottom, alone. I search in myself for envy. I cannot find any. I am too attracted by my own destiny. (18)

In this chapter on mirrors, the old friend becomes an opaque reflection in which similar experiences can be read. Yet, his different, male, superior role transforms a reflection into the portrayal of a judge to whom Luisa's needs must be justified. In the first page of *Group Self-Portrait,* Luisa's affair with a much younger man is described. The result is her somatization of uneasiness, which is transformed into a high fever. This female experience, which mirrors the man's, separates Luisa from rather than connects her to her old "comrade." While he is "riding the waves," Luisa is surrounded by distorting mirrors, illusions of her own youth, and feels that her fate is *andare a fondo* (to sink to the bottom). Even after acquiring a role in the public sphere, Luisa is brought back to becoming the reflecting image of her mother(s) who is/are weighed down, lacking an independent identity as women. Luisa cannot, however, feel any envy for the man's "safe" shortsightedness, which allows him to reject change, to evolve and to ignore difference because he is still attached to a dogmatic definition of a male model of authority and power.

Memories of the "fathers" acquire at this moment in the narrative nightmarish connotations. While Luisa censures her language to please the analyst—"I seem to notice that G. makes imperceptible starts when I use technical terms, even 'analysis.' I stop using them" (19)—history begins to occupy her dreams, which are crowded with symbols of male aggression while Luisa feels trapped, immobilized:

> I dream of shining cockroaches in the dark. I wake up terrified. I do not dare to turn on the light so that I will not see real ones, on the floor, when they suddenly and madly run and then blindly wait. The shining of the color black in the dark, just like SS boots. Black on black. Nazism, Europe/darkness. They will never be harmless, much less friends. They are for me emissaries of darkness, of what is obscene. Blood appears dark, red, almost black. (19–20)

History and women appear here in a dichotomy that seems impossible to destroy. On one hand is male history. On the other is woman as an observer of the violent patterns in history that come to invade her private dreams. Passerini's reaction to such a rigid and threatening vision of history is to supply a plurality of collective histories that describe the early sixties, the student movement, feminism, and terrorism. Such a collective presence of memories is for Passerini the necessary condition to write her own life. In her "Postfazione" to the text entitled *La memoria collettiva* (Collective Memory), Passerini argues:

> Without a shared base in a group, or in the same species, there is no individual memory. Without individual memory, there is no intersubjective comprehension or empathy, and, therefore, no transmission and tradition. . . . What is missing is a more precise investigation of similarities and differences between individual memory and history, and between individual and collective aspects of memory itself.[15]

In the translation of her theory into autobiographical practice, Passerini contributes to the investigation of the similarities and differences between individual and collective history. "From the point of view of historical research," adds Passerini in the "Postfazione," "what we are interested in is the shared ground and the points of friction between two kinds of memory or, even better, between different aspects within one memory."[16] The two forms of memory that she describes are fragmented in *Group Self-Portrait* into a plurality that further problematizes the separation between individual and collective memory by taking into consideration the issue of gendered identities. The agenda is to reject oppositions as the only means to signify difference and to suggest a plurality of interpretations of the concept of otherness as an entity that cannot and must not be essentialized.[17]

In her microhistorical narrative, Passerini creates a multiplicity of voices that are adopted and adapted in order to construct Luisa's identity, which can also partake of the macrohistory narrated in the autobiographical pages:

> In Rome, a series of interviews about '68. Again, the past comes toward me in an unexpected way: one of the youngest men interviewed asks me questions about my situationist period, of which he already knows a few things. An old male friend vividly recalls a painful period, the end of political activism in '73. After the interview, we stay together for a long time into that warm night and we drink his white wine. I end up talking to him too about my cockroaches. (20)

In this chapter on mirrors, male memories present the partly unbridgeable separations between differences. However, in her personal exploration of oral memories, Passerini discovers the complementarity of male and female voices and reproposes the inevitable dilemma of how to construct a private female self by reaccepting traces of male experience.

The double action of rejecting and at the same time rewriting male voices leads the narrator to privilege mirrors that more closely reflect her plural identity: "Strong elements of seduction in each life story. A woman tells me: 'I would like to see you again, and not only during the interview.' I want that too. I tell her fragments of my life; I function as a mirror for her problematic moments" (21). Her metonymic relationship with other women is often represented in this autobiography, which, however, attempts to privilege difference even within sameness in order to avoid an essentializing definition of a universal female identity. The difference between thinking as a woman and thinking as a man consequently becomes an important center of discussion in Passerini's autobiographical discourse on genders:

> The difficulty in thinking what a female entity is, is really nothing other than the inability to accept oneself, the specificity of each individual being. It is because a woman's identity must confront two historical versions of herself, which, however limited, have some consistency that needs to be weighed and which have a lesson to teach. To accept the hardness of the mother who is the head of the family or the only apparent weakness of the housewife is a wealth that must not be lost. It is not even the matter of a set of values now reclaimed,

such as women's intelligence or women's intellectual abilities. No, female identity is the specificity of each woman, the way she is her self (and maybe the relationship with the other within oneself, in men's case). (55)

This antiessentialist definition privileges "women" and consequently "womenhood" because of the diversity inherent in the terms. Her position hinges on the need to include embodied male otherness in a discourse that does not rigidly separate subjectivities, but rather juxtaposes them in order to explore shared grounds of otherness. Such a position is translated in her book *Storie di donne e femministe* (Stories of Women and Feminists), in which Passerini rephrases the statement on female identities supplied in her autobiographical act:

> Female identity cannot be permanently located in any specific behavior or empirical attitude. Neither forms of emancipation alone nor a general definition of the connection to other women are sufficient to shape an identity. This identity lies instead in an *andirivieni* (comings and goings) between different components in women themselves and between women and other subjects by paying critical attention to one's own transformation through communicative relations, which can be more or less successful.[18]

In both passages cited, Passerini stresses the importance of the interrelation between subjects who are able to create a maze-like *andirivieni*, a swinging movement that does not privilege maleness, or a special, definite construction of womanhood. Difference is again brought to the attention of the reader as the necessary catalyst in a "dialectic of similarities and differences" between individuals, necessary to initiate the process of self-definition, which Passerini names *autoriconoscimento* (self-acknowledgment/self-recognition).

Difference, in the construction of "other" identities and in the *autoriconoscimento* of one's voice, filters from Passerini's theoretical work into her practice. Passerini's voice is inscribed as part of a collective oral history. She is interviewed and then inscribed into her own text. My insistence in using terms like "in-scribe," "tran-scribe," translates Passerini's agenda, which is to redefine orality by "writing" it into history. Such a movement focuses the attention of the interpreters of public history on the single individual who, from object of history, becomes subject of a weakened form of historical narrative that can encompass even the historian's personal text, in this case Passerini's autobiographical narrative. In such a redefinition of history, Passerini values minimal contributions and fragmented narratives without privileging the oral stories of the "leaders" of the student movement whose testimonies become only part of a collective autobiographical narrative. In her theoretical essay "Conoscenza storica e storia orale" (Historical Knowledge and Oral History, 1978), Passerini stresses that "the problem cannot only be the fact that one must insist more on the analysis of the leaders or of the base (of a movement) and that we must not dwell only on these oppositions."[19] In the same article, Passerini focuses her critical attention and her search for solutions on the freeing elements inherent in "working on oral history": "We can say that [oral history] has tried to go further in the exploration and analysis of fields such as social interpersonal relations, collective representations, and behavioral norms, that social history had accepted."[20] It is her interpretation of collective and oral history that allows Passerini to gather narratives about historical events that add to the construction of History by fragmenting the traditionally linear narration of "important" moments and (male) heroic protagonists.[21] She also analyzes the complex network of relations between different protagonists of many stories about history: they are seen as interactive characters in parallel historical narratives.

It is in such a light that Passerini approaches even her analysis of transgressive heroes, by placing them in direct contact with what they are attempting to separate from. She pursues those links that remain unsevered and that transform the rebellious heroes into ideological bodies that attempt to separate from tradition but at the same time contain it. In writing her experience throughout the sixties, Passerini elaborates on the androgynous heroes that populate the student movement. "Youth belongs to the father," writes Passerini, "rebellion pursues the myth of the young hero, at times almost ephebic, at other times an androgynous hero" (50). Such a transgressive identity supplies a more tender form of discourse for women involved in the political struggles of the time, but it also displaces attention from difference to a homogeneous and misleading universal identity that cannot be translated into practice, into the still male-dominated hierarchical divisions in the movements of the sixties.[22] In the introduction to the collection of essays entitled *Body Guards: The Cultural Politics of Gender Ambiguity,* Julia Epstein and Kristina Straub contend that "the ambiguous body itself eludes political certainties," but they also remind us of Bakhtin's discourse on the grotesque body to underscore "the recuperability of gender ambiguous bodies into oppressive political and social systems."[23] Their discussion is useful in understanding the undefined position of the androgynous body of the transgressive hero of the sixties who, on one hand, threatens "the tyranny of binary sex oppositions" and, on the other, is still, even in his transgression, recuperable in the patriarchal structures that shaped him in practicing such a tyranny.[24] It is in the sixties that Carolyn Heilbrun's book *Toward a Recognition of Androgyny* (1973) was published.[25] The androgynous model that she presents and traces throughout nineteenth-century literary production is an ideal mediator between male and female characteristics. Heilbrun assigns to an androgynous entity what she calls "our future salvation" and the revision of male-dominated realms.[26] She focuses on the liberating aspects of the new practices of androgyny in the sixties, which Passerini defines in less positive terms. A posteriori, in fact, Passerini reveals that the balance claimed by Heilbrun between the *andro* and the *gyn*, the male and female, has not been translated into practice. In the retrospective narrative of *Group Self-Portrait*, Luisa's dreams bring back the unsettling image of androgyny: "I dreamed of a gigantic woman in a bar, enormous thighs, between them one can see sexual organs that are more male than female, but it is confused: a virago. Many dreams about my homosexual friends, an exchange of roles between them and myself. What's male, what's female? Haven't I been a masculine woman for a long time?" (25). To be an androgynous being means to privilege the *andros*, the man, or, as in Passerini's *virago*, the *vir*.

The attraction of a neutral identity is complicated by the constant presence of "a neutral entity that reveals itself in reality as male," writes Wanda Tommasi.[27] The negativity in the use of the term lies in the betrayal of the intrinsic meaning of the term "neuter, neither one nor the other," adds Tommasi. "Male-female as genders will not exhaust all the possibilities in the discussion, because what is female could not reach the possibility of expressing itself in its irreducible alterity, as subject itself, which is not complementary, which is not contradictory, but rather is irreducible in its difference. It is marked, as a subject itself, by a radical asymmetry."[28] If the only mediating ground, the neutral, is marked as male, Luisa's nightmarish interpretations of the beings, such as the virago, who are neither one nor the other is explained: they appear as monsters because they embody an unresolved struggle between opposites and are saturated with anxiety because they personify an attempt to construct a hybrid entity. An act of mediation is carried out by returning to the term *neutral* not as the "neutralization" of a woman's voice/identity, but as a potentially shared space. Tommasi supplies the concept of the "proximity to the neutral" intended as "absence, silence, emptiness" as a preliminary locus. Tommasi argues that the female subject cannot acquire her own individuality and emerge as subject without a preliminary investigation of the space from which she can surface. It is through writing that "traces of her absence from language can be found."[29] A female voice can surface in this "dangerous, but at the same time necessary proximity to the neutral—listening in silence to the silenced voice, finding the traces of absence."[30] The reintroduction of the concept of the neutral seems to draw the attention to a new language of signification that contains the referent of the reread "space." The insistence on "absence, silence, emptiness" defines the proximity to the neutral as space of women's experiences, the same metaphorical "space" into which Marguerite Duras wants to draw men: "Men must learn to be silent."[31] This theoretical dimension is identified as the space where women can experiment with transforming their selves from objects to subjects of a discourse. The negative side in the reconceptualization of neutrality is, however, apparent because this definition of "silence" echoes the "fertile silence" in Robert's futurist narrative, a silence that belongs to an old rhetoric that entraps otherness within insurmountable marginality. However, in Duras's terms, this silence becomes shared as a space that both men and women inhabit in order to reweave the past of the female other into a new historical narrative. It can be said that this is another version of a space of "hybridity" that is presented in a parallel version in Passerini's autobiographical context. Instead of moving the women into unchanged male roles in a process of emancipation that defines the men as the imitative models, the reverse movement is translated into practice in order to bring a polarized separation into a common ground where woman is at *a* (not *the*) center.

The uneasiness of Luisa's dreams about representations of male hybridity is resolved in the narrative by temporarily abandoning her quest for definitions and by replacing men with women as subjects of the narrative. She chooses the "company of women" and leaves for a holiday "without a man, . . . The women who are with me stroke my head and my shoulders while I cry. . . . But which man do I miss?" (21). The trauma of separation from part of one's own identity is transformed into the mourning for the loss of part of the self. At this moment, memories of "fathers" reappear and need to be integrated into this exploration of opposites: "We used to read Sartre, Camus, Pavese . . . Kant . . ." (33–34). Fragmentation becomes the structure of both form and content in a path to the construction of a transgressive identity, a path that leads to subsequent chapters in a nonlinear, chronologically fragmented narrative that evolves by alternating present and past as connected but nonhomogeneous, complementary but at the same time separate.

In Passerini's autobiographical practice, her personal and public path toward acquiring a voice from the sixties to the eighties constructs the space into which to draw, reread, and rewrite her fathers. In the construction of Luisa's genealogy of political fathers, Passerini devotes a whole chapter to the concept of *orfanità*. The sociopolitical and cultural transgression of the sixties is based on an attempt to separate from the "fathers" and proclaim the right to be "ideological" orphans. *Orfano,* however, in Italian is masculine, directly identifying the transgressor as male and carrying male messages that women have absorbed, but not personalized, as they become guests in the public struggle against "traditional origins." Passerini quotes an interview with Fiorella Farinelli: "I remember very precisely the most beautiful inscription among many on the walls of my college: 'I want to be an orphan.' I shared it, took a picture of it. I brought the poster home. That was the one I liked most: 'I want to be an orphan'" (46). The imitative role played by women stresses, on one hand, the beginning "collective" participation of woman in movements that have "transgression" as the main point in their agenda; on the other, it leads women to separate from the "mothers" in order to privilege male models and integration in a male-dominated order. Passerini explains:

> Inversions and displacements do not remove the apprehension toward what is female and is hard to find, to appropriate, to understand: "I used to think for years that the male figure in the house was that of my mother, not of my father." The female entity is chosen because it is disguised as male: this is the secret of the success of characters such as the vamp, the femme fatal . . . aggressive, "modern." (54)

"Emancipation" in this context is based on the concept of separation among women in the attempt to become a female mirror of masculinity. It involves the rejection and marginalization of women who are not part of the "privileged," public group of female transgressors who displace their attention from a search for an independent subjectivity to a necessary acceptance of male definition of feminine identities and roles that can be part of the public transgression created and guided by men.

To be defined as woman and to internalize and appropriate such a definition is constructed as Luisa's unresolved problem in her middle age. Passerini theorizes about "past mistakes," but she does not construct the protagonist of her autobiography as a superior woman whose experience has elevated her above other women's struggle for self-definition. Luisa is torn between two female models: Durrell's Justine and Boccaccio's Griselda. In the chapter entitled "From Justine to Griselda," Passerini insists in defining her difficult quest through traditional feminine identities constructed by men. This superimposition of models is personalized in a chapter that recounts Luisa's latest love story: "I am still dazzled by a meeting that took place three days ago: his light skin and gray hair, his sometimes slightly effeminate movements, his quiet way of expressing himself with sudden smiles, his big and strong body" (57). The androgynous hero of the past returns to dominate Luisa's daily life. Consequently, Luisa readopts traditional roles: she becomes the woman who waits ("I am torn between the desire to see him and the acceptance of my wait") (59); she is jealous of her lover's wife; she compares her love to Andersen's mermaid's unhappy and unconditional love. Luisa acquires a passive role while her lover is away on business trips that are similar to Luisa's journeys, taken only recently, to conferences and symposiums. "I felt," writes Passerini, "that I was wearing X's head [her lover] instead of mine" (68). Passerini manipulates the traditional separation between mind as male and body as female and close to nature, in order to represent the irreconcilable separation between the public and private identities that she has personified. It is the body now that is claiming attention. It is through the body that her uneasiness becomes visible: "I vomit. Violent revulsions, a kind of vomit that cannot expel the glutinous rice dish I had for lunch. . . . During my convulsions . . . I felt the need to expel both food and this man who is within me. . . . To vomit my desire to devote myself without any limitation, to vomit my absolute availability, the relinquishment of my freedom" (70). Just a few pages after comparing Luisa to Claretta Petacci, famous as Mussolini's lover, Passerini constructs a discourse expressed through the body's violent expulsion of the oppressive "other." To abort "man" and the signifying system that he represents, empties the body and leaves it needing an alternative concept of femaleness to "feed" the body. The passive action of accepting a given identity is replaced by an active search through the discourses created on the body: "I still do not know what to eat," Passerini writes, "and I cannot choose between the two nutritional systems" (72).

Experimenting with food and with a definition of her "self," Luisa once more appropriates her previous roles in the public sphere in order to rewrite them and question their validity. Passerini states: "I begin to work hard again. A split between my ego and my identity is being created. I am nothing definite anymore, I am a mixture of full and empty spaces, a slippery and uneven platform over a river. I am not my work, nor a love interest, nor a political project" (82). While Luisa becomes a member of the official academic public sphere and is named associate professor, the ability to "name" her self through the creation of a homogeneous identity becomes impossible to achieve. The attention shifts from an impossible search for "oneness" and cohesion among the various sides of a female self to the possibility of constructing a dialectic among the often contrasting fragments of a woman's identity. Through the exploration of memories of the past, separation acquires positive connotations as it becomes voluntary exile, a privileged space where Luisa can experiment with "roles." In the early sixties, after her first experiences as a political activist, Luisa leaves the fatherland behind to follow "revolution, guerrillas, the memory of the Resistance movement" (83). She leaves for Africa after attempting to destroy all links with Italy by selling her furniture, her books, her apartment. Luisa departs for a voluntary exile where she can explore other marginalities, first in Kenya, then in Mozambique and Zambia, and finally in Egypt. She experiments with the translation of orality into written documents used then as propaganda for the *Frente de libertação de Moçambique*. She also exploits her European training to collect the literature, "the poems created by militants from any rank, in Portuguese mixed with African languages" (84). This linguistic experimentation creates the locus where a cultural *métissage* can be constructed. It becomes a postcolonial space where the "white intellectual" can actively participate in an intertwining of cultures and languages without limiting them in a hierarchical structure dictated by the supremacy of the "white" languages. "Maybe we hoped," writes Passerini, ". . . that from such a babel a new language could emerge, a language that everybody could speak and understand" (87). The linguistic *métissage* theorized is, however, impossible to translate into practice. It remains an intellectual experimentation that, according to Passerini, mirrors the naive political dreams that had motivated her departure from Italy:

> Even in Cairo I had the growing impression that the role of white sympathizers was weaker and weaker. That showed the limitations of their dedication to a cause, which meant abandoning the cities of the world in order to reach the countries of the oppressed people. (86)

> All the hopes and illusions to found a different world in Africa, a world free from the influences of the blocs, able to launch an African culture aware of previous cultures, have crumbled. (87)

In her voluntary exile, Luisa realizes that her "white" intellectual agenda does not coincide with the revolutionary practice within a historical context in which she can play only a guest role. By displacing her self into a different socioeconomic and cultural context, Passerini attempts an intertextual reading of racial and cultural identities to create a *métissage*, which can, however, acquire only a temporary validity. In her privileged position of voluntary *émigré*, Luisa can abandon the failed utopia, and returns to the land of fathers that she had left behind, a land that is, at that moment, experimenting with transgression, with " . . . '68 . . . [which] is a move from few to many, if not to a majority yet, from the individual to the collective, from private to public" (88).

Passerini witnesses the student movement and its development from a distance while she is involved, in her voluntary exile, in an investigation of national identities, independent from colonialist influences. Anti-imperialism is only one of the themes that acquire priority in the ideology of the movements in the sixties. In 1968, traditional knowledge, the university, and the cultural superstructures are challenged by the student movement, which organizes a collective occupation of public spaces, the traditional symbols of the status quo. The revolutionary potential of such a movement is presented in Passerini's chapter titled "Democracy, Power, Knowledge." However, the movement, which attempts to destroy the hierarchical structure of power, reproduces the rigidity of the structures it is trying to negate. The unofficial but nonetheless evident importance of the "charismatic figure" within the student movement is accompanied by the negation in practice of the democratic ideals that theoretically guide the newly formed movement. Maria Teresa Fenoglio, interviewed by Passerini, defines the paradox inherent in the agenda of the student movement: "We had a bad conscience, because we used to say that we were democratic, but we were very authoritarian, even during the meetings. We greatly despised those who were the famous silent majority, the sheep" (93). In the new alternative public sphere of political transgression, the redefinition of knowledge becomes a priority, and the traditional definitions of *docente* and *discente*, teacher and student, are challenged in order to construct a new "space of knowledge," intended as a dialectical exchange that rejects the dichotomized separation between the "possessor" of knowledge and the receiver of dogmatic truths.

This potentially liberating agenda is reflected in a still hierarchical translation into practice that creates an irreconcilable separation of roles between the gendered identities of the active members of the "transgression." In *Stories of Women and Feminists,* Passerini writes:

> Some [women] underline the feeling of uneasiness, of incomprehension, of heterodirection in their memories of '68. Among the reasons for uneasiness, they mention the duty to the so-called sexual liberation, the difficulty in expressing their disagreements, but mainly the lack of verbal expression, almost the lack of perception in detecting divisions. Very few women only talk about the feelings of uneasiness. Other women date them from a specific moment, maybe even very early, but after they had experienced learning moments in revitalizing group experiences, and in a new political commitment.[32]

Women become subjects in a protest where they can appropriate the liberating use of transgressive language, the unladylike use of the forbidden words, but, on the greater scale, they never appropriate the language that constructs the discussion on transgression.[33] The numerous male leaders of the student movement are not accompanied by a consistent number of women leaders who indeed exist—Barbara Derossi, for instance—and are mentioned in Passerini's autobiographical narrative. Those women, however, are never present with independent agendas that might shift the attention on difference, on female versus male transgression.[34] The secondary role played by women in the student movement is shared by other women in similarly "transgressive" movements in many countries. In her analysis of May 1968 in France, Marguerite Duras contends:

> One has scarcely the time to experience an event as important as May '68 before men begin to speak out, to formulate theoretical epilogues, and to break the silence. Yes, these prating men were up to their old tricks during May '68. They are the ones who started to speak, to speak alone and for everyone else, on behalf of everyone else, as they put it. They immediately forced women and extremists to keep silent. They activated the old language, enlisted the aid of the old way of theorizing, in order to relate, to recount, to explain this new situation: May '68.[35]

What men conquer is the role of hermeneutical heroes appropriating the monopoly of language in the discourse on transgression. In their role as manipulators of signifiers and signifieds, they adopt and slightly adapt old ideologies and traditional discourses on women's bodies and male control over them.

At the time when women were recognized as men's *compagne* (female comrades), the sexual revolution often meant that women had the privilege of choosing the "future revolutionary" hero with whom to sleep.[36] The student movement also appears to acquire the characteristics of a male rite of passage with homoerotic connotations that Passerini describes: "The movement was homoerotic. It was much easier for men to admit their feelings of love toward the leaders, who were mainly men, than for women to find and accept new forms of female authority " (119). It must be said, however, that this movement of male emancipation creates a space in which "the private and the public blended into each other" (126). It allows for the construction of a realm in which the private can be directly drawn into the public in an elaboration of the concept of collectivity and collective history of a group, which has liberating connotations. In such a structure the traditional movement from private to public sphere is not undermined, but at least allows a weakening of the total separation, the dichotomy between spheres.

In the ideological context of the student movement, men "at the margins" succeed in constructing a space within the public sphere where they perpetuate women's marginality in a "transgressive" realm created for and by men.

The need to separate women's agendas from a male discourse of "emancipa-tion that is partly male and partly androgynous" becomes one of the main issues of the women's movement in the early seventies (135). In her book *Sputiamo su Hegel* (Let's Spit on Hegel, 1974), Carla Lonzi argues: "Women . . . realize that the patriarchal world has an absolute need for woman as an element that functions as the rest element for men's freedom struggle. Women's liberation can only be accomplished independently from patriar-chal expectations and from the male freeing process."[37] Lonzi's discussion on women in male movements stresses the restrictive roles assigned to women, who become the reflection of the traditional gendered woman as male private space. Woman is a "space," a "backstage area," writes Alan Ryan in his definition of the "private sphere"—"where one [Man] can wipe off the greasepaint, complain about the audience, worry about one's performance and so on."[38] Ryan's definition of the private realm becomes the accurate de-scription of a woman's body in the public sphere of the student movement, where women's roles are constantly redefined in order to be the "space of rest" for the transgressive hero. Women's realm is therefore enclosed and controlled, a space from which a woman cannot withdraw, because the al-ternative is to return to the even less visible corner of the traditional private sphere: the silence of the *matroneum*.

What, then, is the purpose of the pages devoted to the sixties in Passerini's autobiographical construction of a woman's identity? It appears as a mo-ment of regression, of loss of identity. Passerini, however, continues to elab-orate on her role in the political scene subsequent to the movements of the late sixties. In her text on women and feminists, Passerini articulates the theoretical framework in which she inscribes the narrative, including *Group Self-Portrait*, of her involvement in the (male) far left movements. She argues that, different from the student movement in 1968, women's move-ments "experience important moments marked by radical discontinuity, be-cause they are older and, thanks to their composition, they are more stable. However, women's movements owe something to them, because '68 move-ments propose in a more general sense a freedom movement grounded in their own life conditions."[39] Women's movements are defined here as in-dependent from the male movements of the sixties to avoid the mistake of reading the visibility of the student movement as the origin of women's transgressive quests in feminism. If, on one hand, the student movement contributes to women's agenda by radically changing the relationship between public and private, between the personal and the political, on the other, it perpetuates women's exclusion from the world of politics. "In the last centuries," writes Passerini in *Stories of Women and Feminists*, "European culture has allowed women to gain access to the public sphere of literature and performance arts (the novel, drama), but not to the political sphere."[40] Women's exclusion is signified not by their physical absence from the public sphere of politics but rather by the exclusion of women's discourses on politics, of their agendas, which have always been considered not only different from men's but also of minor importance. The presence of women, therefore, is accepted in the realm of politics if they subordinate their agendas to male political priorities.[41] In Passerini's autobiographical analysis of Luisa's involvement in the extreme left movement in the late sixties and early seventies, considerable space is devoted to the analysis of the acceptance—as part of its ideology—of the "idea of violence" (157).[42] Even if a difference is created between the theoretical concept of the validity of the use of violence and the unacceptable practice of violence, Passerini stresses the presence of the myth of the warrior, the *arbiter iustitiae*, the rightful role of the transgressive male hero. In fact, in their role as active participants in the public sphere of male movements, women have accepted contradictory roles as imitators and emulators of the violent heroes and have also been active participants in the terrorist movements.[43]

Passerini, however, tends to question these apparently simplistic separations between male negative roles, female positive agendas, and negative imitative roles. She stresses the importance of the initial male contribution to the formation of the feminist group known as *Demau* in order to avoid a completely dichotomized representation of male and female transgressions.[44] What Passerini aims to construct is another *métissage* of traces which can accept the contribution of male experiences in the sixties and translate them into the creation of women's independent entities, within and without a feminist movement. Moving from a state of *orfanità*, Passerini shifts her attention to the possibility of constructing a polyhedric identity as daughter of "fathers" and "mothers":

> Now I have begun to accept relationships based on derivation, paternity in some cases, in spite of their imperfection: one of my male professors, my superior at present. I renounce rebelling at all costs. (159)

> Every day I discover a new side to my mother's personality . . . I feel that she loved me, I find again the feeling of being safe protected by somebody's love. . . . Now I can share her pain for dying so young and leaving me . . . Now . . . I can cry for her, and not for myself anymore. Now I can be a mother, too, mainly a mother to myself. A mother can be happy and brilliant, not a terrifying, dark, and judgmental mother. Dancing and playful, just like Mom, my American

mother, who was a girl in spirit and body in spite of her age. This way I can face the final memories, and connect myself to the present. (165)

Matrilinearism constructed in this way privileges the creation of the auto-biographical "I" as daughter of "mothers," and is complicated by the accep-tance of paternal influences intertwined with female traces. A woman's identity becomes, therefore, the result both of a gynealogy and of mixed in-fluences, which construe a braided genealogy. "There are women," writes Passerini, "who are multiple and different subjects searching for their identi-ties, but there is no Woman with her forced models and halting-places" (168). Translated into Passerini's work as a historian, the *métissage* of traces becomes the intertwined traces of male history and women's stories. If one adopts an intertextual reading of her work, Passerini's interest in mediating the traditionally considered "opposites" becomes evident. Her two latest books to date clearly reveal her agenda: one is devoted to "metaphors" of Mussolini, *Mussolini immaginario* (Imaginary Mussolini, 1991); the other is devoted to an analysis of women and feminists, *Storie di donne e femministe* (Stories of Women and Feminists, 1991), which is directly connected with the memories recounted in her *Group Self-Portrait*.

Passerini's plan to "abandon a weak father in order to favor strong women" appears at the beginning of her autobiography (69). Such a statement sub-verts the traditional attributes of the two sexes. In Passerini's discourse, this subversion allows her to articulate a structure in which she inscribes the creation of a gendered identity that does not involve or require an act of subordination on the part of the female subject to preexisting models. The definition of a "weak" father and "strong women" also involves an analysis of the traditional connotations linked to each of the adjectives to which Passerini draws the reader's attention by moving them from their traditional positions (*weak* next to *woman*, and *strong* next to *man*) in order to disrupt the linearity of a discourse on women. She aims to subvert *order* and replace it with *disorder*, which needs to be reorganized according to a new symbolic order, a new approach to the construction of gender identities. In her dis-course on origins, Passerini admits:

> There are unresolved problems with female embodiments. I cannot reconcile some of them, and this provokes conflicts with real women. One of them is my grandmother, who wanted to own me as she had owned my mother. With my mother, instead, I often speak. I wonder what she would be like if she had lived, and an image comes to mind similar to one of the two great-grandmothers I have known. She was shorter than my mother, very wise, not very talkative, very old. Her personality compared with my mother's is more ironic: she

always wears the hint of a smile on her lips because of the obsessions and sorrows that I confide to her. (216)

This matrilinear order temporarily becomes the ideal location for the construction of imitative models in Luisa's life. At the same time, it reopens the discussion on the need for "disorder" in such an "order"—a disordered order ("imperfection" in Montalcini's terms) that can only exist in a "space" which is on the edge, in between worlds. It also mirrors the same space that concludes Cialente's autobiography: a "tongue" of land between the amniotic fluidity of the sea and the patriarchal countries left behind. It is a symbolic space translated into the hybrid space of Passerini's autobiography, which partakes of so many different genres. It is the location where the "symbolic order of the mother" can be verbalized and criticized.

In this context, Passerini's text shares the same theoretical ground with Luisa Muraro and her concept (presented in my introduction) of the symbolic order of the mother. In fact, Muraro displaces the center of feminist discussion from a critical revision of "male thought" to a discussion centered on the construction of maternal models, linked to the personal, the private identity of the woman philosopher. In Muraro's words: "I introduce in philosophy what my mother signifies for me. . . . I affirm that to know how to love the mother makes a symbolic order."[45] To acquire a centrifugal force, which has its center in the symbolic representation of the mother, moves, according to Muraro, the core of the discussion from an analysis of the patriarchal order, which still concentrates on the masculine, to privileging female figures of authority.[46] Such a debate on women can even draw, says Muraro, from the patriarchal discourse on womanhood:

> The logical beginning is that I learn to love the mother. What I learned before is useful and I do not have to make an effort in order to distance myself from systems of being or thinking inferred by patriarchal culture, even if I have been shaped in such a culture . . . there are certainly antimaternal contents in (my) philosophical culture, but they have not been able to enter me deeply for the simple reason that that same antimaternal charge in philosophy has prevented me from learning it properly.[47]

In Muraro's philosophical approach, the attention is placed on subjectivity, on a philosophical discourse that attempts to articulate a theoretical position grounded in the particular and in the personal. The private identity of the thinker becomes part of the public discussion in order to create a philosophical but also personal space on the edge, between a knowledge and respect of the canon, of the official manner in which to talk about philosophy, and the construction of a hybrid and experimental autobiographical context. The attention is placed again on the possibility of accepting definitions, traditionally considered as opposite, that have been too easily separated as dichotomized entities. I do not attempt to define Passerini's and Muraro's theoretical positions as identical. Their stances differ; Muraro speaks from within a feminist context, and Passerini's feminist voice comes from without a movement. Their positioning within or without does not preclude the possibility of a shared creation of an experimental space that can weaken the rigid boundaries of spheres in order to replace them with the plastic space of an autobiographical text. Furthermore, Passerini disagrees with specific positions, such as *affidamento*, theorized by the Libreria delle Donne in Milan, in which Muraro is active. The symbolic mother(s) for Passerini are problematic models who become the personification of tensions articulated on their bodies, their sexuality, their silenced/reclaimed/resilenced voices, which the daughter(s) appropriate and modify. Consequently, both the personal and the theoretical filter each other and constantly call into question the validity of the constructions and articulations of difference and of models of otherness.

In Passerini's narrative, Luisa fulfills the role of a woman who deliberately interrupts those public discourses in which "the mother is *taciuta*." The term *taciuta* lends itself to various interpretations: the mother is silent/silenced/unmentioned. At the same time, Luisa positions her self outside a women's movement in which she has been an activist. In fact, Luisa withdraws from her visible roles as political activist and active feminist and begins a period of "sinking, of petrification, and of hermetic isolation" (169). She chooses self-exile from the political practice that had been her main activity and interest for two decades. In this exile Luisa translates into theory the public roles that she had previously acquired: history becomes elaborated as memory and oral narratives, which are collected to modify the concept of historiography and historiographical research. Yet, the beginnings of her work lie in women's memory, in the collective memory that Luisa transcribes and in which she inscribes herself. When interviewed, Passerini states: "In '75–76, I withdrew from my daily involvement with other women and only participated in a group that investigated our history. The move from active participation to historical investigation was sudden, even if what continued was in the form of women's practice, because the group started from collecting our memories before anybody else's" (169). By privileging oral history, Luisa chooses marginality over the predominant discourses on the narration of history. In her discussion on historical narratives, she inscribes the marginalized dis-

course on women's oral stories into a plural interpretation of history, fragmented in its articulation and theorization. What the narrator constructs is
a *mise en abîme* of "marginality," a multilayered discourse that attempts to
fragment the "idea" of history and to "force the course of history thanks to
an intervention able to interpret it and give back its objectivity through the
achievement of utmost subjectivity" (184). In Passerini's self-portrait in history, voices of women terrorists appear to contribute actively to the direct
construction of a story on history that can accept their direct testimonies
before elaborating a theory of their lives and roles.[48] Difference is the main
subject in her collections of oral testimonies that reflects the plurality of voices
in her group portrait. "The search for an identity," writes Passerini, "through
the other—young people, black people, workers, women—does not seem to
me so different from the search for the other through myself, the search that
I have carried out in these past years" (219). To move from her historical
ritratti (portraits) to a more personal group self-portrait means to translate
theory into a fragmented autobiographical form. This allows Passerini to
remove theory from a public, privileged position and render it complementary to the construction of her private self. In this reverse movement from the
public to the private, the public sphere becomes inscribed in a deliberately
nonhierarchical structure: the nonlinear autobiographical construction of a
woman's identity.

Passerini's fragmented collection of public memories and private stories
is concluded with an "odd" chapter that narrates "the present." The autobiographical text is brought to an end that defies the possibility of closure in her
narrative, not only because it is chronologically impossible to conclude the
life story of a still living person, but because Passerini's narrative flows from
the story of her life to the inscription of the "text" of her self as subject of the
narrative within the book itself. Her autobiographical act is both the story of
a group self-portrait and the story of the writing of an experimental text
that contains the public and the private, the individual and the collective, the
autobiographical and the biographical. This "space of literature" is modified
to create an intermediate, plastic sphere where the public can be inscribed
into the private without transforming such a movement into an act of regression, but on the contrary constructing a woman's act of transgression. In
such a text, Passerini portrays models from her past and locates them in specific sociopolitical contexts that are criticized a posteriori. In doing so, she
debates the validity of creating or accepting models, whether male or female.
Her position seems to be grounded in the assumption that any model needs
to be questioned and its importance subjectively limited so that models do

not become normative and do not lose the initial transgressive/liberating/ empowering charge that they embodied. Also questioned is the validity of creating an autobiographical text in which the modes of representation of the self concur in constructing another identity as a model that invites imitation and emulation. The concept of a "group self-portrait" is instrumental in creating a narrative that can only be structured around a plural sense of the self and that defies any attempt to create other, even if temporary, heroic models.

The discourse on subjectivity is transformed at the end of the narrative into a discussion on the text, the space of literature in which a woman's life is constructed. In the final pages of *Group Self-Portrait,* Passerini states: "I am always divided one way or another: at my worktable I reread the manuscript and I find it shameful, filled with base details. I put a distance between myself and the script during the day and a few good paragraphs come to mind. It seems to me that it is altogether interesting" (223). The autobiographical text is described as a place of imperfection and uncertainty, because it allows one to break the silence and attempt to write the private voice. "I am afraid of being ridiculous," adds Passerini, "and of bad literature. I do not like to betray my professional identity, and I wonder whether silence would not be better" (223). *Group Self-Portrait* ends with this apologetic statement, which seems to complete a circular structure linking Passerini's twentieth-century autobiographical voice to Camilla Faà Gonzaga's apology for the daring act of writing her life. It is not a regression, however; it is the expression of women's awareness of a shared uneasiness in allowing their private voices to surface. Such apologies also reveal the limits of a woman's success in the public sphere, where her visibility does not guarantee her independence from the still male-dominated realm that she is "invading."

"This book is finished," continues Passerini. "I begin again to do serious things such as methodological essays with notes at the bottom of the page and with copious bibliographies" (224). Passerini attributes connotations of inferiority to her autobiographical text as if to negate the previous discourse constructed throughout the narrative. To present the private voice once more as inferior to the public creation of a diligent intellectual identity reopens the discussion on the definition of private and public spheres and offers an invitation to enter the text and supply alternative solutions. This apparent regression is later negated by Passerini's elaboration of her autobiographical text as complementary to and not separated from or inferior to her "other" works. Her subsequent book *Stories of Women and Feminists* adopts her *Self-Portrait* as a pre-text and uses her autobiographical voice as a bibliographic source. To quote from one's own autobiographical voice means, on one hand, to reveal the irony involved in the apologetic tone at the end of the self-portrait and, on the other, to create the possibility of a different relationship between the dominating public sphere and the secondary private realm. The public voice, after being filtered through private memories, becomes one of the subjects in a public sociohistorical narrative that privileges women as protagonists of a weakened public history. In her critical essay "Giochi fuori campo" (Games Out-of-Bounds), about her own autobiography, Passerini makes explicit the connections between theory and practice, public and private.[49] However, it is only five years after the publication of her autobiography that Luisa Passerini writes this essay about it. She has finally come to terms with the fact that the narration of the self is rightfully part of her public production, and that her public self is not at odds with the private identity as they are juxtaposed in the narrative of her life. The act of citing one's own autobiographical narrative in a critical context assures that the voice employed in the construction of a woman's subjectivity will not disappear. Such an act also creates a solution of continuity between identities and their translation into texts as fragmented mirrors.

Beyond Gynealogical Techniques

Writing Private History and Public Stories

On November 12, 1994, Angela Davis presented a public lecture for students and faculty at Dartmouth College, followed the morning after by an informal breakfast with her at the African American Center. The breakfast took place in a room whose walls were decorated with portraits of authoritative models in African American history. Angela Davis sat with her back to Malcolm X, and, as she voiced her awareness of her location in the room, she pointed out to the students that models are valid as long as they do not become the "un-reachable" embodiment of an ideal. Such a personification can make one feel incapable of engaging in activism, because one's success could never match what an extraordinary authority can achieve. Therefore, in her discourse, models become acceptable as a beginning, a support in constructing public and private individual roles. In weakening other models, Angela Davis was, in fact, weakening herself or the representation of her self as model. In defin-ing and stressing the relative value of male and female models alike, Davis articulated a temporary symbolic dis-order that left the students present in the room with the task of appropriating, personalizing, and reconstructing a genealogy of activism.

This practice of dis-order summarizes in part what I have discussed in this book on intersecting genealogies and hybrid constructions of present and future. The assessment of both paternal and maternal legacies is carried out throughout my discussions on autobiographical writing with an eye to the historical and social contexts in which each autobiographer located her search for "origins." In their definitions of the familial sphere, which already contains a certain tension between public and private roles, Cialente, Montalcini, and Passerini describe their attempts to negotiate public and private role definitions. Such attempts share some common ground with Camilla Faà Gonzaga and Cecilia Ferrazzi's narrations of their struggles to modify their position within and without the spheres that they were supposed to inhabit. The topos of modesty, of justifying their appropriation of literary space in order to place their life story in the public sphere of literature, functions as the rhetorical link between all these autobiographies. It is only Passerini who succeeds not only in depicting her search for a well-defined role in the public, but also in creating a balance between her public self and her private identity without attaching connotations of inferiority or superiority to either. She also interrupts, in the end, the long line of justifications constructed by other women autobiographers in order to create and appropriate roles they want to embody. Even so, Passerini can carry out her project only at a distance from her autobiographical act: only years after completing the construction of her self in a text does she validate her act by approaching it from a public position. In such a public position and role, she still has the power to accept or reject the private self mirrored in the public act of portraying a woman's life. Unbalance seems to resurface and to reopen the discussions on limits and boundaries, but also on the challenge to limitations within autobiographical acts.

I would like to return to Angela Davis and her discourse on models, because she embodies a double bind: she enunciates her interpretation of the relativity of authoritative figures, and, at the same time, she personifies a model for many of the students present in the audience. The issue shifts, in this context, from theory to practice, from the mind to the tangible presence of the body of the model within the body politic, the student body , and the academic world. Even Luisa Passerini's text points to such a problematic translation of theory into daily practice and invites a reader's personalization of her life story in order to employ her "traces" in a reader's construction of his or her location within, in this case, academic theory and practice.

Rebecca West has debated the practice of becoming, interpreting, and negotiating female models in Italian studies in her article "Women in Italian."[1] She asserts that in North America "we are indebted more to the pioneering work of some few individual women scholars than to collectives," as is the case in Italy.[2] There are, therefore, figures of authority (including West herself) in the field who have experimented with a public discussion of feminist issues and have established precedents to build upon for those who follow. To develop further the uneven relationship between feminist theory and feminist practice and the issues of isolation in noncanonical research, West analyzes Renate Holub's article "For the Record: The Non-Language of Italian Feminist Philosophy" and elaborates on Holub's influential work on Italian feminism, in particular Holub's discussion of the issue of power relations among women.[3] In doing so, West establishes the theoretical framework authorizing a discourse on the construction of braided genealogical links that now connect many women in the profession (West names some of them in her article) and also connect, as West stresses, a number of men.

The issue, therefore, is displaced from the construction of female models in a matrilinear economy into the articulation of female models in a genealogically hybrid economy in which the models constantly question themselves and are questioned. I would like to quote two short excerpts from West's article to justify the position of my own work in women's studies within the context of Italian studies in the United States:

> Women Italianists . . . have tended, up to the recent past, to struggle in our search for career success in relative solitude and separateness one from the other, and . . . have more typically followed male-authored models of power and hierarchy than have we forged female-authored models of authority and collaboration.[4]

> The concept of *affidamento* or entrustment elaborated by the Milan Feminist Bookstore Collective may be deeply flawed, and it may even prove to be impracticable in the long run, but it has succeeded in shifting value from power to authority, and it could hold the promise of significant pedagogical and institutional revisions for men and women alike.[5]

Rebecca West's interest in the practice of difference in the public sphere of Italian studies underlines the possible revision of the canon by stressing the separation between concepts of power, linked to hierarchy, and concepts of authority, linked to collaboration. The agenda is therefore to privilege female authority in order to construct a revision of an institution toward a recognition of difference within the concept of revisable gynealogy. *Affidamento* is a temporary and revisable tool that is grounded in an initial practice among women, but does not involve a process of ghettoization. In fact, West also contributes to the fundamental discussion of the male presence within this space of difference. The women autobiographers discussed in this book create antecedents to West's argument: their texts are marked by a discontinuity in the positioning of the necessary gynealogical phase in the process of braiding traces. Cialente begins to write her past by creating a maternal biography and later rescues the paternal traces; Montalcini initiates her discourse on her identity by revising the symbolic order of the father and later reconnects with the private domain of her mothers; Passerini's involvement in the movements of the sixties and seventies allows her to join male-dominated movements and to withdraw in order to be part of feminist groups, from which she in turn withdraws, but which she also rescues in her autobiography.

In constructing disparate genealogies in private and public spheres, Passerini demonstrates, essentialism becomes an unacceptable model. However, Silvia Vigetti Finzi reminds us that "even though it is necessary, self-consciousness is not, however, sufficient, because the construction of a female subjectivity cannot only sum up an infinite series of individual narratives. It is necessary that they converge in shared representations, in socialized figures, able to mediate between individual lives and shared experiences."[6] To create the particular in order to connect it to a larger discourse on women without being trapped in the fascination for essentialism is Vigetti Finzi's challenge. It is a challenge that I attempted to incorporate in my discussion, in which connections are made between different women's identities as they are formed in autobiographical texts and are also created with those paternal traces that women can appropriate.

To concentrate on sexual difference helps to articulate a theoretical framework that allows for the possibility of discussing and concentrating on differences, including the issues of racial and cultural difference that are becoming essential in the discussion of contemporary Italian culture.[7] As more and more courses are offered not on Italian literature but on culture, in its many interpretations, the discussion of differences foregrounds the discourse on the meaning of teaching Italian culture. My argument on differences concerns the context of autobiographical writings, because they allow not only for an analysis of the possible revision of the public sphere, as West successfully documents, but also for an analysis of the tensions between private and public spheres—their connections, exchanges, reciprocal influences, and differences beyond a simplistic dichotomization between male and female realms. In doing this, the definitions of male and female identities become more and more difficult to circumscribe.

In her article "Representing Others: Gender and the Subjects of Autobiography," Nancy Miller summarizes the arguments developed by Mary Mason, Domna Stanton, Bella Brodzki, and Celeste Schenck, all of whom define the construction of an autobiographical self who acquires visibility in relation to others, a community, or group as characteristic of women's life stories.[8]

Miller suggests that this "modeling of 'identity through alterity'" may also be traced in men's autobiographical texts, starting from Saint Augustine's *Confessions,* in which Augustine's subjectivity is created through a close relation "to a significant other—who is also a mother."⁹ Miller argues that it is useful to "*expand* the vision of the autobiographical self as connected to a significant other and bound to a community rather than restrict it through mutually exclusive models."¹⁰ She is not decreeing the futility of those investigations that have traced the "modeling of 'identity through alterity.'" Rather, she invites her readers to reread texts such as Augustine's *Confessions,* not to collapse any difference between male and female autobiographical acts, but instead to trace how this technique, which has been considered female, works when it is displaced into male life stories. This interweaving of similarities between male and female autobiographical texts leads Miller to search for differences in the biographical component of autobiography. It is biography that has been a male domain and that has made it possible for everybody to know of Augustine as a universal subject and model, and not of Margery Kemp, since "historically, biography, as the story of public vocation, has been overwhelmingly a male province; and differences are always constructed through hierarchies of power."¹¹ Miller encourages the construction of "a way of thinking flexible enough to accommodate styles of self-production that cross the lines of models we have established."¹²

If we accept Miller's conclusion that "autobiographical practices might be mapped along a continuum of relatedness and autonomy which often but not always coincided with gendered signatures," we move from an emphasis on female autobiographical acts to a genealogical interrelatedness that reflects my agenda in this book, but that could look suspiciously like an attempt to construct a feminist critique that weakens the female components of the subject in the discussion. In Tania Modleski's terms, this can become an act of "gynocidal feminism."¹³ Modleski's question—"What's in these new developments *for feminism* and for women?"—seems to be particularly appropriate in this context.¹⁴ However, the model in this reading of autobiographical texts does not come from a male domain. Feminist studies on autobiography have focused on the shared characteristics and functions in women's autobiographies, which has prompted a revision of the interpretations of male texts of self-representation according to models extrapolated from the relationship between self and alterity. To state that constructions of male subjectivities comply with female techniques of self-representation does not weaken women's constructions of independent selves, but rather weakens the concept of the universal male identity that stood as the center of power and authority to be imitated but not challenged. By drawing male self-representations into the domain of female identity formation also establishes a new direction in the construction of future autobiographical and authoritative models for men and women alike. What is involved is not only a mere displacement between categories, but a realignment of a multileveled discussion that is now based on the opposite of separatism. Such a shift is also based on a privileging of the act of drawing male discourse of self-representation close to the attempted articulations of private and public spheres in women's autobiographical acts.

Miller's discussion of Art Spiegelman's *Maus* illustrates such a shift. Spiegelman creates a patrilinear narrative in which his identity is indirectly constructed in relation to his father's alterity. In his "discovery" of the father's story, Spiegelman narrates the history of the Jews in Poland during the German occupation and his father's internment at Auschwitz. The structure appears parallel to Cialente's construction of the biography of the mother that develops into the autobiography of the daughter, who also reads history into the public and private roles played by her parents. Just as paternal figures also emerge in Cialente's matrilinear narrative, so does the mother in Spiegelman's *Maus*.[15] Art Spiegelman is faced with a double female disappearance, at once physical and symbolic: the mother's death in 1968 is followed by her husband's decision to destroy her war-time memoirs—memories of a time when the "disappearance" of Jews was the norm. The mother's private identity is condemned to remain such, because her "historical narrative" is silenced by the man, her husband, who instead is given a chance to make his life public.[16] It is in the son's act of writing his familial past that the mother's private silence can become eloquent in the public text of a patrilinear genealogy with matrilinear undertones: a braided genealogy from a male point of view.

I do not attempt to perform a synecdochic reading of one specific autobiographical act in order to transform it into the general proof for a universal tendency in contemporary male autobiographical writing. I am merely drawing the reader's attention to the blurring of separations, and I am suggesting that recent critics' attention to women's techniques of self-representation (within and without "feminism*s*") has established "peripatetic" models, open to constant revision, that are consciously adopted by some men in the writing of their identities.[17] This may be too positive and optimistic a portrayal of the future of autobiography (a portrayal that echoes Rebecca West's positive conclusions about the role of women in Italian studies), but it offers an invitation to intertwine threads of Ariadne on the part of both women and men, who will not abandon and silence Ariadne herself.

~

Notes

Introduction

1. Judith Butler, "Imitation and Gender Insubordination," in *Inside/Out: Lesbian Theories, Gay Theories,* ed. Diana Fuss (New York: Routledge, 1991), 14.

2. See Roy Pascal, *Design and Truth in Autobiography* (London: Routledge and Kegan, 1960). Pascal is one of the first critics to consider autobiography as a fictional work and to define an autobiographical narrative not as the locus of "objective" truth but as the place where only "subjective metaphors" of truth can be found. Autobiographies are to be read, therefore, "not as factual truth, but as a wrestling with truth" (75). See also James Olney, *Metaphors of Self: The Meaning of Autobiography* (Princeton: Princeton University Press, 1960).

3. For a historical development of theories on autobiography and autobiographical writing, see: *Life/Lines: Theorizing Women's Autobiography,* ed. Bella Brodzki and Celeste Schenck (Ithaca: Cornell University Press, 1988); Elizabeth Bruss, *Autobiographical Acts: The Changing Situation of a Literary Genre* (Baltimore: Johns Hopkins University Press, 1976); *Women's Autobiography: Essays in Criticism,* ed. Estelle C. Jelinek (Bloomington: Indiana University Press, 1980); Janet Varner Gunn, *Autobiography: Toward a Poetics of Experience* (Philadelphia: University of Pennsylvania Press, 1982); Rita Felski, *Beyond Feminist Aesthetics: Feminist Literature and Social Change* (Cambridge: Harvard University Press, 1989); Georges Gusdorf, "Conditions and Limits of Autobiography," in *Autobiography: Essays Theoretical and Critical,* ed. James Olney (Princeton: Princeton University Press, 1980), 28–48; Philippe Lejeune, *Le pacte autobiographique* (Paris: Seuil, 1975); Françoise Lionnet, *Autobiographical Voices: Race, Gender, Self-Portraiture* (Ithaca and London: Cornell University Press, 1989); Georg Misch, *A History of Autobiography in Antiquity,* trans. E. W. Dickes (Cambridge: Harvard University Press, 1951); *Studies in Autobiography,* ed. James Olney (New York: Oxford University Press, 1988); *Autobiography, Essays Theoretical and Critical,* ed. James Olney (Princeton: Princeton University Press, 1980); James Olney, *Metaphors of Self;* Roy Pascal, *Design and Truth in Autobiography;* Wayne Shumaker, *English Autobiography: Its Emergence, Materials, and Forms* (Berkeley and Los Angeles: Univer-

sity of California Press, 1954); Sidonie Smith, *A Poetics of Women's Autobiography: Marginality and the Fictions of Self-Representation* (Bloomington: Indiana University Press, 1987); Sidonie Smith, *Subjectivity, Identity, and the Body: Women's Autobiographical Practices in the Twentieth Century* (Bloomington: Indiana University Press, 1993); William C. Spengemann, *The Forms of Autobiography: Episodes in the History of a Literary Genre* (New Haven and London: Yale University Press, 1980).

4. On the definition of traditional and transgressive roles in the private and public spheres, see Sandra Burman, ed., *Fit Work for Women* (New York: St. Martin's, 1979).

5. Enif Robert and F. T. Marinetti, *Un ventre di donna: Romanzo chirurgico* (Milan: Facchi, 1919); Fausta Cialente, *Le quattro ragazze Wieselberger* (Milan: Mondadori, 1976); Rita Levi Montalcini, *Elogio dell'imperfezione* (Milan: Garzanti, 1988); for the English translation, see Rita Levi Montalcini, *In Praise of Imperfection* trans. Luigi Attardi (New York: Basic Books, 1988); Luisa Passerini, *Autoritratto di gruppo* (Florence: Giunti, 1988). The translation of Passerini's autobiography will be published by Wesleyan University Press. All translations from Italian into English are mine.

6. See Margaret George, "From 'Goodwife' to 'Mistress': The Transformation of the Female in Bourgeois Culture," *Science and Society* 38 (1973).

7. Leigh Gilmore, *Autobiographics: A Feminist Theory of Women's Self-Representation,* ix–xv. In this book, Gilmore explores the strategies of "concealment and disclosure" in order to engage with "'truth' and 'lying'" as "determinants of autobiographical authority" (xi). She is also focusing on what she calls "a feminist theory of autobiographical production" (x).

8. See Olney, *Metaphors of Self,* and Lea Melandri, *Lo strabismo della memoria* (Milan: La Tartaruga, 1991).

9. Mary Kelley, preface, *Private Woman, Public Stage: Literary Domesticity in Nineteenth-Century America* (Oxford and New York: Oxford University Press, 1984), viii.

10. Ibid.

11. Ibid., viii–ix.

12. Ibid., ix.

13. Linda Nicholson, *Gender and History: The Limits of Social Theory in the Age of the Family* (New York: Columbia University Press, 1986), 102.

14. Michelle Rosaldo, "A Theoretical Overview," in *Woman, Culture, and Society,* ed. Michelle Rosaldo and Louise Lamphere (Stanford: Stanford University Press, 1974), 23.

15. Michelle Rosaldo, "The Use and Abuse of Anthropology: Reflections on Feminism and Cross-Cultural Understanding," *Signs* 5 (Spring 1980): 400.

16. Joan B. Landes, "Women and the Public Sphere: A Modern Perspective," *Social Analysis* 15 (1984): 28.

17. See Renate Bridenthal, "The Family: The View from a Room of Her Own," in *Rethinking the Family,* ed. Barrie Thorne and Marilyn Yalom (New York: Longman, 1982).

18. Alan Ryan, "Private Selves and Public Parts," in *Public and Private in Social Life,* ed. S. I. Benn and G. F. Gaus (New York: St. Martin's, 1983), 151.

19. Ibid. The definition of the role of the bourgeois Man in the public sphere and in the domestic realm is a controversial issue, and it is differently constructed by various authors. In his *Fall of Public Man* (New York: Knopf, 1977), Richard Sennett states: "The public for a bourgeois man had a different moral tone. By going out in public, or 'losing yourself in public,' as the phrase occurred in ordinary speech a century ago, a man was able to withdraw from the very repressive and authoritarian features of respectability which were supposed to be incarnated in his person, as father and husband, in the home. So that for men, the immorality of public life was allied to an undercurrent of sensing immorality to be a region of freedom" (23). Both Ryan and Sennett, even in their different portrayals of the relationship between man and the public

sphere, agree in describing Man in his "freedom of movement" between the spheres, which allows him to choose which one to inhabit.

20. Carole Pateman, "Feminist Critiques of the Public/Private Dichotomy," in *Public and Private in Social Life*, ed. S. I. Benn and G. F. Gaus (New York: St. Martin's, 1983), 296.

21. See Patricia Meyer Spacks, *Imagining a Self: Autobiography and Novel in Eighteenth-Century England* (Cambridge: Harvard University Press, 1976).

22. Becoming an "honorary man," writes Carolyn Heilbrun in "Non-Autobiographies of 'Privileged' Women: England and America," in *Life/Lines: Theorizing Women's Autobiography*, ed. Bella Brodzki and Celeste Schenck (Ithaca: Cornell University Press, 1988), 62–76, involves a "fantasy of feminine strength" embodied in a "token woman" who is accepted into a man's world. It also involves a struggle on the part of a woman to become "like a man" in order to be welcomed by men. The "honorary man" distances herself from a common perception of woman as confined to the private sphere; this positive evolution of her role is, however, accompanied by a necessary separation of herself as "privileged woman" from womankind. In her isolation in the public realm, the "token woman" is a controllable entity that has exchanged the enclosed world of the private sphere for a new entrapment in the male realm.

23. Jürgen Habermas, *The Structural Transformation of the Public Sphere: An Inquiry into a Category of Bourgeois Society*, trans. Thomas Burger (Cambridge: MIT Press, 1989).

24. Craig Calhoun, "Introduction: Habermas and the Public Sphere," in *Habermas and the Public Sphere*, ed. Craig Calhoun (Cambridge and London: MIT Press, 1992), 3.

25. Habermas, *The Structural Transformation of the Public Sphere*, 27.

26. Ibid.

27. Ibid., 56.

28. Nancy Fraser, "Rethinking the Public Sphere: A Contribution to the Critique of Actually Existing Democracy," in *Habermas and the Public Sphere*, ed. Craig Calhoun, 109–42.

29. Ibid., 110.

30. Ibid., 137.

31. Ibid., 123.

32. Ibid., 134.

33. Ibid.

34. Judith Butler, *Gender Trouble* (New York: Routledge, 1990), ix.

35. Pateman, "Feminist Critiques of the Public/Private Dichotomy," 299.

36. See Françoise Lionnet, "*Métissage*, Emancipation and Female Textuality in Two Francophone Writers," in *Life/Lines: Theorizing Women's Autobiography*, ed. Bella Brodzki and Celeste Schenck, 260–81; and Françoise Lionnet, *Autobiographical Voices*.

37. Ibid., 16–17.

38. Ibid., 17.

39. Michel Foucault, "Nietzsche, Genealogy, History," in *The Foucault Reader*, ed. Paul Rabinow (New York: Pantheon Books, 1984), 79–81.

40. Sidonie Smith, *A Poetics of Women's Autobiography*, 19.

41. Ibid.

42. Habermas, *The Structural Transformation of the Public Sphere*, 55.

43. Much theoretical work has been done on mothering, matrilinearism, and mother-daughter relationships. Issues on such themes will be discussed more specifically in each chapter of this book. For recent scholarship on mothering, see *Mothering: Ideology, Experience, and Agency*, ed. Evelyn Nakano Glenn, Grace Chang, and Linda Rennie Forcey (New York and London: Routledge, 1994); *Representations of Motherhood*, ed. Donna Bassin, Margaret Honey, and Meryle Mahrer Kaplan (New Haven and London: Yale University Press, 1994); Sara Ruddick, *Maternal Thinking: Toward a Politics of Peace* (Boston: Beacon Press, 1989).

44. Carol Lazzaro-Weis, *From Margins to Mainstream: Feminism and Fictional Modes in Italian Women's Writing* 1968–1990 (Philadelphia: University of Pennsylvania Press, 1993), 41.

45. Luisa Muraro, *L'ordine simbolico della madre* (The Symbolic Order of the Mother) (Rome: Editori Riuniti, 1991). This text is not translated into English. Therefore, all translations from this text are mine. However, in recent years, many books and articles have been published either as translations of feminist theory from Italian into English or as essays on Italian feminism. See Lucia Chiavola Birnbaum, *Liberazione della donna: Feminism in Italy* (Middletown: Wesleyan University Press, 1986); *Sexual Difference: A Theory of Social-Symbolic Practice*, trans. Teresa de Lauretis and Patricia Cicogna (Bloomington: Indiana University Press, 1990); *Italian Feminist Thought: A Reader*, ed. Paola Bono and Sandra Kemp (London: Blackwell, 1991); *The Lonely Mirror: Italian Perspectives on Feminist Theory*, ed. Sandra Kemp and Paola Bono (London and New York: Routledge, 1993); Carol Lazzaro-Weis, *From Margins to Mainstream*. For articles, see Renate Holub, "Towards a New Rationality: Notes on Feminism and Current Discoursive Practices in Italy," *Discourse* 4 (1981–82): 89–107; Teresa de Lauretis, "The Essence of the Triangle or, Taking the Risk of Essentialism Seriously: Feminist Theory in Italy, the U.S and Britain," *Differences* 1.2 (1989): 3–38. Renate Holub, "For the Record: The Non-Language of Italian Feminist Philosophy," *Romance Languages Annual* 1 (1990): 133–40; Renate Holub, "The Politics of Diotima," *Differentia* 5 (Spring 1991): 161–71.

46. The "Narrow Door" was presented at the conference "Gendered Context 2" held at Johns Hopkins University in 1992. Copies of Muraro's talk were distributed among the conference participants, but the essay has not been published.

47. I interviewed Lea Melandri in December 1993. The interview is still unpublished. The debate between Muraro and Melandri takes place in books and in their journals. Luisa Muraro is editor of *Via Dogana: Rivista di politica* (Via Dogana: Journal of Politics), published by the Libreria delle Donne, Milan. Lea Melandri is editor of *Lapis*, published by La Tartaruga.

48. A literal translation of the title would be "Don't Think You Have Any Rights." The book has been translated into English with the title *Sexual Difference: A Theory of Social-Symbolic Practice*, see note 45.

49. Lazzaro-Weis, *From Margins to Mainstream*, 50.

50. Ibid., 44.

51. Lea Melandri, *Come nasce il sogno d'amore* (Milan: Rizzoli, 1988).

52. It is again Carol Lazzaro-Weis who eloquently summarizes the positions of the critics of affidamento: "Critics of affidamento also propose that . . . the theory not only reproposes old structures and schemata but avoids dealing with women's inherited problems. One critic argues that although the practice of affidamento claims to empower the mother, it is done at the expense of stifling the daughter. The figure of the older mentor woman who replaces the Omnipotent Goddess that feminists deconstructed also reiterates the standard good mother (me) versus bad mother (them) categories" (54).

53. Muraro, *L'ordine simbolico della madre*, 9.

54. Ibid., 18.

55. Ibid.

56. Ibid., 21. Here, Muraro attempts a discussion on female psychology that comes close to both Nancy Chodorow's and Dorothy Dinnerstein's theories that revise the Freudian discourse on the female process of individuation in early childhood. Chodorow writes that "a girl's libidinal turning to her father is not at the expense of, or substitute for, her attachment to the mother" (*The Reproduction of Mothering*, 127). Muraro narrates her turning to a symbolic order of the father at the expense of what she calls "female greatness." See Nancy Chodorow, *The Reproduction of Mothering: Psychoanalysis and the Sociology of Gender* (Berkeley and Los Angeles: University of California Press, 1978); Dorothy Dinnerstein, *The Mermaid and the Minotaur:*

Sexual Arrangements and the Human Malaise (New York: Harper and Row, 1976); Marianne Hirsch, "Mothers and Daughters," *Signs* 7 (Winter 1981): 200–222.

57. Ibid., 28.

58. Diotima, *Il pensiero della differenza sessuale* (Milan: La Tartaruga, 1987); *Mettere el mondo il mondo: Oggetto e oggettività alla luce della differenza sessuale* (Milan: La Tartaruga, 1990); *Il cielo stellato dentro di noi: L'ordine simbolico della madre* (Milan: La Tartaruga, 1992).

59. Renate Holub, "Weak Thought and Strong Ethics: The 'Postmodern' and Feminist Theory in Italy," *Annali d'Italianistica* 9 (1991): 136–37.

60. Muraro, *L'ordine simbolico della madre*, 35.

61. Fraser, "Rethinking the Public Sphere," 135.

62. Hannah Arendt, "What Is Authority?" in *Between Past and Future: Eight Exercises in Political Thought* (London: Penguin Books, 1993), 91–142.

63. Ibid., 94.

64. Ibid., 95.

65. Ibid., 92, 95.

66. Ibid., 122.

67. Ibid., 119–20.

68. Ibid., 121.

69. Ibid., 123.

70. Ibid., 122.

71. Lazzaro-Weis, *From Margins to Mainstream*, 50.

72. See Philippe Lejeune, *Le pacte autobiographique* (Paris: Seuil, 1975).

73. See Brodzki and Schenck, eds., *Life/Lines: Theorizing Women's Autobiography*. I am using the term "life/lines" as Germaine Bree defines it in the foreword of the book: "Life/Lines: the metaphor is ambiguous and invites us to ponder its relation to the subtitle. Lifelines, ropes thrown to ships or persons floundering in deep waters nearby; lifelines, ropes that link the deep-sea diver to the mother-ship; lifelines, more metaphorically, essential routes of communication between mutually dependent communities; but again, and differently, lifelines, those lines in the palm of the hand that in palmistry, dictionaries tell us, supposedly reveal facts about a person's life to the person who can decode the meaning" (ix). The multifaceted metaphor of life/lines allows a wide range of interpretations and use in the discussion of female autobiographies. Bree calls it "more than a metaphor; it defines a critical space or scene and suggests a purpose" (ix). It is a loose metaphor that encompasses the various techniques and strategies adopted by women to translate their lives into the fictional world of autobiographical writing. It is a "polyvalent metaphor" (ix) that describes the translation and transformation of life roles into "invented" lives, newly created roles and female identities in autobiography. Life/lines supplies the "metaphorical" context in which "gynealogy" can be created. Constructing "gynealogy" involves the redefinition of a woman's past, which is reflected into the narrative of her present life and is translated into a new metaphor of a female future.

74. Cialente, *The Four Wieselberger Girls*, 175.

75. See Shirley Nelson Garner, Claire Kahane and Madelon Sprengnether, eds., *The (M)other Tongue* (Ithaca: Cornell University Press, 1986). The book contains essays that "point to the following topics as inhibited or absent in dominant cultural expression: relationships among women as mothers and daughters, as sisters, friends and lovers; . . . and portrayals of motherhood as a source of cultural as well as biological creativity" (10).

76. Marianne Hirsch devotes a chapter of her book *The Mother/Daughter Plot: Narrative, Psychoanalysis, Feminism* (Bloomington: Indiana University Press, 1989) to the description of a "feminine" language of the brother, which she calls the "brother tongue." The brother, the character who acquires feminine "traces," is only one of the examples of the possibilities of constructing a "braided genealogy" by gathering softer traces from the male and female charac-

ters in a woman's retrospective narration in order to create an identity that defies separation and dichotomization.

77. Montalcini, *In Praise of Imperfection*, 11.

78. Mary Mason has noted that women often created portrayals of selves through relationships with others. Leigh Gilmore adds that it is limiting to essentialize women's autobiographical writing by establishing a new dichotomy between women, individuals characterized by fluid ego boundaries, and men, characterized instead by rigid ego boundaries. I am not stating that women autobiographers construct their selves by creating metonymic relationships with surrounding others. However, such a technique is sometimes present as one of the many other techniques adopted by some of the authors in this book. See Mary Mason, "The Other Voice: Autobiographies of Women Writers," in *Life/Lines*, ed. Brodzki and Schenk, and Leigh Gilmore, *Autobiographies: A Feminist Theory of Women's Self-Representation* (Ithaca and Cornell: Cornell University Press, 1994).

79. Primo Levi's words are quoted by Montalcini at the beginning of the final chapter in the Italian edition of the book: "I beg the reader not to look for messages. It is a term that I detest because it puts me in a critical position, because it gives me a role that does not belong to me; a role that belongs to a human type I distrust: the prophet, the bard, the seer. I am none of those" (212). (My translation). Levi's reading practice of his own text is elaborated by Montalcini, who translates his "weak message" into the autobiographical context and into science and states: "Today terms 'message' and 'messengers' have lost their sacred aura and have acquired a human and secular dimension" (212).

80. Montalcini, *In Praise of Imperfection*, 197.

81. Carolyn G. Heilbrun, *Writing a Woman's Life* (New York: Norton, 1988).

82. Butler, "Imitation and Gender Insubordination," 13–14.

83. Teresa de Lauretis, *Technologies of Gender: Essays on Theory, Film, and Fiction* (Bloomington and Indianapolis: Indiana University Press, 1987), 2.

84. Ibid.

85. Louis Althusser, *Lenin and Philosophy* (New York and London: Monthly Review Press, 1971), 175–76.

86. De Lauretis, *Technologies of Gender*, 9.

87. Ibid., 10.

One. Camilla Faà Gonzaga: Public and Private in a Woman's Autobiography

1. The Italian version of Faà's narrative consulted is "Historia della Sig.ra Donna Camilla Faà Gonzaga" in Fernanda Sorbelli Bonfà, *Camilla Gonzaga Faà: Storia documentata* (Camilla Gonzaga Faà: Documented History) (Bologna: Zanichelli, 1918). The translated text is quoted from Valeria Finucci, "The Italian Memorialist: Camilla Faà Gonzaga," in *Women Writers of the Seventeenth Century*, ed. Katharina M. Wilson and Frank J. Warnke (Athens and London: University of Georgia Press, 1989). Finucci's translation uses the first published edition by Giuseppe Giorcelli, "Documenti storici del Monferrato," in *Rivista di storia, arte, archeologia della provincia di Alessandria* 10.4 (1895): 75–93. There are some small discrepancies between Bonfà's Italian text and Finucci's translation from Giorcelli, but they are not such that the meaning of whole sentences is completely different.

2. Juliana Schiesari, "In Praise of Virtuous Women? For a Genealogy of Gender Morals in Renaissance Italy," *Annali d'Italianistica: Women's Voices in Italian Literature* 7 (1989): 66. For a discussion of the private roles of women in the Italian Renaissance, see Joan Kelly Gadol, "Did Women Have a Renaissance?" in *Women, History, and Theory: The Essays of Joan Kelly* (Chicago: University of Chicago Press, 1984), 19–50.

3. I use the name Camilla whenever I am indicating the protagonist of the autobiographical narrative created by Faà.

4. Valeria Finucci, "Re-Membering the 'I': Faà Gonzaga's *Storia* (1622)," *Italian Quarterly* 28 (1987): 22.

5. Franco Fido, "At the Origins of Autobiography in the 18th and 19th Centuries: The *Topoi* of the Self," *Annali d'Italianistica* 4 (1986): 168–80.

6. Ibid., 168.

7. We do not know the exact year when Camilla wrote her memoir. However, it seems that it was written after 1622, when she became a nun. Camilla was born in 1599 and became a lady-in-waiting to the duchess Margherita of Savoy when Camilla was only thirteen. In 1615 she met the duke, who it seems had already noticed her, and they married in 1616. In 1618 she entered the convent as a *secolare* and became a nun in 1622. She lived in the cloister for forty years and died in 1662.

8. See Maurizio Viano, "Ecce Foemina," *Annali d'Italianistica* 4 (1986): 223–41. Many books on autobiography and autobiographical acts in Italian literature have been published in the past two decades. However, very little has been said on women's autobiographical works and constructions of female selves in women's memoirs, autobiographies, and autobiographical novels. See Angelica Forti Lewis, *Italia autobiografica* (Rome: Bulzoni, 1986); Marziano Guglielminetti, "L'autobiographie en Italie XIV–XVII siècles," in *Individualisme et autobiographie en occident*, ed. Claudette Delhez-Sarlet and Maurizio Catani, Colloques du Centre International de Cerisy-La Salle, 1983 (Brussels: Ed. de l'Université de Bruxelles, 1983); by the same author, *Memoria e scrittura* (Turin: Einaudi, 1977). See also Lina Unali, *Descrizione di sè* (Rome: Lucarini, 1979).

9. Faith E. Beasley, *Revising Memory: Women's Fiction and Memoirs in Seventeenth-Century France* (New Brunswick: Rutgers University Press, 1990).

10. Ibid., 73.

11. Camilla comments upon the bishop's role: "The gallant bishop (may God forgive him) was not the last to be against me, and he should really be given the most blame because he had to tell me the truth when I asked him, or defend his actions with all his strength" (Finucci, "The Italian Memorialist: Camilla Faà Gonzaga," 133).

12. Ibid., 129. Antonio Passevino in *Historia belli Monferratensis* (Mantua, 1637) writes about Camilla's tormented life. Her memoir was published, for the first time, by Paolo Giorcelli in *Camilla Faà da Casale* (Florence: Libreria Filodrammatica, 1850). Faà Gonzaga's memoir, transcribed by Fernanda Sorbelli Bonfà, is a copy of the manuscript preserved in the private archives of the *Clarisse Francescane* in the convent of Corpus Domini, Ferrara. Other authors, mainly romantic writers, have been inspired by Camilla's tragic life; however, they often ignored the document left by the unofficial duchess. P. Giacometti wrote the historical drama *Camilla Faà da Casale* (Florence: Libreria Filodrammatica, 1846). Another romantic writer, Carlo d'Arco, published *Degli amori sfortunatissimi di Camilla Faà* (Mantua: Negretti, 1844). G. B. Intra wrote *La bella Ardizzina* (Milan: Tipografia della Perseveranza, 1881). Intra's novel is still an important source of documentation; it contains, in fact, the transcription of some of Camilla's and Ferdinando's letters.

13. In her *Camilla Gonzaga Faà: Storia documentata*, Fernanda Sorbelli Bonfà writes: "After overcoming his reluctance, Ardizzino [Camilla's father] allowed his daughter to return to Mantua. The ladies-in-waiting took residence in the palace, with the stipend of 20 liras . . . pleasing the cardinal who was waiting impatiently to have 'balls and other gallant activities'" (15).

14. Finucci, "The Italian Memorialist: Camilla Faà Gonzaga," 132.

15. Ibid., 130.

16. Ibid.

17. Bonfà, *Storia documentata*, 123. This line is my translation.

18. Ibid., i. The translation is mine.

19. Beasley, *Revising Memory: Women's Fiction and Memoirs in Seventeenth-Century France*, 4.

20. In her autobiography Camilla quotes the duke's words: "Now I cannot publicize this matter for the best because it is necessary that I reach an agreement with my brother and Madama di Ferrara. However, this should not worry you because the thing has been done. Were I to change my mind, I pray God not to let me kiss the Cross at my death and thus have my soul damned" (Finucci, "The Italian Memorialist," 131).

21. Bonfà, *Storia documentata*, 128–29. This translation is mine, because part of the Italian text in Bonfà's transcription is not present in Finucci's translation.

22. Finucci, "The Italian Memorialist," 132.

23. Ibid.

24. Diane Bornstein, "Women's Public and Private Space in Some Medieval Courtesy Books," *Centerpoint: A Journal of Interdisciplinary Studies* 3.3/4 (1980): 68.

25. Gaye Tuchman, "Some Thoughts on Public and Private Spheres," *Centerpoint: A Journal of Interdisciplinary Studies* 3.3/4 (1980): 112.

26. Finucci, "The Italian Memorialist," 135. In the Italian text the word is *Padroni*, and Finucci translates it as "masters." It means both masters and lords.

27. Seventeenth-century women writers translate into their prose the portrayal of the convent as a female prison chosen by men in order to control and silence women. Camilla's autobiography does not reveal any detail of her life in the cloister, but other contemporary women eloquently describe their imprisonment in convents. Elena Tarabotti, who was destined to become a nun even as a child because she was a cripple, wrote in her book entitled *Semplicità ingannata* (Simplicity Deceived): "So these unhappy women, born under an unlucky star, spend the years of their simple childhood: with their tongues still stained by milk, they whimper with love, and their tender arms make pretty gestures. They please the ears and the soul of their hard parents who, deceitful, weave treacherous plots. They do not think about anything besides how to . . . bury them alive for the rest of their lives in cloisters where they are tied by indissoluble knots and where, while they are still breathing, they say, and with reason, *circumdederunt me dolores mortis*. The divine majesty never thought (I think) of ordering such excesses . . . , men's temerity is what allows such a big sacrilege." In Natalia Costa, ed., Zalessow, *Scrittrici Italiane dal XIII al XX secolo* (Ravenna: Longo, 1982), 158–59.

Suor Angelica Tarabotti wrote a second book on life in a convent, and she entitled it *Inferno monacale* (Monastic Hell). It has been recently published as "*L'inferno monacale*" *di Arcangela Tarabotti* (The Monastic Hell by Arcangela Tarabotti), ed. Francesca Medioli (Turin: Rosenberg and Sellier, 1990). Even Galileo Galilei's daughter proclaims, however indirectly, that she is trapped in the prison of a convent. In a letter to her father, Virginia Galilei sympathizes with her imprisoned father and states: "I would have very willingly volunteered to live in a stricter prison than the one in which I live if that could free you" (Zalessow, 138). Women writing from the isolation of the convent create complementary texts. What unites their works is an intertextual link that ignores the differences in genre privileged by each individual author. Galilei's letters, Tarabotti's treatise, and Camilla's autobiography construct, on one hand, a transgressive female voice that breaks the silence imposed on their exile; on the other, women writers create coherent replies to the misogynist literature of the time, such as *Donneschi difetti* (Women's Faults) by Giuseppe Passi (1595), which appeared in four editions in twenty-three years, and the controversial *Disputatio nova contra mulieres, qua probatur eas homines non esse* by Valente Acidalio (New Discussion against Women, 1595, translated into Italian in 1648 with the title *Che le donne non siano della specie de gli uomini*), who developed in his book the thesis that women do not have a soul. Through their voices, women writers of that century indeed succeeded in creating their "literary soul," a corpus of writings that strongly transgresses patriarchal rules. In defense of women, Lucrezia Marinelli Vacca wrote *La nobiltà e l'eccellenza delle donne e i difetti e mancamenti degli uomini* (The Nobility and the Excellence of Women and the Faults and Shortcomings of Men, 1600), and Sara Copia Sullam defended in her letter entitled

Manifesto (1621) her identity as an intellectual and her determination to proclaim her public and religious identity as a Jew. At the same time, she responded to Baldassare Bonifacio's *Discorso sull'immortalita' dell'anime* (Discourse on the Immortality of the Soul, 1621), in which he attempted to accuse Sara Copia Sullam of believing in the mortality of the soul: "Even allowing that in a discussion I might have supported some theological or philosophical difficulty, it was not because of any doubt or wavering that I have ever had in my faith. It was only for curiosity in order to hear from you . . . some curious and peculiar doctrine. I thought that that was permitted to any person who practices as a student, besides being permitted to a Jewish woman, who is often placed in such discussions by people who try hard to bring her, as you know, into the Christian faith" (Zalessow, 126). What becomes evident, even after reading only these few excerpts, is women's attempt to initiate a discourse which can create a dialogue with the dominant discourse on theology, history, philosophy, and femininity. However, these potentially disruptive texts, briefly and insufficiently quoted in this note, have been silenced in the construction of a linear history of literature from which they have been excluded.

28. In a note to Camilla Faà Gonzaga's *Historia*, Fernanda Sorbelli Bonfà writes: "Here Camilla's memory was not accurate. By vaguely indicating [the time as] "four days later," she maybe means the ratification of her marriage, which she does not mention at all. . . . But the ratification was carried out in the presence of Count Bruschi, not Barutti. She either confused one with the other, or she is not even vaguely mentioning the ratification" (125). (The translation from *Storia documentata* is mine). Later, Bonfà, in a different note to the text, indirectly makes the reader realize the extent to which Camilla succeeded in creating a plausible document, which, however, is mocking the pretense of truthfulness of patriarchal history. Bonfà argues: "Camilla says that the bishop of Casale, Monsignor Pasquali, went to test her about the marriage after the birth and the christening of her son, Giacinto. But that cannot be true, because Camilla herself talks about the 'testimony signed by her' in a letter to the duke dated November 1, and Giacinto was born on December 4. Furthermore, she stated that the notary did not write the truth and that he forged the document and her signature, because 'she never signed any document.' However, in the letter mentioned above, she assured the duke that she had signed her name in order to obey him. The document itself is signed by her with the wording: 'I state what is written above.' She certainly was confused about one 'fatto,' the document filled out by Iberti and Baruti, who made her sign it, and the 'atto,' which contained her deposition made before the court of Monsignor Pasquali, bishop of Casale. This second document was the one drawn after Giacinto's birth. She could have entirely forgotten about the first document, which still exists and about which she writes in her correspondence to the duke" (129). (The translation is mine.)

29. In *La bella Ardizzina*, G. B. Intra quotes the document written by Ferdinando: " I, Ferdinando Gonzaga, Duke of Mantua and Monferrato, promise to God and to Donna Camilla Faà to marry her and to take her as my lawful wife. In demonstration of my irrevocable decision, this document will be written and signed [scritta e sottoscritta] by myself. February 18, 1616" (23). (The translation is mine.) The duke demands the return of the document so that he can marry Caterina. Camilla, therefore, is deprived of the official proof that her marriage is valid.

30. Finucci, "The Italian Memorialist," 134.

31. Ibid., 130.

32. Isabella Canali Andreini, "Del nascimento della donna" (About the Birth of Women), in Zalessow, ed., *Scrittrici Italiane dal XIII al XX secolo*. The translation is mine.

33. Zalessow, ed., *Scrittrici Italiane dal XIII al XX secolo*, 14.

34. Fernanda Sorbelli Bonfà gives a short biography of the frightening Madama di Ferrara. She was the third wife of Alfonso II of Este and became a widow at thirty-three (1597). She was then sent by her brother Vincenzo to govern Monferrato during his absence. After returning to Mantua, she founded the church of Sant'Orsola and the monastery of Orsoline, where she spent

the last fifteen years of her life. While in the convent, however, she continued to influence the political decisions made by the rulers of Mantua. In her *Historia*, Camilla describes both Madama di Ferrara's and the Queen of France's influence on her life: "Madama di Ferrara and the counselors started to pester His Highness. They had the Queen of France write fiery letters in order to persuade him to leave me and marry a princess" (Finucci, 132). On April 12, 1622, Caterina de' Medici writes a letter to her counselor in which she describes her rival; the letter is quoted by Fernanda Sorbelli Bonfà: "Not only she [Camilla] makes a fool of us, but also of the duke himself. . . . This woman has shown her evil nature by even pretending to be ill so that the matter could be silenced . . . I will personally tell you about her foolish actions and her impertinence. She does not want to leave her marquisade to Signor Don Giacinto, but rather to her brother. Imagine: she loves her son so little. In a word, you cannot draw wine from an empty cask. So she has shown how very shameless she is. She would want to bleed His Highness, my lord, white by asking for money, the usual attitude of women" (77). (The translation is mine.)

35. Bonfà, *Storia documentata*, 88.

36. For a discussion on forced vocations, see E. Cattaneo, "Le monacazioni forzate tra cinque e seicento" (Forced vows between 1500 and 1600), in *Vita e processo di suor Virginia Maria de Leyva monaca di Monza* (The Life and Trial of Virginia Maria de Leyva, Nun in Monza) (Milan: Garzanti, 1985), 145–95. See also Giorgio Chittolini and Giovani Miccoli, eds., *Storia d'Italia. Annali 9: La chiesa e il potere politico dal medioevo all'età contemporanea* (History of Italy. Annals 9: The Church and Political Power from the Middle Ages to Today) (Turin: Einaudi, 1986).

37. After entering the convent, Camilla Faà Gonzaga assumes the name of "Suora Caterina Camilla Gonzaga Faà." She appropriates Ferdinando's second wife's name in an attempt to destroy the forced separation between her new role as an unwilling nun and her rightful place as a marchioness. In "Re-Membering the 'I,'" Finucci comments on Faà Gonzaga's act of renaming herself: "The addition of the name of Caterina . . . to Camilla metaphorically dismembers the Duke's triangular tie with his two wives before proceeding to deform, reform and transform it. In re-christening herself for a life of self-erasure, Camilla re-members both her sexual being (Camilla) and her legal past (Gonzaga). Not yet satisfied, she inscribes and publicizes her sociolegal punishment as a nun with the peculiar semantic choice of prioritizing the name of the Duke's powerful second wife over her own. Ironically, this carefully wrought *adnominatio* is useless in the very moment that she appropriates it. The existential program to which monastic life subscribes requires, as Camilla well knows, the voluntary renunciation of all forms of secular self-authentication" (29). Even when destined to subside into silence, Camilla attempts to speak by using her self as a text in order to occupy a linguistic space.

38. For a historical introduction to cloistered life since the Middle Ages, see Penelope D. Johnson, "The Cloistering of Medieval Nuns: Release or Repression, Reality or Fantasy?" in *Gendered Domains: Rethinking Public and Private in Women's History*, ed. Dorothy O. Helly and Susan M. Reverby (Ithaca and London: Cornell University Press, 1992), 27–39.

39. Fiora Bassanese, "What's in a Name? Self-Naming and Renaissance Women Poets," *Annali d'Italianistica: Women's Voices in Italian Literature* 7 (1989): 104.

40. Elissa Weaver, "Convent Comedy and the World: The Farces of Suor Annalena Odaldi (1572–1638)," *Annali d'Italianistica: Women's Voices in Italian Literature* 7 (1989): 190.

41. Ibid.

42. Finucci, "The Italian Memorialist," 136.

43. Fido, "At the Origins of Autobiography in the 18th and 19th Centuries," 171.

44. Cecilia Ferrazzi, *Autobiografia di una santa mancata*, ed. Anna Jacobson Schutte (Bergamo: Pierluigi Lubrina, 1991). All subsequent references to this edition will be indicated by the page number in parenthesis following the quotation.

45. Ferrazzi writes: ". . . and because marriage filled me with disgust, I ran away from home" (21).

46. Ferrazzi states: "And little by little, a homeless girl was entrusted to me, then another, and

then another so that gradually, counting the number of girls there when I left . . . I had 120 girls, with whom I went to Saint John the Evangelist, and there I remained two or three years to guide those girls, who grew in number" (23). (The translation is mine.)

47. Weaver, "Convent Comedy and the World," 182.

48. Ferrazzi, *Autobiografia di una santa mancata*, 47. (The translation is mine.)

49. Ferrazzi talks about the "presents" given to her by her protector and feminine guide: "The Holy Mother appeared to me. She gave me the above-mentioned little chain and she put it around my right arm. It was so tight that it could only be removed by breaking it. It was broken and removed, causing me great pain, by the above mentioned discalced Carmelite" (87). (The translation is mine.) The pain she refers to is both psychological and physical as the confessor forcefully pulls the jewel off her arm. She is violated by a man's will aimed at destroying her privileged relationship with her Mother. The father confessor symbolizes the male desire to replace the maternal influence on Cecilia with a more traditional patriarchal control on female destiny. This relationship, however, cannot be disrupted. Mary returns in Ferrazzi's narrative to oppose Cecilia's decision to cut her hair, to become a nun, to agree to taking part in a religious institution easily controlled by male religious hierarchies: "I remember that when I was among the Capuchin nuns I once took a pair of scissors in order to cut my hair, because I desired to take the veil and remain among them. I was almost cutting it when the very Holy Virgin appeared to me. She removed the scissors from my hands and said: 'Is this in my hands that obedience you promised me?' I bowed to her, asked for forgiveness, and told her that I would be happy to stay there without becoming a nun" (97). (The translation is mine.)

50. The father confessors play a power game with her, of which Ferrazzi seems aware, a game that could only be called a "confessional ping-pong." In her description of their "game," Ferrazzi adopts a subtle, humorous tone, which does not appear in any other part of her narrative: "After becoming the confessor of the nuns of Saint Laurence, he [the parish priest] sent somebody to tell me that I had to go and see a Jesuit father confessor and that I had to answer all the questions he would ask, and so I did. Initially, this father asked me to describe how I had found those girls and then, in order to guide my soul, he asked me [to tell him] how the confessor was guiding me. And he added: 'Daughter, if you remain with that confessor, he will drive you crazy.' Afterward, I went to see the parish priest, who asked me as a token of obedience to tell him everything that Chiaromonte had told me and everything that I had told him. And the parish priest gave me a new order: I had to go back to Chiaromonte in order to reconcile, and, if he asked me other questions, I had to come back and talk to him. If he ordered things that Chiaromonte, instead, prohibited, I had to obey Chiaromonte. The parish priest ordered me in confession to remove the rings I used to wear. Afterward, I went to Chiaromonte, who, seeing me without my rings, asked me why I was not wearing them. I answered that I had to obey the parish priest's, my confessor's, order to remove them. He replied: 'What does that mean? He allowed you to wear them for nine consecutive years and now he wants you to remove them.' And he ordered me to put the rings on and wear them. Then, I fearfully went to the parish priest and told him. He answered that I had to do what he [Chiaromonte] had ordered. I continued in this fashion, going from one to the other, for three or four months" (68–69). (The translation is mine.)

Two. Speaking through Her Body: The Futurist Seduction of a Woman's Voice

1. A shorter version of this chapter is published with the title "The Transparent Woman: Reading Femininity within a Futurist Context," in *Feminine Feminists: Cultural Practices in Italy*, ed. Giovanna Miceli Jeffries (Minneapolis: University of Minnesota Press, 1994).

2. Elaine Showalter, "Hysteria, Feminism, and Gender," in *Hysteria beyond Freud*, ed. Sander L. Gilman, Helen King, Roy Porter, G. S. Rousseau, and Elaine Showalter (Berkeley, Los Angeles, London: University of California Press, 1993), 335.

3. *The Laws of Plato*, trans. Thomas Pangle (New York: Basic Books, 1980), 6, 781 C–D, 170.

4. Ibid.

5. Silvia Vegetti Finzi, "The Female Animal," trans. Giuliana de Novellis, in *The Lonely Mirror: Italian Perspectives on Feminist Theory,* ed. Sandra Kemp and Paola Bono (London and New York: Routledge, 1993), 141.

6. Ibid., 139.

7. Ibid.

8. F. T. Marinetti and Signora Enif Robert, *Un ventre di donna: Romanzo chirurgico* (A Woman's Womb: A Surgical Novel) (Milan: Facchi, 1919). All subsequent references to this edition are indicated by the page number, following the quotation in the text. The name Enif will be used to indicate the protagonist of Robert's autobiographical act. The full name Robert will be used to indicate the author or, when specified, the narrator. All translations are mine.

9. Sidonie Smith, *Subjectivity, Identity, and the Body: Women's Autobiographical Practices in the Twentieth Century* (Bloomington and Indianapolis: Indiana University Press, 1993), 3.

10. Judith Butler, *Bodies That Matter: On the Discursive Limits of "Sex"* (New York and London: Routledge, 1993), 2.

11. Ibid., 7.

12. Alice Jardine, "Death Sentences: Writing Couples and Ideology," in *The Female Body in Western Culture: Contemporary Perspectives,* ed. Susan Rubin Suleiman (Cambridge, Mass., and London: Harvard University Press, 1985), 84.

13. Louis Althusser, *Lenin and Philosophy* (New York: Monthly Review, 1971), 162.

14. Smith, *Subjectivity, Identity, and the Body,* 10.

15. In her book *Tabù e coscienza* (Taboo and Conscience) (Florence: La Nuova Italia, 1978), Anna Nozzoli devotes a chapter to futurist women, where she analyzes both the relationship between women writers and the avant-garde by looking at texts by Enif Robert, Rosa Rosà, Valentine de Saint Point, and Maria Ginanni, and the relationship between women's futurist works and Marinetti's literary production. Nozzoli stresses the problematic entrapment of female creativity within the dominating male ideology of the movement. She concludes by creating a triangular structure in which the link between futurism and fascism is presented by the work of a futurist woman who wrote predominantly in the late forties. Maria Goretti's creative effort is a pillar in the construction of what Nozzoli calls "the new aesthetics of the Mussolinian war" (63), and it also concludes Nozzoli's panorama of women writers in Marinetti's movement.

In her article "The Scarred Womb of the Futurist Woman" (*Carte Italiane: A Journal of Italian Studies* 8 [1986–87]), Cinzia Blum concentrates her critical attention on F. T. Marinetti and Enif Robert's *A Woman's Womb*. Her intention is to reject the common assumption that "the women in the movement [futurism] are seen as having a simply mimetic, entirely subordinated relation to the male Futurists" (15). Blum stresses that "the Futurist experience is a significant episode in women's activity on the Italian cultural and literary scene at the beginning of the twentieth century" (15). However, throughout her analysis of Robert's autobiographical act, she must recognize what she calls "the limits of the strategy adopted by the Futurist women: to follow an avant-garde practice prescribed by a male centered movement which does not seriously threaten the social organization of gender" (26).

The theme of entrapment of female creativity within an artistic movement seems to be the common denominator of both Anna Nozzoli's and Cinzia Blum's articles. In her essay "Futurism and Feminism" (*Annali d'Italianistica* 7 [1989]: 253–71), Lucia Re focuses her attention instead on the feminist potential of futurist women's writings. In regard to the *questione femminile* within the futurist movement, Re describes the often contradictory, but always prescriptive definitions of Woman in futurist works by men and women writers. Her article ends, like Nozzoli's essay, with Maria Goretti's literary homage to fascist ideology. Re's reading of this female "involution" offers a solution to the problematic of the "female creative entrapment" in Marinetti's literary movement. She argues that "Maria Goretti's book—along with some other works by futurist women written in the period of the fascist 'involution' of the movement—could be read as the locus where, in the face of the fascist regimentation of the female subject and of her discourse, a new 'ventriloquized' form of expression developed whose 'secret' resistance-function is precisely that of carrying out a poetic deconstruction of the fascist myth of femininity" (271). For an exhaustive analysis of futurist women and their writings, see Claudia Salaris, *Artecrazia: L'avanguardia futurista negli anni del fascismo* (Florence: La Nuova Italia, 1991) and *Le futuriste* (Milan: Edizioni delle Donne, 1982).

16. In his *Prosa e critica futurista* (Milan: Feltrinelli, 1973), Mario Verdone argues: "Next to totally invented characters, the author [Marinetti] circulates with extreme ease. . . . Besides, most of Marinetti's work is autobiographical. . . . And at the center there is always him: F. T. Marinetti, like in that small and delightful treatise of *ars amandi* which is *How to Seduce Women*. . . . In short, . . . to Flaubert's 'Madame Bovary c'est moi,' Marinetti countered with 'Marinetti c'est moi'" (13). In *A Woman's Womb*, Marinetti not only supplies the framework for Enif's story of her life, but also, as a more experienced "autobiographical writer," he leaves his imprint in the relationship between theory and autobiographical practice.

17. Fillia (Luigi Colombo), "La morte della donna" (The Death of Woman), in *Prosa e critica futurista*, 177. All subsequent references to this work are indicated by the page number, following the quotation in the text.

18. Ibid., 178.

19. In *Come si seducono le donne e si tradiscono gli uomini* (How to Seduce Women and Betray Men) (Milan: Sonzogno, 1933), a woman tells Marinetti: "I like you as you are, so much! But I think that I mean very little to you. Much less than your latest labor: your poem, your magnificent fetus" (118).

20. Ruggero Vasari, "L'angoscia delle macchine," *Teatro Italiano d'avanguardia*, ed. Mario Verdone (Rome: Officina, 1970), 180.

21. In *How to Seduce Women*, Marinetti states.

—You think of women as train stations.

—Sometimes they are nothing but tunnels! . . . It is a matter of habit. (64)

Most of the quotations from *How to Seduce Women and Betray Men* are taken from the 1933 edition. However, Marinetti's manual of seduction was first published in 1916 with the title *How to Seduce Women* (Florence: Edizioni da Centomila). A polemic followed the publication of Marinetti's book, and women's reactions were published in the magazine *Italia Futurista* (Futurist Italy), 1917. In 1918 a new edition of Marinetti's book of seduction was published (Florence-Rome: Rocca di San Casciano, 1918). The book contains a new chapter entitled "Polemiche sul presente libro" (Polemics about this book), which contains some women's polemic writings from *Italia Futurista*. The writers are Rosa Rosà, Shara Marini, Enif Robert, and a man, VOLT. Robert's two contributions included in this edition are "How To Seduce Women (Open Letter to F. T. Marinetti)" and "A Serene Word," and they are both signed "Enif Robert, Parolibera Futurista." In 1920, Marinetti's *How to Seduce Women* became *How to Seduce Women and Betray Men* (Milan: Sonzogno, 1920). The men betrayed are certainly not the futurist men. Marinetti writes: "A woman's complete and long-lasting devotion is justified and beautiful when this man [i.e., the futurist man] completely absorbs all her faculties and a priori overcomes all other men, eliminating in the woman the desire to search further up and farther away" (194). The 1920 edition only contains Enif Robert's reelaborated comment to Marinetti's book, entitled "To Seduce or to Be Seduced"; the other female voices have disappeared and do not reappear in other editions.

22. Smith, *Subjectivity, Identity, and the Body*, 10.

23. In their introduction to *How to Seduce Women* (1933), Corra and Settimelli write: "We sincerely believe that when talking about women it is impossible to generalize too much" (17). Marinetti disagrees: "Consider women like sisters of the sea, of the wind, of the clouds, of electric

batteries, of tigers, of sheep, of geese, of carpets, of sails. Do not ever consider them as sisters of the stars. . . . They all have a soul, which, however, depends upon the length of their hair, wires of the hurricane" (166).

24. The image of the uterus as a self-contained representation of woman appears also in Marinetti's addenda to his manual of seduction entitled "How to Betray Men," published in 1920. Marinetti seems to want to continue his discourse on women's disturbances of the womb and writes: "Women, tired, exhausted by life's hardship, are deprived of their sensitivity by disturbances of their uteri and their too frequent and pathological pregnancies. They pretend to follow men through the various degrees of yearning to the moment of tender prostration that follows the embrace" (190). In this later writing, disease represents woman's defeat and the unveiling of her pretense to "keep up" with the superior futurist man. The futurist cure has not therefore succeeded in canceling man's preoccupation with the elusive female diseased body.

25. In her "Open Letter to F. T. Marinetti," published in the 1918 edition of *How to Seduce Women*, Enif Robert writes: "I open the dictionary (and please suppress your terrified reaction!) to find the term—To Seduce.

'To dissuade someone from Good, and attract him toward Evil, it often refers to allurements that others use to attract a woman who can fulfill their desires. . . .'

That old belief, which has been popular for centuries, according to which women are *cunningly* won by men and they are subdued by the control of the stronger will, has no more meaning. Nothing of the kind! Stories! Men invent them in order to create for themselves the illusion of being in command, of being superior, because they have the aggressive instinct always to conquer someone or something. Women allow them to believe that that is true because almost always women find that it is to their advantage to use their apparent weakness as one of the most effective weapons" (iii). This statement appears unchanged in the next and modified edition of Marinetti's manual of seduction, and it reveals Robert's preoccupation with the definition of the concept of seduction and her intent to negate its existence.

26. Judith Butler, "Variations on Sex and Gender: Beauvoir, Wittig, and Foucault," in *Feminism as Critique: On the Politics of Gender*, ed. Seyla Benhabib and Drucilla Cornell (Minneapolis: University of Minnesota Press, 1987), 133.

27. This statement is in Robert's contribution, entitled "A Serene Word," to Marinetti's 1918 edition of his manual of seduction (vii). It also appears in the 1920 edition in the addendum entitled "To Seduce or to Be Seduced" (210).

28. Enif's unsatisfactory relationship with her lover, Giulio, makes her desire a change in her life. Such a change is, however, reduced to a search for "another" man: "Giulio has done everything in his human and superhuman power to be adored by me. In reality, I do adore him. However, my ironic, unhappy spirit runs abruptly away when he kisses me tenderly, and it runs somewhere else, looking, searching, far, near, in the past, in the future, deep down in myself, for another happiness, a shapeless whim, another man without a body and without a voice, an abstract type . . . an act of madness, in short" (4). Her initial investigation of her past, present and future, which seems the beginning of an autobiographical analysis and a pre-text to her decision to write her life, becomes subordinated to the desire for the personified superhero that Marinetti will come to represent.

29. Alice Yaeger Kaplan, *Reproductions of Banality: Fascism, Literature, and French Intellectual Life* (Minneapolis: University of Minnesota Press, 1986), 79.

30. Ibid.

31. Julia Kristeva, "Stabat Mater," *Poetics Today*, 6, no. 1–2 (1985): 151.

32. Ibid.

33. Ibid.

34. Luisa Muraro, "Le ragioni che una donna può avere di odiare la sua simile" (The Reasons

Why a Woman Can Hate Another Woman), introduction to Patricia Highsmith, *Piccoli racconti di misoginia* (Milan: La Tartaruga Nera, 1984), 97–104.

35. Ibid., 98.

36. Ibid.

37. Ibid., 104.

38. Ibid., 101.

39. Butler, *Bodies That Matter*, 17.

40. Nancy Miller, *Getting Personal: Feminist Occasions and Other Autobiographical Acts* (New York and London: Routledge, 1991), 21. The interest in the personal as part of the theoretical, which is redirected (seduced) by Marinetti in Robert's autobiographical act, has been an object of interest for Italian women writers throughout the century. I am not attempting to supply an exhaustive list here, but just a few examples of such an interest in Italian literature.

Like Enif Robert, Dacia Maraini is concerned with the relationship between public theory and private practice. In a recent article in *Corriere della sera*, "Una scrittura segreta per il dolore delle donne" (Secret Writing of Women's Sorrow)(October 13, 1991), Dacia Maraini writes: "I have always thought that there is a secret and deep relationship made by necessity and modesty, between women's bodies and writing, which, in its institutionalized forms has always been used, if not exactly against her, certainly without her" (3).

In her *Come nasce il sogno d'amore* (How the Dream of Love Is Born) (Milan: Rizzoli, 1988), Lea Melandri introduces with pages of her own diary her critical work on Sibilla Aleramo. The subsequent chapters of Melandri's book are constructed so that the personal writings are closely intertwined with Aleramo's autobiographical works. In this *mise en abîme* of autobiographical writings (Melandri's autobiographical notes on Aleramo's autobiographical works), the critical is constructed as inseparable from the personal.

In *Autoritratto di gruppo* (Group Self-Portrait) (Florence: Giunti, 1988), Luisa Passerini creates a "group autobiography," which alternates sections created as a personal diary with chapters dedicated to developing political issues, including interviews of ex-members of the student movement to which Passerini had belonged. Her private life, a love relationship, and psychoanalytic sessions are closely connected to the public interviews and to her past involvement in a political movement in order to reveal the complexity of the translation into an autobiographical text of public and private memories.

In *Pubblici segreti* (Public Secrets) (Milan: Mondadori, 1965), Maria Bellonci experiments with form and content. In the private form of a diary, Bellonci elaborates public issues.

41. Hélène Cixous, "The Laugh of the Medusa," in *New French Feminism*, ed. Elaine Marks and Isabelle de Courtivron (Amherst: University of Massachusetts Press, 1980), 251.

42. Kaplan, *Reproductions of Banality*, 78. She is here quoting from F. T. Marinetti, *Mafarka le futuriste, roman africain* (Paris: E. Sansot, 1909).

43. Mary Ann Doane, *The Desire to Desire: Women's Film of the 1940s* (Bloomington: Indiana University Press, 1987), 38.

44. Aretaeus, *The Extant Works of Aretaeus, the Cappadocian*, ed. and trans. Francis Adams (London: Sydenham Society, 1856), 285.

45. Galen, "How to Detect Malingerers," in *Greek Medicine: Being Extracts Illustrative of Medical Writers from Hippocrates to Galen*, trans. and ann. Arthur J. Brock (London: J. M. Dent and Sons, 1929), 184.

46. In their introduction to *How to Seduce Women*, Corra and Settimelli openly call Marinetti "an observer and a psychologist" (23).

47. See Ellen Bassuk, "The Rest Cure: Repetition or Resolution of Victorian Women's Conflicts?" in *The Female Body in Western Culture*, 139–51.

48. Philip Rieff, introduction to Sigmund Freud, *Dora: An Analysis of a Case of Hysteria*, ed. Philip Rieff (New York: Collier Books, 1963), 11.

49. Showalter, "Hysteria, Feminism, and Gender," in *Hysteria Beyond Freud*, 316. This volume contains essays that trace the history of interpretation of hysteria. On the history of hysteria see also Martha Noel Evans, *Fits and Starts: A Genealogy of Hysteria in Modern France* (Ithaca and London: Cornell University Press, 1991).

50. On June 27, 1994, Elaine Showalter presented, at the School of Criticism and Theory, Dartmouth College, a paper entitled "Hystories: Hysteria, Narrative, and the Memory of Feminism."

51. Showalter, "Hysteria, Feminism, and Gender," 321.

52. In the first chapter of *How to Seduce Women and Betray Men* (1933), Marinetti states: "I sketched the first part of this book while in a military hospital bed in Udine, where I was immobilized because of eleven wounds in my groin and legs. . . .
To multiply a hundredfold the patriotism of young fighters, a super-enjoyable book had to be written. Therefore, I thought right away of an essay about the art of seducing women, which could demonstrate, through a number of very comical, erotic, and sentimental adventures, how courage and assault make up an irresistible form of charm for the fair sex" (26).

53. The quotation is taken from VOLT's "Open letter to Maria Ginanni," published at the end of the 1918 edition of Marinetti's manual of seduction (xv-xvi).

54. In *How to Seduce Women*, Marinetti comments on his meetings with a woman writer: "Very intelligent . . . less than a futurist man, though (108). . . . Everything that a beautiful literary woman does [is] in order to decrease momentarily the undisputed superiority of an Italian futurist poet. Erotic confessional" (109).

55. Jean Baudrillard, *Seduction* (New York: St. Martin's, 1990), 20.

56. Aretaeus, *The Extant Works of Aretaeus, the Cappadocian*, 285.

57. Friedrich Nietzsche, *The Genealogy of Morals* (New York: Doubleday, 1956), 260.

58. Other futurist women present female sickness and female monsters in their narratives. In Rosa Rosà's *Una donna con tre anime* (A Woman with Three Souls) (Milan: Edizioni delle Donne, 1981), the protagonist, Giorgina Rossi, is an acquiescent housewife who breathes strange fumes and consequently acquires different personalities that allow her to break away from her monotonous life. She therefore needs a "cure" and becomes an object of study for "male doctors." I am not implying that Giorgina Rossi's disease mirrors Enif's hysterical womb. The two novels are very different, but they share the portrayal of female changing roles accompanied by disease.
Benedetta Marinetti's *Viaggio di Gararà* (Voyage of Gararà) (Milan: Morreale, 1931) contains the description of a haunted journey populated by strange beings. The journey could be both a dream and a nightmare in which many of the monsters are female. Marinetti writes the introduction to this "romanzo cosmico per teatro" (cosmic novel for the theater) and talks about women's writings as inferior because they are inevitably autobiographical (vii). Marinetti argues: "You go up with her [Benedetta] to the inebriating atmospheres of the highest abstract poetry. Women rarely elevate themselves to such heights. Almost all of them, because they are women, when they write, narrate in detail—great and little—spiritual or material experiences of their daily lives (straightforward love, sexual eccentricities, husband, lover, children, luxuries, parties, rivalries, careers)" (vii). What Marinetti is stating is that Benedetta's abstract poetry is "better" than what other women usually write, because women can only talk of what is autobiographical, linked to their everyday reality (sexual eccentricities!). The reason that Benedetta can be "as abstract as a man" is skillfully disguised in the following statement by Marinetti: "I admire the geniality of Benedetta, my equal, not my disciple. Critics will search in vain for my mark on her very original cosmic novel for the theater: *Voyage of Gararà*" (v). By inviting critics not to look for his mark on his wife's work, Marinetti draws attention to the relationship between himself (master) and his wife (disciple) and actually invites critics to see that Benedetta's "superior work" is such because of his influence and imprint on it.

59. Barbara Spackman, *Decadent Genealogies: The Rhetoric of Sickness from Baudelaire to*

D'Annunzio (Ithaca and London: Cornell University Press, 1989), 173. Spackman adds in a note: "For Freud, of course, the terror of Medusa is a terror of castration that is linked to the sight of 'something,' and that 'something' is the woman's lack of a penis" (173). Enif as Medusa is a doubly threatening monster as she is doubly lacking, a woman lacking the lack, a double castration.

60. Claudine Hermann, *The Tongue Snatchers* (Lincoln and London: University of Nebraska Press, 1989).

61. In his letters to Enif Robert, Marinetti assigns meaning to their epistolary relationship, which is a complementary to Marinetti's discourse on violence, cure, and the hygienic war: "To hit the target by firing a cannon is equal to an epistolary love: you cannot see it and neither can you feel the kissed mouth, far away. To hit the target by throwing bombards is, instead, equal to a furious radio-telegraphic embrace, or better, a telephonic kiss" (139–40).

62. Luce Irigaray, *Speculum of the Other Woman* (Ithaca: Cornell University Press, 1985), 71.

63. See Juliet Mitchell, "Femininity, Narrative, and Psychoanalysis," in *Women: The Longest Revolution* (London: Virago, 1984).

64. Hélène Cixous and Catherine Clément, *The Newly Born Woman*, trans. Betsy Wing (Minneapolis: University of Minnesota Press, 1986), 154.

65. See Luisa Muraro, *La posizione isterica e la necessità della mediazione*, ed. Mimma Ferrante (Palermo: Donne Acqua Liquida, Biblioteca delle Donne, 1993); and *In Dora's Case: Freud-Hysteria-Feminism*, ed. Charles Bernheimer and Claire Kahane (New York: Columbia University Press, 1990). See also Monique David-Ménard, *Hysteria from Freud to Lacan*, trans. Catherine Porter (Ithaca and London: Cornell University Press, 1989), and Hannah S. Decker, *Freud, Dora, and Vienna 1900* (New York: Free Press, 1991).

66. Robert insists on the relationship between a woman's physical ugliness and her inability to "think the right way," that is, to accept the futurist doctrine. She elaborates her essentialist description of an intellectual woman: "Here is a case that makes one think. An ugly woman, made even worse by a barbarian outfit, has her mind cluttered by erudite solemnities. Therefore, she is the least suitable to understand the very modern simplifiers of life and art. She keeps instead, with funny skill, at least two of them at a time tied to her clownlike pom-pom on her absurd little hat" (202–3). In *How to Seduce Women*, Marinetti presents a similar portrayal of the intellectual woman: "On my right [there is] a very famous woman writer, liquefied by thirty years of literary teas. [She has] large prowlike breasts, which are foolishly wrapped in garnet red velvet, a Far East-like hat that looks like the swinging mast of a ship" (143).

67. He described autobiography as *the* female mode of expression in his introduction to one of his wife's books, *Viaggio di Gararà* (see note 58 for this chapter).

68. Robin Pickering-Iazzi, "The Politics of Gender and Genre in Italian Women's Autobiography of the Interwar Years," *Italica* 71, no. 2 (1994): 176–97.

69. F. T. Marinetti, "Contro il lusso femminile" (Against Female Luxuries), in *Teoria e invenzione futurista*, ed. Luciano de Maria (Milan: Mondadori, 1983), 476. The image of the woman who offers herself naked, which penetrates into Robert's autobiographical work, is often repeated in Marinetti's writings. In his *How to Seduce Women*, Marinetti describes his "erotic" trip to Hungary: "I had the pleasure of judging aesthetically the lower belly and the thighs of hundreds of women farmers. . . . Once when my car had a mechanical problem I could witness the slow distracted toilette of a girl who was combing her hair at the window, wearing nothing on her breasts, naked down to her belly. Evidently, women's modesty is not necessary for man's desire" (42–43).

70. Kaplan, *Reproductions of Banality*, 81.

71. On the relationship between seduction and hysteria as part of a male discourse on women's bodies, see Martha Noel Evans, "Hysteria and the Seduction of Theory," in *Seduction and Theory: Readings of Gender, Representation, and Rhetoric*, ed. Dianne Hunter (Urbana and Chicago: University of Illinois Press, 1989), 73–85.

Three. From Genealogy to Gynealogy and Beyond:
Fausta Cialente's *Le quattro ragazze Wieselberger*

1. Thomas Laqueur, "The Facts of Fatherhood," in *Conflicts in Feminism*, ed. Marianne Hirsch and Evelyn Fox Keller (New York and London: Routledge, 1990), 205.

2. Sara Ruddick, "Thinking about Fathers," in *Conflicts in Feminism*, 223.

3. Alice A. Jardine, *Gynesis: Configurations of Woman and Modernity* (Ithaca and London: Cornell University Press, 1985), 25.

4. Fausta Cialente, *Le quattro ragazze Wieselberger* (Milan: Mondadori, 1976). All future references to this text will be indicated by the page number following the quotation in the text. The name Fausta will be used to indicate the protagonist of Cialente's autobiographical act. The name Cialente will be used to indicate the author or, when specified, the narrator. All translations are mine.

5. I am using the term "life/lines" as Germaine Bree defines it in the foreword to *Life/Lines: Theorizing Women's Autobiography*, ed. Bella Brodzki and Celeste Schenck (Ithaca: Cornell University Press, 1988). See also note 69 in my introduction.

6. Fausta Cialente has been a very prolific writer. Her first novel, *Natalia*, was published in 1929. *Cortile a Cleopatra* (Courtyard in Cleopatra) was written in Egypt and published in 1936. Between 1930 and 1939, Cialente wrote short stories later collected in two volumes, *Pamela o la bella estate* (Pamela or the Beautiful Summer, 1935) and *Interno con figure* (Characters in Interior Spaces, 1976), the latter of which includes the stories in *Pamela* and others written after Cialente left Egypt in 1947. In the late 1930s and early 1940s, Cialente abandoned fiction writing in order to become actively involved in antifascist propaganda by becoming a broadcaster for Radio Cairo. She also contributed to *Fronte Unito*, a publication for Italian prisoners. After leaving both Egypt and her husband, Cialente traveled in Europe and the Middle East, spending most of her time with her daughter. Cialente returned to fiction writing in 1961 with *Ballata Levantina* (*The Levantines*, trans. Isabelle Quigly [London: Faber and Faber, 1962]), another "Egyptian novel." *Il vento sulla sabbia* (Wind on the Sand, 1972) is the last novel centered on the lives of émigrés in Egypt. Until 1966, *Natalia* was the only novel whose story unfolds in Italy. Then, in 1966, Cialente published *Un inverno freddissimo* (A Very Cold Winter), in which she recounts the story of one of the characters in *The Levantines* who leaves Egypt at the end of World War II and moves to Milan. This novel was made into a film for Italian television entitled *Camilla*.

7. The narration of the mother's life is not only a biography in Fausta Cialente's autobiography, it is also the daughter's indirect autobiography. To create another woman's biography, transforming it into an "indirect autobiography," is a technique used by several writers. The most famous is Gertrude Stein's *The Autobiography of Alice B. Toklas*. Rosellen Brown's *The Autobiography of My Mother* (New York: Doubleday, 1976) can be considered a parallel text to Fausta Cialente's autobiography. The mother, described as same and at the same time other, becomes the character through which a daughter can construct her self. The mother's life becomes the starting point in the construction of an independent female self in an autobiographical act.

On matrilinearism and matrilinear constructions, see Stephanie A. Demetrakipoulos, "The Metaphysics of Matrilinearism in Women's Autobiography: Studies of Mead's *Blackberry Winter*, Hellman's *Pentimento*; Angelou's *I Know Why the Caged Bird Sings*; and Kingston's *The Woman Warrior*," in *Women's Autobiography*, ed. Estelle C. Jelinek (Bloomington: Indiana University Press, 1980), 180–202.

8. Judith Butler, *Gender Trouble: Feminism and the Subversion of Identity* (New York and London: Routledge, 1990), 13.

9. Lynda Boose, "The Father's House and the Daughter in It: The Structures of Western Culture's Daughter-Father Relationship," in *Daughters and Fathers*, ed. Lynda Boose and Betty Flowers (Baltimore and London: Johns Hopkins University Press, 1989), 24.

10. Sandra Gilbert, "Life's Empty Pack: Notes toward a Literary Daughteronomy," in *Daughters and Fathers*, 257.

11. Ibid., 258.

12. Ibid., 259.

13. Boose, "The Father's House and the Daughter in It," 21.

14. Marianne Hirsch, "Maternity and Rememory: Toni Morrison's *Beloved*," in *Representations of Motherhood*, ed. Donna Bassin, Margaret Honey, and Meryle Mahrer Kaplan (New Haven and London: Yale University Press, 1994), 94.

15. Nancy K. Miller, "Autobiographical Deaths," *Massachusetts Review* (Spring 1992): 19–47.

16. Mary G. Mason, "The Other Voice: Autobiographies of Women Writers," in *Life/Lines: Theorizing Women's Autobiography*, 22.

17. Carolyn Heilbrun, *Writing a Woman's Life* (New York: Norton, 1988), 18.

18. Luce Irigaray, *Speculum of the Other Woman* (Ithaca: Cornell University Press, 1985), 35.

19. James E. Breslin, "Gertrude Stein and the Problems of Autobiography," in *Women's Autobiography*, ed. Estelle C. Jelinek, 162.

20. I am here referring to Carolyn Heilbrun's statement: "But, at least insofar as women's lives are concerned, it is wrong. Lines can be cancelled and washed out" (*Writing a Woman's Life*, 19).

21. I would like to thank Lionella Muir Terni, Fausta Cialente's daughter, for reading this chapter. I am grateful to her for pointing out to me that it was her mother who chose to have that specific portrayal of the grandfather reproduced on the cover of the book (letter dated April 8, 1993).

22. Marianne Hirsch, *The Mother/Daughter Plot: Narrative, Psychoanalysis, Feminism* (Bloomington: Indiana University Press, 1989), 73.

23. Ibid., 79.

24. Ibid., 80.

25. I am borrowing the definition of patrimony as paternal inheritance in a large sense from Philip Roth's *Patrimony: A True Story* (New York: Simon and Schuster, 1991), in which he writes about his troubled relationship with his sick parent.

26. See Françoise Lionnet, "*Métissage*, Emancipation and Female Textuality in Two Francophone Writers," in *Life/Lines: Theorizing Women's Autobiography*, ed. Bella Brodzki and Celeste Schenck (Ithaca: Cornell University Press, 1988), 260–81; and Françoise Lionnet, *Autobiographical Voices* (Ithaca: Cornell University Press, 1989).

27. Gilbert, "Life's Empty Pack," 276.

28. Sandra Petrignani, *Le signore della scrittura* (Milan: La Tartaruga, 1984), 87.

29. Ibid.

30. Ibid., 85.

31. Paola Malpezzi Price, "Autobiography, Art, and History in Fausta Cialente's Fiction," in *Contemporary Women Writers in Italy: A Modern Renaissance*, ed. Santo Aricò (Amherst: University of Massachusetts Press, 1990), 109–22.

32. Homi Bhabha, *The Location of Culture* (London and New York: Routledge, 1994), 2.

33. Ibid., 9.

34. Angela Ingram, Introduction to *Women's Writing in Exile*, ed. Mary Lynn Broe and Angela Ingram (Chapel Hill: University of North Carolina Press, 1989), 5.

35. Sara Ruddick, *Maternal Thinking: Toward a Politics of Peace* (Boston: Beacon Press, 1989), 157.

36. Hirsch, *The Mother/Daughter Plot*, 167.

Four. Rita Levi Montalcini's Perfect Imperfection

I would like to thank Rita Levi Montalcini for reading this chapter and for her valuable suggestions. All translations in this chapter are mine. Montalcini's autobiography is available in translation: *In Praise of Imperfection: My Life and Work,* trans. Luigi Attardi (New York: Basic Books, 1988).

1. Rita Levi Montalcini, *Il tuo futuro: I consigli di un Premio Nobel ai giovani* (Your Future: Advice of a Nobel Prize Winner to Young People) (Milan: Garzanti, 1993), 20.

2. Helen Longino and Evelyn Hammonds, "Conflicts and Tensions in the Feminist Study of Gender and Science," in *Conflicts in Feminism,* ed. Marianne Hirsch and Evelyn Fox Keller (New York and London: 1990), 164.

3. Ibid., 165.

4. Ibid., 180.

5. Ibid.

6. Ibid., 173. See also Sandra Harding, *The Science Question in Feminism* (Ithaca and London: Cornell University Press, 1986) and, by the same author, *Whose Science? Whose Knowledge? Thinking from Women's Lives* (Ithaca and New York: Cornell University Press, 1991).

7. Rita Levi Montalcini, *Elogio dell'imperfezione* (Milan: Garzanti, 1988). All future references to this text will be indicated by the page number in parentheses following the quotation in the text. The name Rita will be used to indicate the protagonist of Montalcini's autobiographical act. The full name Rita Levi Montalcini will be used to indicate the author or, when specified, the narrator.

8. Montalcini writes: "The pact of allegiance that was established very early in our lives between Paola and me alleviated, but did not free us from, the anguish we felt in our childhood. It was an anguish that had its roots in extreme shyness, lack of confidence in myself, fear of adults, in general, and of my father in particular" (22).

9. Alan Ryan, "Private Selves and Public Parts," in *Public and Private in Social Life,* ed. S. I Benn and G. F. Gaus (New York: St. Martin's, 1983), 151.

10. Marianne Hirsch, *The Mother/Daughter Plot: Narrative, Psychoanalysis, Feminism* (Bloomington: Indiana University Press, 1989), 65.

11. Carolyn G. Heilbrun, *Reinventing Womanhood* (New York: Norton, 1979), 178.

12. Chiara Zamboni, *L'azione perfetta* (Rome: Edizioni Centro Culturale Virginia Woolf, 1993), 11.

13. Evelyn Fox Keller, *Reflections on Gender and Science* (New Haven: Yale University Press, 1985), 77.

14. Ibid., 79.

15. Rita Levi Montalcini states: "After so many years, I have understood that my father, much more than my mother, to whom I felt close because of the love I felt for her, was a major influence in my life because of the genes he had passed on to me and because of our daily relationship, which aroused contrasting feelings in me. I admired his tenacity, his energy, and his intelligence, but I also silently disapproved of other sides of his personality about which I will talk later" (23).

16. Hirsch, *The Mother/Daughter Plot,* 80.

17. Ibid.

18. Keller, *Reflections on Gender and Science,* 86. Many women who are involved in the medical profession identify the father as the model that inspired their choices. It is the case of Emanuela Mecca, professor at the University of Verona, who is interviewed by Luisa Muraro: "Una scienziata medica: Intervista a Emanuela Mecca," in *Autorità scientifica, autorità femminile* (Rome: Editori Riuniti, 1992), 13–24. This volume was created by Ipazia, the name of a group of women involved in the medical profession who meet regularly at the Libreria delle Donne in Milan. They are named after Ipazia, a mathematician and philosopher who lived between the fourth and fifth centuries c.e. In this volume women scientists are interviewed, and they elaborate on their roles in science, on their models and authoritative figures, and on their "female" approach to medicine.

19. Pier Aldo Rovatti, "Elogio del pudore," in *Elogio del pudore: Per un pensiero debole,* ed. Alessandro dal Lago and Pier Aldo Rovatti (Milan: Feltrinelli, 1990).

20. I am here borrowing the idea of a "dialogue" between texts and between opposites from Gianni Vattimo's *La società trasparente* (Milan: Garzanti, 1989), where the author writes: "The logic according to which one can describe and critically measure the knowledge in human science, and the possible 'truth' in the world of mass media communication, is a 'hermeneutical' logic, which searches for truth intended as continuity, 'correspondence,' dialogue between texts, and does not search for a truth intended as conformity to a mythical condition" (40). The construction of "truth" as a dialogue among minor "truths" destroys the concept of truth as "strong," that is, unchangeable and eternal. Truth as a "continuity" reveals its weakness, as it is an ever changing entity constructed on a plurality of "weak" truths.

21. Maurizio Viano, "Sesso debole, pensiero debole," *Annali d'Italianistica* 7 (1989): 418.

22. Elisabetta Donini, professor of physics at the University of Turin (contribution without title), in *Donne e scienza*, ed. Anna del Bo Boffito (Milan: Guerini Studio, 1990), 26. Her essay connects discussions on science and gender developed in the United States by Evelyn Fox Keller, Sandra Harding, and Vivian Gornick to the discourse that Italian women scientists are elaborating. See Vivian Gornick, *Women in Science: Portraits from a World in Transition* (New York: Simon and Schuster, 1983); Sandra Harding, *Feminism and Science*, ed. Nancy Tuana (Bloomington and Indianapolis: Indiana University Press, 1989); Sandra Harding, ed., *The "Racial" Economy of Science: Toward a Democratic Future* (Bloomington and Indianapolis: Indiana University Press, 1993); Jonathan Cole, *Fair Science: Women in the Scientific Community* (New York: Free Press, 1979).

23. Donini, *Donne e scienza*, 30.

24. The relationship among women after years of *autocoscienza* is one of the centers of interest in Italian contemporary feminist thought. I indicated the possibility of assigning to Montalcini's fictional construction of a self the role of female guide to enter the public sphere. Italian feminism has developed a parallel theory and practice of a feminist exchange among women. The theory and practice of "entrustment," or *affidamento*, is summarized by Teresa de Lauretis in her article "The Essence of the Triangle, or Taking the Risk of Essentialism Seriously: Feminist Theory in Italy, the U.S. and Britain," *Differences* 1.2 (1989). De Lauretis states: "The relationship of entrustment is one in which one woman gives her trust or entrusts herself symbolically to another woman, who thus becomes her guide, mentor, or point of reference—in short, the figure of symbolic mediation between her and the world. Both women engage in the relationship . . . not in spite, but rather because and in full recognition of the disparity that may exist between them in class or social position, age, level of education, professional status, income, etc. That is to say, the function of female symbolic mediation that one woman performs for the other is achieved, not in spite but rather because of the power differential between them, contrary to the egalitarian feminist belief that women's mutual trust is incompatible with unequal power" (22). Montalcini's Ariadne's threads acquire a larger meaning as they come to symbolize the mutual exchange among women who are helping one another in order to destroy the traditional marginalization of a single isolated woman who struggles to create her "own" space in the world.

25. Rita Levi Montalcini does not define herself as a feminist, but her voice has been heard on a recent important issue regarding women's health. She has taken a clear position in favor of the pill RU 486, invented by Emile Baulieu, because it supplies a "safe alternative" to the traditional abortion practices. On this matter, Montalcini was interviewed by Gianni Bonadonna, who includes the conversation with Montalcini in his book *Donne in medicina* (Milan: Rizzoli, 1991). Montalcini states: "After being tested, the pill received the approval of the French health authorities. In a country like ours, which has recognized since 1978 the right to the interruption of a pregnancy in the first months, provided that there are valid reasons, a pill of this kind embodies a safe, pain-free, risk-free alternative if you compare it to the surgical methods now employed. I declared that I am in favor of the use of such a pill under strict medical supervision, even if some people had misunderstood my reasons and wrote that I had taken a position against the

Vatican. Whoever knows me is aware that I am a free spirit and that I am too tolerant to allow myself any intolerant practice" (240).

26. Pier Aldo Rovatti,"Elogio del pudore," 44–45.

27. Ibid., 44.

28. Ibid., 31.

29. Gianni Vattimo, *La società trasparente* (Milan: Garzanti, 1989), 11.

30. Ibid., 14.

31. Rovatti, "Elogio del pudore," 32.

32. Ibid., 46.

33. When Rita reveals her intention to attend the university to her father, "he listened to me with a serious look on his face, an expression that made me fear him. He asked me if I knew what I wanted to do" (44). When Rita answers, the father gives his consent: "If this is really your wish. . . . I will not stand in your way, but I have doubts about your choice" (44).

34. Eugenia's approach to mathematics echoes Rita's earlier experience with "imperfect definitions" that contribute to create her reputation as *sensitiva* within her family (23). Montalcini writes: "In second grade, a teacher asked us to write a composition explaining the use of our ten fingers. I made my brother Gino and others who had heard about it laugh when I wrote: 'To send kisses to mom.' They were still kisses in the air, but the difference from those I sent my father was that these had a very precise target. They revealed not only the love for my mother, but also my lack of practical sense, a lack that persisted in the future" (20).

35. Heilbrun, *Reinventing Womanhood,* 212.

36. Rovatti, "Elogio del pudore," 41.

37. Montalcini quotes from a manifesto published in 1941: "The Jews are: Da Verona, Pitigrilli, Moravia, Loria, Segre, Momigliano, Terracini, Franco, [Gino] Levi-Montalcini, Einstein, Blum, La Pasionaria, . . . Karl Marx, . . . Lenin, . . . Modigliani, . . . Roosevelt, . . . the Negus, . . . The leaders of the free masons are Jews. . . . The most despicable cowards, the spreaders of panic-provoking news, the hoarders, and those who are the cause of other people's starvation, the most resilient defamers, the most perverse among the defeatists, those who exploit women and men are Jews. Homosexuals, those who have never felt sweat on their brow, those who have never worked, those who have always betrayed their land, those who are responsible for the sanctions are Jews" (96–97).

38. Helen Longino and Evelyn Hammonds, "Conflicts and Tensions in the Feminist Study of Gender and Science," 175.

39. In the narrative, Montalcini hints at her sister's work during the war. After leaving Turin in search of a safer place to live, Rita, Paola, and their mother rent rooms in Florence, where they remain until the end of the war. Montalcini comments on Paola's paintings of that time: "The mass movement of people, before the final expulsion of the Germans and the arrival of the allied forces, was the subject of one of Paola's most beautiful paintings of that time: the city that walks" (111).

40. I am adopting the psychoanalytic terms that describe the early relationship between mother and child as symbiotic. In her book *The Reproduction of Mothering: Psychoanalysis and the Sociology of Gender* (Berkeley: University of California Press, 1978), Nancy Chodorow greatly contributed to the feminist revision of psychoanalysis by attracting attention to the preoedipal phase and its consequences in the development of the child. She has therefore displaced the attention from the oedipal time, when the father is the point of reference, to a preoedipal time, when the mother and her symbiotic relation with the child become the point of reference. On this same subject Evelyn Fox Keller writes in *Reflections on Gender and Science:* "Many psychoanalysts have come to believe that, because of the boy's need to switch his identification from the mother to the father, his sense of gender identity tends always to be more fragile than the girl's. On the other hand, her sense of self identity may be comparatively more vulnerable. . . .

Although she too must disentangle her 'self' from the early experience of oneness [with the mother], she continues to look toward her mother as a model for her gender identity. Whatever vicissitudes her relation to her mother may suffer during subsequent development, a strong identification based on common gender is likely to persist—her need for 'disidentification' is not so radical" (89).

Five. Luisa Passerini's *Autoritratto di gruppo:* Personalizing Theory

I would like to thank Luisa Passerini for reading this paper, for her helpful suggestions, and for her friendship.

In this chapter, all translations from Italian into English are mine.

1. Luisa Passerini, *Autoritratto di gruppo* (Group Self-Portrait) (Florence: Giunti, 1988), 227. All future references to this text will be indicated by the page number in parentheses following the quotation in the text. The name Luisa will be used to indicate the protagonist of Passerini's autobiographical act. The full name Luisa Passerini will be used to indicate the author or, when specified, the narrator. Passerini's autobiography is forthcoming in English translation and will be published by Wesleyan University Press.

2. In her article "La tentazione del neutro," in *Il pensiero della differenza sessuale* (Theories of Sexual Difference), ed. Diotima (Milan: La Tartaruga, 1990), Wanda Tommasi writes: "Is there anything that can guarantee us that the neutral in science and philosophy suits well both women and men? . . . The fact is that in psychoanalysis, more clearly than in other fields, we have a neutral which proves to be male in reality" (85).

3. Jürgen Habermas, *Theory and Practice* (Boston: Beacon Press, 1973), 9.

4. Nancy Miller, *Getting Personal* (New York and London: Routledge, 1991), 1.

5. Ibid., 2.

6. Ibid., 4.

7. Ibid., 21.

8. Adele Cambria, "Gli anni dei movimenti" (The Years of the Movements), in *Scritture, scrittrici,* ed. Maria Rosa Cutrufelli (Milan: Longanesi, 1988), 41.

To experiment with hybrid structures and often with the translation of autobiographical theory into practice is part of the feminist agenda of several Italian women writers. In her book *Come nasce il sogno d'amore* (How the Dream of Love Is Born) (Milan: Rizzoli, 1988), Lea Melandri creates a hybrid context in which a critical approach to Sibilla Aleramo's work is transformed by Melandri into an autobiographical text. Melandri adopts Aleramo's style and thematics in order to gradually filter her own voice through another woman's, Aleramo's, auto-biographical narrative. Melandri writes a woman's biography by experimenting with redefining the boundaries between biography and autobiography. She weakens the separation between genres and, at the same time, between women's voices. In her book *Lo strabismo della memoria* (The Crooked Eyes of Memory) (Milan: La Tartaruga, 1991), Melandri continues her discourse on autobiography in a text that creates a personal and public path from the sixties to the eighties by, once more, adopting a hybrid structure that partakes of different genres: autobiography, biography, fiction, and nonfiction. It contains articles on politics, personal memoirs, and the development of her theoretical discourse on her literary experimentations.

9. Cambria, "Gli anni dei movimenti," 41.

10. Luisa Passerini, "Don Benedetto e l'ego-storia," *Belfagor* 44.5 (1989): 575.

11. Ibid., 577.

12. Luisa Passerini, "Conoscenza storica e storia orale" (Historical Knowledge and Oral History), in *Storia orale,* ed. Luis a Passerini (Turin: Rosenberg and Sellier, 1978), xxxiv.

13. Luisa Passerini, *Storia e soggettività: Le fonti orali, la memoria* (History and Subjectivity: Oral Sources and Memory) (Florence: La Nuova Italia, 1988), 12.

14. Passerini, *Storia e soggettività,* 12.

15. Luisa Passerini, postfazione (afterword) to Maurice Halbwachs, *La memoria collettiva* (Collective Memory), ed. Paolo Jedlowski (Milan: UNICOPLI, 1987), 191–92.

16. Passerini, Postfazione to *La memoria collettiva*, 195.

17. Thinking about difference is an important part of the agenda of the Italian feminist movement and above all of the members of Diotima, which has published a book entitled *Il pensiero della differenza sessuale*. The various sections of the book are entitled: "Sexual Difference: To Be Discovered and Engendered," "For a Theory of Sexual Difference," and "The Temptation of Neutrality." The contribution that is complementary to Passerini's choice of privileging difference is Adriana Cavarero's chapter "Per una teoria della differenza sessuale" (In Favor of a Theory of Sexual Difference). Cavarero concludes: "By recognizing the original duality as an inevitable assumption, the theory of sexual difference excludes a logical assimilation of the other. In women's theory of difference, the other is theoretically an entity that has not been investigated yet. Probably, the other cannot be investigated by employing only the methods allowed by the logic of duality, which is for now the only one considered as correct and necessary, but not developed yet. However, even now, such a logic presents itself as conflicted in relation to the logic of oneness, which suffocated its historical potential. It is a conflict that is not carried out with sticks (maybe, I do not know), but rather requires a suspension of trust, a distrust of theory when there is a confrontation with the whole construction of the conceptual logic of oneness. We, women, are right now within and not without such a construction: therefore, it is necessary to refine the strategies of mistrust in ourselves. That does not mean that we reach a stage of paralysis caused by our own self-censoring, and, by all means, it also does not mean that we paralyze other women by labeling them as 'sexist' or something similar. What it really means is that we must distrust the apparent neutrality of language, in its scientific objectivity, and even in its beauty. So that in this beauty, to be a woman does not involve a spell on a mute creature when she is confronted by language" (78).

18. Luisa Passerini, *Storie di donne e femministe* (Stories of Women and Feminists) (Turin: Rosenberg and Sellier, 1991), 80.

19. Luisa Passerini, "Conoscenza storica e storia orale. Sull'utilità e il danno delle fonti orali per la storia" (Historical Knowledge and Oral History: A Discourse on the Positive and Negative Influences in Utilizing Oral Sources in History), *Storia orale: Vita quotidiana e cultura materiale delle classi subalterne* (Oral History: Daily Life and Material Culture of the Subaltern Classes), ed. Luisa Passerini (Turin: Rosenberg and Sellier, 1978), x.

20. Ibid., xv.

21. Ibid., xvii.

22. Passerini describes the androgynous image of one of the most admired leaders of the student movement, Guido Viale: "Viale was skilled in voicing the most radical points of view in the movement. He could gather and express confused aspirations . . . , and not only the theoretical position, but also the values. . . . On the symbolic level, what played a role was the use of certain signifiers: his body, lean and androgynous. His long blond hair—besides his identity as an orphan—contributed to turn him into a character who did not accept compromises with the existent world; he was legendary and rebellious" (116). In her book *Storie di donne e femministe*, Passerini elaborates on the "role of androgyny" in the sixties: "One of the characteristics of '68 recognized then and now is androgyny, which manifested itself in the fact that certain models were privileged. . . . It is obvious that androgyny, as it is embodied in relations in which there is not a precise adoption of gender differences, is expressed in male models. However, these models are not marked by omnipotent and arrogant virility. On the contrary, they are marked by nostalgia for the feminine, in a process of convergence that draws together the models of the young male and of woman that are characteristic in a patriarchal culture" (146).

23. Julia Epstein and Kristina Straub, "Introduction: The Guarded Body," in *Body Guards:*

The Cultural Politics of Gender Ambiguity, ed. Epstein and Straub (New York and London: Routledge), 9.

24. Ibid., 21.

25. Carolyn G. Heilbrun, *Toward a Recognition of Androgyny* (New York and London: W.W. Norton, 1973).

26. Ibid., ix.

27. In "La tentazione del neutro," Tommasi is referring to psychoanalysis, but it can be translated into the historical context narrated by Passerini (85).

28. Ibid., 93.

29. Ibid., 96.

30. Ibid.

31. Marguerite Duras, "Smothered Creativity," in *New French Feminism: An Anthology*, ed. Elaine Marks and Isabelle de Courtirvron (Amherst: University of Massachusetts Press, 1980), 111.

32. Passerini, *Stories of Women and Feminists*, 150–51.

33. On the liberating aspect of the use of transgression in language, Luisa Passerini writes in *Group Self-Portrait*: "The widespread use of obscene, irreverent, and blasphemous language must be remarked on. The fact that young people used together expressions of that kind was nothing new. What was new was that they employed that language openly, using it in their speeches at meetings or in daily conversations together with sexual terms and swear words. It was above all new that women used such language, which marked a stage in their emancipation and which, by passing through a peer group, carried a prevalent male influence. Some women, who have now stopped using such language, remember the equalizing charge it had then, for example among the comrades who, when they used it among themselves, would quickly apologize whenever they mentioned a forbidden word in front of a woman" (114).

34. Interviewed by Passerini in *Group Self-Portrait*, even Barbara Derossi, who lived her experience in the movement in a relatively privileged position as leader, states: "My equality ended with the movement. In the movement, I never felt even for a second that I was different, had fewer rights, could do fewer things. After the movement I always felt that, if somebody had to be chosen to write a document, to deliver a speech, it was automatic that I would not be chosen" (137).

35. Duras, "Smothered Creativity," 111.

36. I paraphrased in the main text from an interview with Bettina Berch that is quoted in *Stories of Women and Feminists:* "At the time, the idea of sexual liberation seemed very promising and also very enjoyable. However, for most of us women it meant that we could choose which future revolutionary hero we wanted to go to bed with" (139). Bettina Berch's experience refers to the student movement at Columbia University in 1968. Her statement expands Passerini's observation on women and sexual transgression to women's international experiences in the "liberating" sixties. See also Ronald Fraser et al., *1968: A Student Generation in Revolt* (New York: Pantheon, 1988).

37. Carla Lonzi, *Sputiamo su Hegel: La donna clitoridea e la donna vaginale* (Let's Spit on Hegel: the Clitoral Woman and the Vaginal Woman) (Milan: Scritti di Rivolta Femminile, 1974), 64.

38. Alan Ryan, "Private Selves and Public Parts," in *Public and Private in Social Life*, ed. S. I. Benn and G. F. Gaus (New York: St. Martin's, 1983), 151.

39. Passerini, *Stories of Women and Feminists*, 155.

40. Ibid., 60.

41. In writing the introduction to Clara Zetkin's *La questione femminile e la lotta al riformismo* (The Female Question and the Fight against Reformism) (Milan: Mazzotta, 1972), Passerini analyzes how Clara Zetkin considered "the female question" in her discourse on Marxism. Woman is, in Zetkin's ideology, first a proletarian and only secondarily the carrier of a "woman's agenda." Passerini writes: "Clara Zetkin approaches the female question according

to the classical terms in Marxist tradition. She positions it within the 'social question,' whose solution could include, without any doubts, the solution of specific contradictions. The fight for the emancipation of the proletarian woman 'is a fight together with men of the same class against the capitalist class . . . the final objective in her fight is not free competition with men but rather the proletarian class and the acquisition of political power . . . that does not mean that she does not have to support the demands of the bourgeois women's movement. However, the fulfillment of such demands represents for the proletarian woman only a means toward an end, in order to enter the fight side by side with the proletarian class.'

"One can infer that the specific aspects of women's oppression are not changed by women's socialist fight. These women's duty cannot be that of estranging the proletarian woman from her duties as mother and wife. On the contrary, the fight must make it possible for women to perform their mission better than ever before, and this is carried out in the interest of proletarian emancipation. This aims to create a 'red wife,' a devoted comrade to her proletarian husband and to the proletarian class. She is, as always, a secondary being whose improved conditions within the family are instrumental in strengthening the proletarian class itself and its decision to fight" (13).

42. Many novels have been written about the Italian *anni di piombo* (lead years). The most famous is probably Renato Curcio's *WKHY* (Rome: Fatamorgana, 1984). He has also founded a publishing company, Sensibili alle Foglie, which published Curcio's autobiography entitled *La soglia* (The Threshold, 1993). Curcio has also published a collection of essays, *La mappa perduta* (The Lost Map) (Rome: Sensibili alle Foglie, 1990), that elaborate on the material created by terrorist groups in the seventies and on the socioeconomic conditions in which terrorism developed. The publishing company he founded is devoted to publishing texts that are traditionally ignored: memoirs from prison, autobiographical texts by AIDS patients, narratives written by immigrants.

Many other novels on the lead years have concentrated on developing the problematic relationship between women and violence not only in the terrorist movement but also, from a theoretical point of view, in the movements of the seventies that did not actively practice violence. Luce d'Eramo's *Nucleo Zero* (Milan: Mondadori, 1981) is followed by other works on the role of women in the terrorist movements, including one of her latest short stories entitled "Tra i pensieri d'una terrorista rossa" (Within the Mind of a Red Woman Terrorist), *Tuttestorie* 1: (1990). The protagonist of the short story states: "It is not by chance . . . that terrorism has so many women among its members. As everybody knows, women are more irrational than men. Introduced too quickly into the world of male thought—above all in Italy in the past decades—of course they have contributed to degrading it. They have no familiarity with abstract thinking. . . . They have not been taught how to separate theory from practice" (37). This short story is followed in the same collection by Ida Farè's story "Come voi" (Just Like You), which appears as a long monologue by a woman terrorist. In her novel *La mia signora* (My Lady) (Milan: SugarCo, 1986), Ida Farè recounts the story of a woman's experience through the left-wing movements in the seventies and her theoretical *simpatizzare* (sympathizing) for the terrorists and their movements. Farè has also published the book *Mara e le altre: Le donne e la lotta armata* (Mara and the Other Women: Women and Terrorism) (Milan: Feltrinelli, 1979). Farè's analysis of a generation is also echoed in other novels, such as Melo Freni's *Le passioni di Petra* (Petra's Passions) (Florence: Vallecchi, 1985), which tells the story of a woman's involvement with the student movement, her later detachment from politics, and her life both as a mother and as the wife of a terrorist. In *Generazione* (Generation) (Milan: Garzanti, 1987), Giorgio Von Straten constructs a "generational path" through the last thirty years. Similarly, Sandro Medici's *Via Po* (Rome: Cooperativa il Manifesto anni 80, 1987) investigates a generation's uneasiness in facing their daily life and public roles after their political involvement in the sixties.

43. In *Stories of Women and Feminists*, Passerini comments on one aspect of the complex

problem of the presence of women in the public sphere: "The process responsible for the growing presence of women in the public sphere also involves a deeply unsettling and contradictory aspect: their extensive participation in the phenomenon of terrorism in Italy in the seventies. It was a tragic moment of equality within the existing domain" (157). The problem seems to become even more complex in the early nineties as the still surviving terrorist movements in Europe are constituted by a prevalence of women. See Ellen MacDonald, *Shoot the Women First* (New York: Random House, 1991).

44. In *Stories of Women and Feminists,* Passerini draws her conclusions on the relationship between the student movement and women's movements: "The conclusive hypothesis is that '68 movements have had a great importance for women, whether they lived them firsthand or not. They accelerated and exposed contradictions; at the same time, they proclaimed the possibility of becoming the subject of one's own discourse and life, often in ways that did not have a direct consequence in praxis itself. It should have been the duty of the women's movement to go beyond such consequences. In a way, they should have adopted what '68 had promised in terms of a radical change in the relationship between public and private, between individual and collective" (159). On the history of the feminist movement in Italy, see Judith Adler Hellman, "The Originality of Italian Feminism," in *Donna: Women in Italian Feminism,* ed. Ada Testaferri (Ottawa: Dovehouse, 1989), 15–23; Teresa de Lauretis, "Eccentric Subjects: Feminist Theory and Historical Consciousness," *Feminist Studies* 16.1 (1990); Renate Holub, "For the Record: The Non-Language of Italian Feminist Philosophy," *RLA: Romance Languages Annual* 1 (1990): 133–40; Linda Hutcheon, "Feminism and Postmodernism," in *Donna: Women in Italian Culture,* 25–37; Carol Lazzaro-Weis, "Gender and Genre in Italian Feminist Literature in the Seventies," *Italica* 65.4 (1988): 293–307.

45. Luisa Muraro, *L'ordine simbolico della madre* (The Symbolic Order of the Mother) (Rome: Editori Riuniti, 1991), 20–21. In "La tentazione del neutro," Wanda Tommasi constructs a definition of the symbolic order of the mother, mediated through a dialogue with the female "other," the same and different at once. She states: "The voice of the other woman comes to break this silence: her words, her representations, begin to shape by crossing with mine, an interweaving of meaning, a web of signification. Between my silence, which attempts to gain a voice, and what has already been said in language, lies, as a form of mediation, a preliminary distance from what is immediate. Such a form allows the acquisition of a voice, the Third, until now excluded from discourse: that of the symbolic mother. It is a pattern of representations and significations that are exchanged between the other woman and myself and that allow us to speak, to Say words that are no more Echoes of a distant voice" (100–101). The idea of a symbolic order of the mother is the necessary component to an elaboration of the concept of *affidamento* (entrustment) intended as a derivation of the construction of a mother/daughter relationship beyond a biological-familial relationship. *Affidamento,* analyzed by Elvia Franco in "La scuola dell'affidamento" (The School of Entrustment) contained in the same anthology as Wanda Tommasi's article, becomes a key concept in the development of the construction of a female order based on privileging "the company of women." Such a theoretical program has found a translation into practice in books such as *Le lettere del mio nome* (The Letters of My Name) (Milan: La Tartaruga, 1991), in which author Grazia Livi constructs a personal and public path through private memories and portrayals of her literary mothers, the group voices that she can personalize.

The discussion surrounding the idea of *affidamento* and of Muraro's construction of the "symbolic order of the mother" has emerged also in an issue of the journal *Via Dogana,* published by the Libreria delle Donne in Milan. Entitled "L'amore femminile della madre" (Women's Love for the Mother), the December 1991 issue contains contributions by many Italian feminists. In her article "Dalla parte della madre" (On the Mother's Side) in *Via Dogana* 3 (December 1991): 3–4, Alessandra Bocchetti writes: "What motivates a woman toward maternal love is the necessity of finding meaning in her existence (the order of the father is too confused for her, too basically offensive, here and there flattering, but only superficially).

"I want to explain, however, the following: the order of the father is not a rival. Even if it ends up being a rival of the symbolic order of the mother, it is only a secondary order just like the father is in the eyes of the child. He is a secondary figure mediated through the mother; he is an order of partial truths. In positioning ourselves on the side of the mother in order to look at ourselves as men and women and at the world, we realize that there is a wider point of view, that we can see farther away" (3). To privilege the maternal and at the same time to inscribe it into an order signified by an act of *métissage* is the common agenda that links Passerini's work to the ongoing discussion on difference, which is attempting a total separation from the dangers of a possible reconstruction of a dichotomized portrayal of gendered identities.

In the same December issue of *Via Dogana*, Luisa Muraro, who is its editor, contributes to the discussion with an article entitled "L'amore come pratica politica" (Love as Political Practice) (18–19). Her discourse on "mothers," here, responds to some negative reactions from women who had translated her theory into a personal practice, restricted to individual relationships with single mother-daughter relationships: "Women's love for the mother is *not* the name of a feeling that could be or could have been between a woman and her mother. It is the name of a necessary mediation, that is, the way that the mind must cross in order to be able to practice its power. Therefore, a woman reaches maternal love thanks to the same movement that allows this woman to realize the necessity of this mediation. That means that if we look at our history, thanks to techniques of self-consciousness that, from the description of the relationship with men, has now moved on to the description of families of origin, in which the relationship with the mother is at the center . . . maternal love exists. Places such as the Virginia Woolf Center in Rome, Diotima, the Women's Bookstore in Milan, UDI, and others are spaces where female genealogy exists. These places would not have been created if the mothers of those women who created them had only passed on misery, a sense of abandonment, and hatred" (19). In her statements, Muraro manages to include women as identities in the public and the private, active in public movements, nurtured in the private within a movement that easily allows them to move from one sphere to the other. In this construction Muraro presents the idea of female genealogy as a hybrid entity that partakes of public and private.

Muraro's journal, *Via Dogana*, has now been renamed *Via Dogana: Rivista di politica* (Via Dogana: A Political Journal). In the issue of March-April 1993, Rosetta Stella writes: "With this issue, *Via Dogana* changes its formula: instead of articulating each issue around a single topic, it is now an ordinary journal of politics" (2). The discourse on entrustment that had been at the center of the feminist debate in the pages of *Via Dogana*, is now inscribed among a wide range of issues that expand the concept of feminist themes and the realms to which they belong. This change locates women's issues not at the margins of contemporary Italian political life, but at its center.

46. In "The Laugh of the Medusa," in *New French Feminism: An Anthology*, ed. Elaine Marks and Isabelle de Courtivron (Brighton: Harvester, 1981), Hélène Cixous writes: "Their 'symbolic' exists, it holds power—we, the sower of disorder, know it only too well" (255). Such a statement seems to constitute the pre-text to Muraro's insistence on the importance of constructing a symbolic order of the mother as an act of empowerment. See also the analysis of Cixous's essay in Morag Shiach's article "Their 'Symbolic' Exists, It Holds Power—We, the Sower of Disorder, Know It Only Too Well," in *Between Feminism and Psychoanalysis*, ed. Teresa Brennan (London and New York: Routledge, 1989).

47. Muraro, *Symbolic Order of the Mother*, 18.

48. Passerini collects women's voices in many of her texts on oral history. See, for instance, her text *Torino operaia e fascismo* (Working-Class Turin and Fascism) (Turin: Laterza, 1984). She also collaborates in an anthology, *Interpreting Women's Lives: Personal Narratives*, ed.

Personal Narrative Group (Bloomington and Indianapolis: Indiana University Press, 1989). In her essay, entitled "Women's Personal Narratives: Myths, Experiences, and Emotions," included in the anthology, Passerini analyzes the role of transgression in women's oral recounting of their youth. Transgression, as filtered through the imaginary, also becomes one of the important themes in the chapter dedicated to women terrorists in her book *Stories of Women and Feminists*. The important role of the collector of oral memories is brought to the attention of the reader of her work. In fact, creating a collective history based on oral testimonies allows Passerini to redefine the role of the historian. In "Conoscenza storica e storia orale: sull'utilità e il danno delle fonti orali per la storia" (Historical Knowledge and Oral History: On the Advantages and Negative Aspects in Using Oral Sources in History), in *Storia orale: Vita quotidiana e cultura materiale delle classi subalterne*, Passerini writes: "Oral history was believed to be revolutionary only because it stressed the role of the masses, instead it became such because it stresses the role of the historian" (xvii). More than a decade later, similar words introduce the concluding section of the anthology *Interpreting Women's Lives:* "All autobiographic memory is true. It is up to the interpreter to discover in which sense, where, for which purpose" (261). The problem is indeed related to the gendered identity of the "interpreter" and on her agenda in discussing gender issues in an analysis of autobiographical texts. Reduced to minimal terms, the question one could ask is: what does it mean to be a woman who interprets other women's oral autobiographical interpretations of their lives? The relative answer can be found in the inscription of such a study within a feminist agenda, which has been investigated in the book *Women's Words: The Feminist Practice of Oral History*, ed. Sherna Berger Gluck and Daphne Patai (New York and London: Routledge, 1991). In their introduction to the book, the editors analyze the validity of a feminist approach to oral history that is narrated by women. They state: "The appeal of oral history to feminists is easy to understand. Women doing oral histories with other women in order to recover their stories and revise received knowledge about them have seen their work as consistent with the principle of feminist research later codified in the phrase 'research by, about, and for women'"(1–2). This discussion about women performed through other women's voices within the autobiographical work authored by a woman can create what Patai and Gluck would call "a double act of empowerment." In fact, they write: "The telling of the story can be empowering, validating the importance of the speaker's life existence. This, indeed, is one of the reasons that oral history work with women was assumed to be inherently feminist" (2).

49. See Luisa Passerini, "Giochi fuori campo," *L'asino d'oro*, no. 8 (November 1993): 174–83.

Conclusion. Beyond Gynealogical Techniques

1. Rebecca West, "Women in Italian," in *Italian Studies in North America*, ed. Massimo Ciavolella and Amilcare A. Iannucci (Toronto: Dovehouse Editions, 1994), 195–214.

2. Ibid., 202.

3. Renate Holub, "For the Record: The Non-Language of Italian Feminist Philosophy," *Romance Languages Annual* 1 (1990): 133–40.

4. West, "Women in Italian," 209–10.

5. Ibid., 210.

6. Silvia Vigetti Finzi, *Il bambino della notte: Divenire donna divenire madre* (The Child of the Night: Becoming a Woman Becoming a Mother) (Milan: Mondadori, 1992), 210.

7. On the subject of migration and multicultural Italy, see Rosi Braidotti, *Nomadic Subjects: Embodiment and Sexual Difference in Contemporary Feminist Theory* (New York: Columbia University Press, 1994); Armando Gnisci, *Il rovescio del gioco* (Rome: Sovera, 1993); Graziella Parati, "Strangers in Paradise: Foreigners and Shadows in Contemporary Italian Literature," in *Designing Italy: "Italy" in Europe, Africa, Asia, and the Americas*, ed. Beverly Allen and Mary Russo (Minneapolis: University of Minnesota Press, forthcoming), and Graziella Parati, "Looking through Non-Western Eyes: Immigrant Women's Autobiographical Narratives in Italian," in

Writing (New) Identities: Gender, Nationalism, and Immigration in New European Subjects, ed. Sidonie Smith and Gisela Brinker-Gabler (forthcoming).

8. Nancy Miller, "Representing Others: Gender and Subjects of Autobiography," *Differences* 6, no. 1, (Spring 1994): 1–27. See also Mary Mason, "The Other Voice: Autobiographies of Women Writers," in *Life/Lines: Theorizing Women's Autobiography,* ed. Bella Brodzki and Celeste Schenck (Ithaca: Cornell University Press, 1988).

9. Ibid., 9.

10. Ibid.

11. Ibid., 16.

12. Ibid., 17.

13. Tania Modleski, *Feminism without Women: Culture and Criticism in a "Postfeminist" Age* (New York and London: Routledge, 1991).

14. Ibid., 5.

15. See Art Spiegelman, *Maus: A Survivor's Tale* (New York: Pantheon, 1986) and *Maus, A Survivor's Tale II: And Here My Troubles Began* (New York: Pantheon, 1991). See also Marianne Hirsch's construction of a personal/critical narrative on Spiegelman's texts: Marianne Hirsch, "Family Pictures: *Maus,* Mourning, and Post Memory," *Discourse* 15.2 (Winter 1992–93): 3–29.

16. Marianne Hirsch comments on the construction of a father-son text in which the son is the interpreter of the paternal oral narrative about the mother: "In *Maus,* father and son together attempt to reconstruct the missing story of the mother, and by extension, the story of women in Auschwitz. They do not go to Mala, Vladek's second wife, for assistance, even though she too is a survivor. Mala, in fact, is disturbingly absent as a voice and even as a listener in the two volumes" (21). It is still correct to name Spiegelman's narrative as patrilinear, in the end.

17. I borrow the term "feminisms," intended as "feminism as a plural phenomenon," from Liz Stanley, "Feminist Auto/Biography and Feminist Epistemology," in *Out of the Margins: Women's Studies in the Nineties,* ed. Jane Aaron and Sylvia Walby (London: Falmer Press, 1991), 204–19.

Index

Compiled by Eileen Quam and Theresa Wolner

Graziella Parati received her Laurea in English literature and language from the Università Statale in Milan, her M.A. in Italian literature from the University of Washington, and her Ph.D. from Northwestern University. She has taught at Lancaster University, England, at the University of Colorado, Boulder, at the University of Pennsylvania, and is currently an assistant professor in the Department of French and Italian at Dartmouth College. Graziella Parati is the author of articles on Italian women writers, African Italian literature, and Italophone studies. She has edited a special issue of the journal *Italian Studies in Southern Africa* devoted to contemporary African Italian texts.